mean and lowly things

mean
and
lowly
things

Snakes, Science, and Survival in the Congo

Kate Jackson

Harvard University Press

Cambridge, Massachusetts, and London, England ◇ 2008

Library of Congress Cataloging-in-Publication Data
Jackson, Kate, 1972–
Mean and lowly things : snakes, science, and survival in the Congo /
Kate Jackson.—1st ed.
p. cm.
ISBN-13: 978-0-674-02974-3 (cloth: alk. paper)
1. Jackson, Kate, 1972– 2. Herpetologists—Canada—Biography.
3. Poisonous snakes—Congo (Brazzaville)—Anecdotes.
I. Title.
QL31.J23A3 2008
597.96096724—dc22
2007041327

*To understand the world, we must understand
mean and lowly things.*

Aristotle

contents

Color illustrations follow page 184

prologue

I went to the Congo for the snakes mostly, though for the frogs and lizards and toads as well. When I set out to spend two rainy seasons camped in the swamp forest of northern Congo, I had nothing in mind except documenting the species diversity of animals neglected by science, in a part of the world where they had never been studied before.

But what I found there were a lot of things I hadn't counted on. Reconstructed from the mud-spattered pages of the journals I kept, this is the story of what went into producing a brief report of a survey of amphibians and reptiles, for publication in a scientific journal—the bureaucratic frustrations, disgusting food, parasites, diseases, linguistic confusion, complicated personalities, civil war, isolation, miserable living conditions, cultural misunderstandings, fear, danger, narrow escapes—and also great kindnesses. In short, all the things they didn't prepare me for in graduate school at Harvard.

It will be clear when you read the story that I owe a debt of thanks to a great many individuals and organizations. These are listed in the Acknowledgments at the back of the book and implicitly throughout the text.

chapter 1

how
it
all
started

It is my fifth day in the Republic of Congo. The war broke out yester-day, the beginning of my first independent expedition to collect am-phibians and reptiles for Harvard's Museum of Comparative Zoology, where I am a student. Yesterday morning I was on a plane taking off from Brazzaville, the capital, en route to Ouesso, in the forested north-ern part of the country. I had no idea that at the same time a coup was taking place which was to throw the country into a brutal civil war. This morning, in Brazzaville, dead bodies line the streets. Buildings that I was inside just two days ago are being leveled by gunfire, and foreign embassies are desperately rounding up their citizens for evacuation.

But here at my remote field station, 450 miles north of the capital, my morning is starting more calmly, over coffee and baguettes.

My relaxed breakfast is interrupted by the arrival of a man from the nearby Pygmy village, frantic and out of breath. "Madame, there is a snake in the village!" I leap up in excitement, pausing only to stuff a snake bag into the waistband of my cargo pants and to grab my snake hook. My first specimen so soon? I run after the man back to the village. There is no difficulty locating the snake, since all the villagers are standing in a cautiously wide ring around a tree that doubles as the corner of somebody's house. They step aside to let me through. Tangled around the tree's roots is a nondescript brownish snake about 3 feet long. As I approach, it hisses and strikes at me, hoping to scare me off. Is it venomous? My snake hook is going to be absolutely useless here.

I crouch over the snake to get a good look at the head, and the crowd gasps. I see the snake's head scales and my stress level drops a couple of notches—this is *Lamprophis,* the harmless house snake. I know it from the drawings I studied and the preserved specimens I examined in preparation for this trip. It is unmistakable. It shouldn't be too difficult to unravel from the tree. I will let it bite my left hand with its tiny teeth. That will keep its head still while I use my right hand to untangle the body. But as I reach toward the snake, the spectators shriek with alarm.

"Don't touch it, Madame!"

"It is deadly poisonous!"

"It will kill you!"

I hesitate. Aren't indigenous people supposed to know all about the animals and plants they share the forest with? But no! There is no question that this is *Lamprophis,* one of the easiest snakes to identify. I reach toward the snake again and it darts forward, clamping its jaws down on my hand. Now the villagers are screaming. This has to be *Lamprophis.* It all made sense back in the lab at Harvard, but that seems long ago and far away. This is the first snake I've caught in Africa, and although I cling to what I know to be rational, it is hard to keep the reaction of those around me from undercutting my confidence in what I know to be true. It doesn't take me long to unwind the snake's body from the roots of the tree. The snake lets go of my hand and I quickly drop it into my white cotton snake bag, which I tie shut. A ring of tiny pinpricks on my left hand—the mark left by the bite of any harmless snake—is bleeding slightly. I lick the blood away, and tuck the knot of the bag into my belt with satisfaction.

The people are looking at me with suspicion, and perhaps a bit of hostility? "It's a harmless snake," I explain, not sure how much French they understand—"a kind of snake that has no poison."

I had been looking forward to telling the story over dinner with the other researchers, but by dinner time everyone within miles has already heard about it. Apparently, the Pygmies don't believe that the snake is harmless. They think that I must be a witch. A snake is frightening, but a witch is even more terrifying.

Being thought to be a witch is a great nuisance. I need to hire two Pygmies as guides to accompany me when I venture far from the base camp to another camp known as Ndoki. My offer of employment elicits absolute terror. Only much later do I learn that *ndoki* is the Lingala word for "sorcerer." Imagine being asked to venture into the forest, to a place called Sorcerer, to accompany a witch who will be catching snakes. No wonder they're afraid.

Eventually, though, I set out with two very reluctant employees. I spend 4 weeks working on my survey of the local herpetofauna. Although the war is still raging in the south, it hasn't reached our remote location. But my expedition is cut short anyway. The two Pygmies persuaded to work for me have reputations as the worst guides in the village. Their cooking often includes rotting fish, which they serve cold for breakfast if I don't finish it at dinner. They are supposed to do my laundry, but they find women's underwear too embarrassing to contemplate. They won't go out after dark, and they consider wading in the swamp to be absolute folly. So I'm alone late one night when I fall over a log and scrape my left leg, on my way back from the swamp with a bag of treefrogs.

I think nothing of the scrape until 5 days later, when my temperature shoots to 104°F and my leg swells and turns red. Some microbe from the swamp has entered through the scrape and spread to infect my whole body. Perhaps the Pygmies had some sense in refusing to wade in the swamp. I try everything in my first-aid kit to stop the upward creeping of the redness and swelling, but nothing works. The skin on my leg is so stretched from swelling that it looks in danger of splitting. I don't want to end my expedition with an amputated leg, so instead my trip ends with a medical evacuation, by a small plane from a lumber company 7 hours downstream by pirogue (dugout canoe). As I watch the forest disappearing beneath the clouds through the airplane window, I am certain of one thing. I will be back.

Collecting for natural history museums is not a branch of science that receives much press. I came to it only gradually. Although I have been obsessed with amphibians and reptiles for most of my life, it wasn't until Career Day in my final year at my Toronto high school that I saw my first museum collection. In preparation for Career Day, we were each asked to fill out a slip of paper naming a career we were interested in. The guidance counselor collected the slips and had to do his best for each student, tracking down surgeons, journalists, and corporate lawyers willing to have a teenager tag along with them for a day. On my slip of paper, I wrote "herpetologist," and handed it in without much hope.

Now a herpetologist can be many different things. A zoo curator may be a herpetologist. A pet store owner might be a herpetologist at heart. A biology professor could specialize in amphibians. A veterinarian could focus on "exotics" and care for sick reptiles. And then there are many accomplished and knowledgeable amateur herpetologists—people in entirely different professions—taxi drivers, plumbers, engineers—who keep basements full of terrariums. But the herpetologist who got saddled with me on that day was the collections manager of the Herpetology Department at the Royal Ontario Museum.

He met me at the museum's back entrance at 9:00 a.m., where he filled in some elaborate paperwork to get me a badge that said "Visitor." I was surprised that security was so tight, and said so. "Well, there are a lot of valuable things in this museum's collections," he explained. "If we didn't have a security system, anyone might just come in off the street and walk out with a Ming vase or a pickled toad."

Most people, including me until that day, only know about the public galleries of natural history museums—the part of the museum that provides educational entertainment. That is the place you take your kids to every weekend until they outgrow their dinosaur phase. Old-fashioned museums are simply rooms full of glass cases of seashells, stuffed birds, or rocks and minerals, each carefully labeled. Many modern museums have more ambitious exhibits, such as interactive games, designed to educate while at the same time increasing ticket sales. But in any major natural history museum, the public display is nothing but window dressing—window dressing, to be fair, that has inspired many a young biologist. But a much larger part of the museum, the part where the serious action takes place, is given over to collections, libraries of species—essential to the scientific study of the natural world.

Once we'd negotiated the security desk, the collections manager led me through a warren of hallways and elevators to the Herpetology Department. I had never seen anything like it. As large and high-ceilinged as a gymnasium, the room was divided by rows upon rows of metal shelving which held thousands of jars of amphibians and reptiles in preserving fluid. As I stared in awe, the collections manager explained to me how it all worked. The specimens in the jars had been collected over many years by herpetologists working all over the world in remote and exotic places. Each one of them was carefully labeled with a number tag corresponding to a card in a catalogue with detailed information of where, when, and how it had been collected. "So," he said, ready to show the cataloguing system in action, "name a species you've always wanted to see, and we'll see if we can find one."

"A forest cobra," I answered without hesitation, and the collections manager led me down the aisles until we found one in an enormous jar. "A Japanese giant salamander" was my next demand. Here we struck out, but I made do with a hellbender, the largest salamander found outside of Japan. "A tuatara," and so on. But the collections manager was a busy man, and couldn't play this game with me all morning, so he set me to work "skeletonizing."

In addition to the specimens in jars of preservative, the museum maintains a collection of skeletons. The collections manager led me to a freezer chest full of animals that had died at the zoo and were destined to become skeletons. To make a skeleton specimen, the first step is for somebody (me!) to cut as much flesh as possible off the carcass. Then, to remove the last tiny bits of flesh, the skeleton is left in the "bug room"—a small room swarming with flesh-eating dermestid beetles which greedily nibble the remaining fragments of flesh until all that's left is a shiny white skeleton. I spent a blissful day taking apart a monitor lizard, a cobra, and a small crocodile. When the collections manager came in to tell me that it was 5:00 p.m. and time to stop, I felt as if I'd hardly begun.

That day, it never occurred to me to ask a question that might seem obvious: What was the purpose of the collection? Who used it, for what, and why? But to a girl mad about reptiles, a herpetology collection needed no more purpose to justify its existence than, say, an art gallery did.

My next experience of a natural history museum was a summer I spent as an undergraduate intern in the Herpetology Department of the Smithsonian Institution, using scanning electron microscopy to study the fangs of snakes. I loved every minute of it. "The undergraduate intern training program is all about getting kids excited about science," said the curator who had supervised my independent project, "and you really bit the hook."

My work that summer led me on to graduate school at Harvard. Harvard's Museum of Comparative Zoology has a collection that rivals even the Smithsonian's in size. When I arrived in September, I was given a key to the herpetology collection and a room in a dorm next door to the museum. I could let myself in at 3:00 in the morning and take a snake out of a jar if I wanted to, and often I did.

As I started the research for my doctoral dissertation, I finally began to think, for the first time, about the purpose of natural history collections. Natural history museums go back a long way, and their nature and purpose have changed over the centuries. I suppose there have always been people with the impulse to collect and catalogue bits of the natural world. In eighteenth-century Europe there was a vogue for "cabinets of curiosities," private collections of odd assortments of interesting specimens—an ostrich egg, a two-headed sheep embryo, a flint arrowhead thousands of years old. Today's great natural history museums owe their beginnings to a later movement. "Natural History" became a popular hobby among Victorian gentlemen (and sometimes ladies), often, interestingly, clergymen. A collector might specialize in seashells or birds' eggs, or the general flora and fauna of the place where he lived. These were collections lovingly assembled and painstakingly studied and labeled. What was their purpose? To display the wonderful diversity of God's creation. Though the work of today's museum biologists certainly has nothing to do with God or creationism, they continue to marvel at the wonderful diversity of living organisms—at biodiversity.

"Documenting biodiversity" was the answer I got from everyone when I asked what each thought was the main purpose of a natural history museum today. Protecting biodiversity is a high priority for scientists, as it ought to be for everyone else as well. Unfortunately, the parts of the planet richest in biodiversity—the rainforests, the coral reefs—tend to be located in the world's poorest countries, where people are more occupied with getting enough food for their families than with protecting the great biodiversity that surrounds them. But to maintain that great biodiversity, we must save species from becoming extinct.

To me the importance of saving species from extinction was completely obvious, as it was to all the other zoologists at the museum. We loved amphibians and reptiles, and all other animals and plants. We delighted in the thousands of species of each, and agreed that the world would be a sadder place if any were driven to extinction. But that explanation alone made me uneasy. It made species sound like luxury items, to be protected only for aesthetic reasons. I wanted an explanation that would convince a nonscientist—even someone who did not consider snakes irresistibly attractive.

And so I brought the question to the Herpetology Department's weekly coffee and doughnut hour. "Why," I asked the assembled professors, graduate students, and technicians around me, "should biodiversity be protected?" Was a simple love of animals and plants reason enough?

"There's more to it than that," another graduate student immediately pointed out. "Every species has a place in an ecosystem, and if you remove one, you risk having the whole ecosystem collapse."

"It's true," chipped in a postdoc, "and our planet depends on functioning ecosystems to maintain life—certainly human life. If we destroyed enough ecosystems by removing species, new ones might establish themselves, but they might be ones that didn't include us—the cockroaches might not mind." This got a laugh. The Herpetology Department had been struggling for years with a cockroach infestation.

"But how does what we do help?" I asked. "Collecting and identifying specimens in different parts of the world, describing new species . . ."

"Well, we need to know what species are where in order to protect them," explained my supervisor, stirring coffee whitener into his mug. "We can't protect what we don't know. We're identifying the areas of highest biodiversity, figuring out which are the most important ones for us to protect."

"But what we're really trying to do, as scientists," said an elderly visiting researcher, wiping powdered sugar off his chin, "is find out *everything*. Identifying the species is the very first step. Once we know what they are, we can begin to study what they do. If we understand everything about an ecosystem we will know which are the keystone species, everything, and we will be well placed to see that the balance needed to hold it all together is maintained. But it's a huge job," he reflected. "At this point we've described about 1 percent of the species on the planet—just *described* them, not learned anything about their natural history. Here in the Herpetology Department we complain that our animals are neglected by science, but you should just go down the hall to Invertebrate Zoology and ask them what they think. An enormous job. I certainly won't live to see it finished."

I drained my coffee cup and set off back to the lab with a lot to think about. Now I understood better what I was being trained to do and why.

Sometimes late at night, as I worked in the collection, surrounded by thousands of jars, my mind drifted. Every specimen in each of those jars had been collected by someone—usually someone long forgotten.

But for each jar, there must be a story—a story of a lucky grab in a muddy swamp in New Guinea or a quick job with a snake hook in the Kalahari Desert. My dissertation work consisted entirely of describing the anatomy of preserved snakes, but I longed to study the real thing in the wild.

I had chosen Harvard as the place to do my doctoral degree because of a particular professor. The man I wanted to learn from was a recently hired assistant professor who had never supervised a graduate student before. But I had heard stories of his adventures in the field. That he went off to Peru and Madagascar in search of snakes; that he had contracted the flesh-eating disease, leishmaniasis, in Peru and had been struck by lightning in Madagascar; and that, in both cases, he had bravely refused to be sent home. Other stories he volunteered himself—the time a terrestrial leech crawled up his nose while he was sleeping, the time he caught his first cobra, grabbing it by the tail and then, in a panic, flinging it up into the air. He was the kind of herpetologist I wanted to be, and I longed to accompany him on his adventures. I spent hours sitting with him in his office, talking about fieldwork. I was sure that he would take me as his assistant on his next expedition.

It took me almost a year to realize that this man was never going to take me, or anybody else, for that matter, into the field with him. He was essentially a loner, and didn't want anybody tagging along after him. I needed to just get out there on my own, he eventually told me. Make my own arrangements, go somewhere that had interesting reptiles, and figure it out for myself. That was how he had learned.

I was bitterly disappointed at first, and afraid of just setting out alone, not really knowing what I was doing. But most of all I was afraid of not living up to the example set by my professor. I had a recurrent nightmare in which, working by myself in some remote part of the world, I mistook a venomous snake for a harmless one and got bitten by it. The worst part of this dream was a horrible dilemma: If I didn't go and try to get help I would die, but if I did go for help, the professor I admired so much would find out that I had misidentified a snake. I couldn't decide which fate would be worse.

But eventually, I did organize my own expedition. I leafed through an atlas, poring over the possibilities. I found myself drawn to central Africa and the vast and mysterious forest that follows the path of the Congo River. Compared to the forest around the Amazon River, it was a virtual blank spot on the herpetological map of the world: most of it had never been studied by herpetologists. Perhaps in some small way I could make a difference there.

So in the end I did set off on my own as my professor had told me to. I made mistakes, I did things wrong, I did things that were dangerous—and I figured it out for myself. That expedition was my first experience of the Congo, an expedition which began with a civil war and ended with a medical evacuation—a medical evacuation and an altogether irrational longing to return.

chapter 2

back
to
the
congo

Seven years fly by. I complete my dissertation on snake anatomy, and follow it up with a postdoctoral fellowship studying crocodile physiology. But soon my thoughts drift back to that vast central African forest that drains into the Congo River. The amphibians and reptiles in that forest are still among the most poorly known in the world. The Congo, less stable and more dangerous than Cameroon or Gabon where other scientists are working, is an empty niche. My postdoctoral fellowship ends and I have no job. It is time to return to Africa.

I should explain here that there are two Congos. The larger of the two is the Democratic Republic of Congo (DRC), formerly Zaire, and before that the Belgian Congo. The capital city is Kinshasa. The DRC

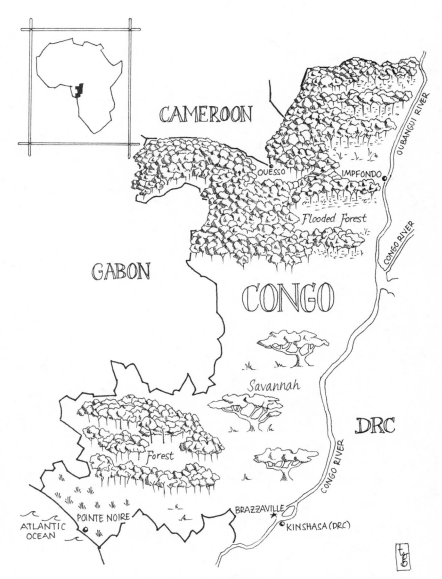

The Republic of Congo, bordering on the Democratic Republic of Congo (DCR) to the southeast, Gabon to the west, and Cameroon to the northwest

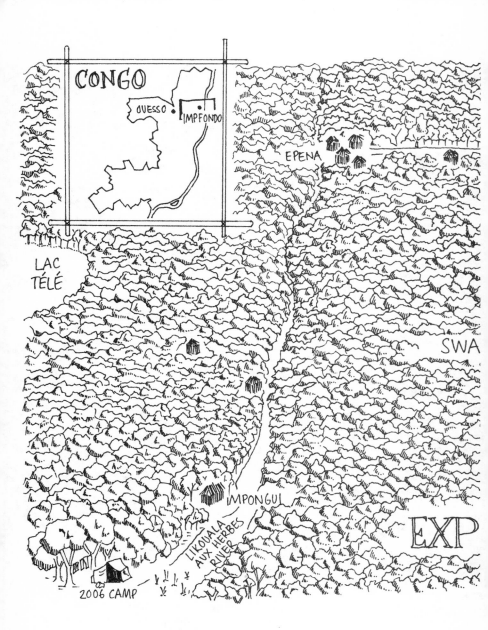

CONGO

OUESSO • IMPFONDO

EPENA

LAC TÉLÉ

SWA

IMPONGUI

LIKOUALA AUX HERBES RIVER

EXP

2006 CAMP

IMPFONDO

2005 CAMP

FLIGHT TO IMPFONDO

MP FOREST

OUBANGUI RIVER

EDITIONS 2005/2006

The area around Lac Télé, with the site of my 2005 camp at the top right
corner and the site of my 2006 camp at the bottom left

covers more than 1.5 million square miles in the center of Africa and has a population of almost 60 million. The other, smaller Congo is where I do my work. This is the Republic of Congo (I know it's confusing), formerly the French Congo. The capital city is Brazzaville, across the Congo River from Kinshasa. Congo-Brazzaville (as the Congo is often called, to avoid confusion) is roughly northwest of the DRC, with much of the border between the two countries formed by the Congo River. Congo-Brazzaville covers only 200,000 square miles and has a population of just under 3 million. The northern third of the country is forest—part of the enormous forest of the Congo River drainage basin.

An expedition to the Congo takes an unbelievable amount of organizing. To start with, I will need funds for an expedition, even working as cheaply as I possibly can. I can think of one institution to turn to. The Smithsonian. Maybe people there will remember that undergraduate intern from so many years ago. I e-mail George Zug, a senior curator of herpetology, and offer him all the snakes, lizards, and amphibians I collect in exchange for a contribution to my expedition fund. I get a reply within minutes. Of course he remembers me, he says, and he's very excited about getting the specimens. He will scrape together as much money as his department can spare. Good old Smithsonian.

Harder to find, and just as crucial as funds, are connections in the country I want to go to. My first expedition to the Congo had left me with the impression that civil wars were a regular occurrence there, but this turns out not to be the case. The "War of 1997," as I hear the war that coincided with my arrival in the Congo called, devastated the country. Everything destroyed is being gradually rebuilt, and what contacts I had there are gone. So I start a search by e-mail that takes many months. I e-mail a herpetologist who has worked in east Africa. He gives me e-mail addresses for two botanists in Gabon, one of which bounces. The one whose address doesn't bounce knows of a herpetologist who worked in Cameroon 15 years ago. And so it goes on. Each helpful person who responds gives me a list of other contacts. Some e-mails bounce, some are never answered, and some send me another list of names. I make a big chart on the wall of my office to keep track of who's who. It is on about the sixth iteration of e-mails that I make contact with Claude Laveissière.

Claude is in charge of a branch of a French organization, the IRD—Institute of Research for Development—at Pointe Noire, the second-largest city in the Congo. He replies, with detailed logistical advice, to every e-mail I send, and is willing to help my project in any way he can. Claude knows his way around the political structure of the country well. He tells me that the best thing I could get is the approval of the DGRST, the top government office in charge of science and technology in the country, and urges me to submit a research proposal to that office, asking for permission to collect amphibians and reptiles anywhere in the country for the next 3 years. I put together a proposal. Claude tactfully asks if I would mind allowing him to correct my French, and polishes my effort into a masterpiece of eloquence. He also encourages me to add the promise that I will train Congolese graduate students in herpetology as one of my objectives. The Congo is badly in need of trained scientists. The application is a success, and my permit is all arranged long before my arrival. Moreover, Claude will accompany me to Brazzaville, where he will introduce me to all the important people he thinks it would be useful for me to know.

As my departure date approaches I become absorbed by logistical minutiae: How many batteries will I need for headlamps? What is the French word for "graduated cylinder"? Will Ziploc plastic bags leak, and would I be better off using regular freezer bags for storing specimens wrapped in formalin-soaked cheesecloth? The success of this expedition rests on details. A single signature missing from a permit, a single item overlooked in the first-aid kit, and the whole project may fail.

This vulnerability to details neglected, I reflect, is not unlike that of a complex tropical ecosystem, where disaster may result from removing the species of bat that pollinates the species of tree on which a species of moss grows, which is eaten by . . . I worry about every single detail in spite of well-meant reassurances from my exasperated friends that everything will work out if I just calm down.

I begin packing an entirely unnecessary 2 months in advance of the trip. Every inch of floor space in my tiny studio apartment is soon piled high. The senior curator in the Herpetology Department at the Smithsonian sends me no fewer than seven fascinating parcels—cheesecloth to wrap specimens in and soak with formalin, to keep them moist and preserved in transit; little plastic screwtop vials for preserving tissue samples for DNA extraction; disposable syringes and hypodermic needles in an assortment of sizes, for use with formalin and ethanol; hundreds of plastic bags, for uses too numerous to list; numbered field tags, ready to tie around the neck of a snake or the knee of a frog; and much more. Toronto's Chinatown sells lots of useful things. I buy plastic trays for use in hardening formalin-fixed specimens, and wonderful folding scissors that cost 99 cents and work surprisingly well for everything from cutting through wire mesh to snipping a tiny fragment of liver tissue from a treefrog. Field clothing is another necessity I buy: cargo pants—cotton trousers with lots of pockets for storing equipment. Sleeveless undershirts to wear on top, and bandannas to cover my head and keep the sweat out of my eyes, and my hair, as it grows longer, out of my face. Thinking of Claude's mention of several days spent in Brazzaville, meeting "dignitaries," I realize that perhaps I ought to pack a more formal outfit than just cargo pants and undershirts. "YES!!!" says Claude when I casually ask him this, 2 days before my departure. He sounds appalled by the possibility that I almost neglected to pack a dress, an item so essential to a study of snakes in an African forest. It is the end of summer in Toronto and I easily find one on sale: sleeveless and with a hem just above the knee, made of cotton in a bright pattern of tropical flowers. Just the thing.

I buy benzocaine gel at the local pharmacy. It is an anesthetic intended for toothaches, but I have found it very effective as a humane way of euthanizing frogs. You put a dab of it on the frog's head, and it appears to just fall asleep and never wake up. When I was in junior kindergarten, my love of frogs was so intense that the older boys would corner me in the playground and say, "Hey, Kate, I killed a frog yesterday," just for the fun of watching me cry. Now I sometimes wonder what I'm doing—hunting down the amphibians and reptiles that I love and killing them. Some people ask why I don't just take a photograph. But working in an area where the animals are so poorly known, "voucher" specimens are essential. That means bringing back the entire animal, in preservative, to be exhaustively studied at the museum. These specimens are absolutely necessary in order to confirm identifications. A tissue sample has no value unless later researchers can verify the identification of the specimen from the whole preserved animal. So the need for voucher specimens is a reality of working on the front lines of museum collecting, and can't be avoided. I often envy my colleagues who study well-known species in the United States. The biology of rattlesnakes is now so well known that people studying them are interested not in identifying their species, but in learning the details of their behavior. They follow the snakes around by radiotelemetry, looking at the snakes each day without having to disturb them. One day perhaps we'll get to that stage with central African snakes.

I make an appointment with the travel doctor at the local clinic. He asks me where I'm going and for how long, and starts consulting books. I'm excitedly filling him in on details when he cuts me off. "Look, you're going to the Republic of, of, I don't know what, you're going to be wading in swamps and handling poisonous snakes. I *don't* want to hear any more—I'm used to dealing with people who are going to a resort in Belize for two weeks!" He prescribes big capsules of doxycycline against malaria and Cipro in the event of traveler's diarrhea, and sends me for seven assorted injections.

Arranging a visa to enter the country is the first truly Congolese experience of this expedition. I need a visa to allow me to spend 2 and 1/2 months in the Congo, which has to be obtained from the Congolese embassy, in Washington, D.C. "Ambassade du Congo," says the man who answers the phone. I am reminded that from here on I must function in French. The Congolese embassy turns out to have a website from which I am able to download a visa application form, a document that looks as if it has been photocopied 10 times at an assortment of angles. I fill this in and send it in, accompanied, with some misgivings, by my passport, a check for $70, and a FedEx return envelope. When my passport returns, relief gives way to frustration. The embassy official has written in a departure date of November 19, not November 29 as I had requested. The visa is a stamp in my passport with various blank spaces to be filled in with dates. I phone the Congolese embassy again. I get the same man who answered the phone the last time and explain the problem. He pulls out my visa application. "Yes, it is true you did put the 29th. Oh dear, this is very serious, very serious." But his obvious distress gives way to delight as he hits on a solution to the problem. "I filled in the number 19 in black ink, didn't I? Well get a black pen and very carefully change the 1 to a 2."

On the eve of my departure, Claude asks me, in an e-mail, to describe myself so that I can be easily recognized at the Pointe Noire airport. "Well, I'm smallish, brown hair down to my chin, thick glasses," I begin to type . . . oh, forget it—"I'll wear an orange t-shirt," I tell him. The very last e-mail from Claude before I leave is a reminder to be sure to wear the orange t-shirt. I'm already beginning to get the sense of a man accustomed to nobody else in the world being as efficiently organized as he is. And I soon discover that I have seriously underestimated Claude.

Arriving in Pointe Noire, I am expecting to be met by a man called Roland, who will know me by my orange t-shirt. Of course I don't know what he looks like. No Roland appears. I show my passport. I show my yellow-fever vaccination card. I follow the rest of the crowd leaving the plane outside the terminal, and suddenly find myself face to face with a white man about 60 years old. We're face to face because he's short, though burly. "Ket Jacksonne?" he asks.

"Claude?" Even after almost a year of frequent, friendly, casual e-mails he is not at all what I had imagined. I had expected someone about my own age, hired to run a small field station for a few years. But for Claude, Director of the IRD at Pointe Noire, going to the airport to meet someone is clearly a task to be delegated to an underling, and from the indignant cell phone conversation I am overhearing one side of, it sounds as if that underling is in serious trouble.

"But what do you mean you are in bed? It is 7:00 a.m. and the plane landed at 6:30! I made it perfectly clear yesterday that you were to be at the airport by 6 a.m. at the *latest!* I am here *myself* greeting the re-searcher!" He turns his attention back to me. "So you have arrived!" he says with a genuinely warm and welcoming smile. "Did you sleep on the plane? No? Well, never mind. I have booked you a room for 3 nights at the Hotel Azul. You can sleep this afternoon."

When we arrive at the hotel it becomes clear that if I have underesti-mated Claude, he has overestimated me. The unfamiliar euros that I am carrying still feel like Monopoly money to me, but even so I calcu-late the cost of the room to be about $100 a night. The scary thing about money in this country is that everything works entirely by cash. No trav-eler's checks, no credit cards. I will have to carry all the money I have, for the entire 2-and-1/2-month expedition, on my person. The currency here is cfa: Central African Francs. It takes me a while to start thinking of things in terms of cfa. Now 500cfa is equal to about 1 U.S. dollar. So the cost of the hotel is about 50,000cfa ($100) per night. A taxi ride in Brazzaville costs 700cfa ($1.50), a pack of cigarettes 500cfa ($1), a bar of soap 300cfa (60¢), and a ballpoint pen 100cfa (25¢). When I finally get to the forest, a machete costs 2,500cfa ($5), and a generous wage for a villager hired as a guide is 3,000cfa ($6) per day.

I soon become aware that the dress, which seemed fine in Toronto, is really so short as to verge on indecent here. In fact I feel almost as exposed as if I were wearing no dress at all, when I change into it and come out into the hotel lobby, thinking of going for a walk to explore Pointe Noire. I find I am attracting the unwelcome attention of several men. "Mademoiselle," says one, sidling up to me, "I can show you around Pointe Noire in my car. I know all the sights." I decide against the walk and hurry back to my room.

In spite of my exhaustion and the comfortable hotel, I never do manage to sleep. During my 3 sleepless days in Pointe Noire, Claude and his Congolese wife, Sylvie, are wonderful hosts, and treat me to great luxuries. At one restaurant, as I eat escargots, followed by crayfish on a skewer, followed by crepes with fresh strawberries, I wonder what my friends back home would think of such extravagance. They all imagine me hacking my way through the jungle with a machete and living on manioc and sardines. Where on earth do they find fresh strawberries in Pointe Noire?

It soon becomes clear that finding suitable students to bring with me into the field is not possible at such short notice. Perhaps in some later expedition. I have arranged to work in the Lac Télé Wildlife Reserve, run by the American organization WCS (Wildlife Conservation Society). It is in the Likouala Region, the northeast part of the Congo, which is mostly flooded forest. I am disappointed that the director there doesn't want me to arrive for another week, but Claude assures me that a week in Brazzaville making political contacts will be a week well spent. I already have that crucial research permit from the DGRST, which Claude went to so much trouble to obtain for me. But Claude's plan is that I will make "courtesy visits" to a confusing number of important people, and there are certainly enough of them to fill a week. There are also some people I made contact with on my own, scientists at the National Laboratory of Public Health, who are interested in reducing deaths from snakebite in the country. Tomorrow, Monday, Claude will accompany me to Brazzaville to get me started.

Claude can spare only one day in Brazzaville, so it is going to be a busy one, introducing me to various "dignitaries"—powerful men in the branches of the government dealing with science or environmental conservation. Claude is miserable dressed in a jacket and tie, which must be unspeakably hot, and I am wearing the embarrassing Toronto dress. We rush off for a long series of appointments. Always with intimidating, overweight men in suits. I have trouble keeping track of who's who, and I quickly realize that I should have brought twice as many business cards as I did. Luckily these men all have business cards, so I am able to sort out who's who later on by the cards. Claude keeps introducing me as "*Madame* Jackson," and I take the opportunity, in a waiting room between appointments, to tell him it should be "*Docteur* Jackson." He tells me sternly that this is how things are done here and that I should count myself lucky that he is not introducing me as "*Mademoiselle.*"

I'm doing my best in complicated conversations in French on 3 nights without sleep. Claude tolerates my ineptitude except for one mistake he can't stand to hear me make over and over again: apparently the word for *arboreal* is not *arboréale,* but *arboricole.* It's not only my French that's suffering from my lack of sleep. After I leave my folder of documents in a restaurant after twice almost leaving it in a taxi, he says grimly to the man we're having lunch with, "Kate has these little moments of cloudiness."

After the scary government officials, it is a great relief to meet my contacts at the National Public Health Laboratory. Jean Akiana, a junior scientist there, has been my main e-mail contact. I suspected that there might be some confusion over my name because he kept writing to me as "Dear Mr. Kate." I guess Jackson is a possible man's first name, and Kate is a totally unfamiliar name in French, besides which there's the sexist assumption that the venomous snake specialist you're corresponding with is male. Anyway, Jean is in for a great shock when Mr. Kate arrives in a dress. We all have a good laugh over it, but thereafter I start using my full name, Katherine. Claude and Jean and I meet with Dr. Parra, who is the director of the lab, as well as with the biomedical director, and after all the government officials of the morning I feel immediately at ease with friendly fellow scientists. I say of our morning that it seems that in the Congo permits are harder to catch than mambas. "Permits! Mambas! Harder to catch! That's not bad!" laughs the biomedical director, "Hey, that's not bad!"

I had originally made contact with Jean because of a study he had conducted on human deaths from snakebite in the Congo. Surveying remote villages throughout the country, he talked to villagers and filled out questionnaires. He wanted to find out how people throughout the country—from those in the cities to those in the most remote villages—dealt with snakebite, and how well equipped the country was to treat snakebite victims. The results of his study were sobering. Of people bitten by snakes (there was no way of separating out species, or even distinguishing between venomous and harmless snakes, when he was interviewing villagers), half the victims went to the nearest clinic for treatment, while the other half chose to stay in the village and take traditional medicine. The mortality rate for both groups was the same—you were just as likely to die if you went to a modern hospital as you were if you simply took some useless placebo sold in the village. This didn't say much for the hospitals! Jean continued his study with a country-wide survey of antivenom availability. Though he scoured the country he found only one clinic and one pharmacy that stocked antivenom.

Antivenom is complicated. In contrast to the popular "traditional" treatments for snakebite, and it seems every village has someone who makes one, it is not a single, simple and effective cure for the bite of any snake. You need to use an antivenom against the venom of the species of snake that you have been bitten by, or something closely related to it, or it won't work. And antivenom is tricky to administer. It is not like most of the traditional cures, which the victim just drinks or pours on the bite wound. It requires an intravenous injection, and is complicated in various other ways, which really makes it usable only in a hospital setting, with the supervision of a physician. So the problem goes much further than making antivenom available in remote clinics. I wonder how many clinicians there are in the Congo who are actually experienced in the use of antivenom. Dr. Parra shows me an ampoule of the kind of antivenom that is available in the few places that have it. Reading the label, I find that it is a polyvalent antivenom: a combination of antivenoms against the venoms of several species. But the list of species it is good for is four species of viper, only one of which exists in the Congo. It is an antivenom that might help a patient bitten by a Gaboon viper (if the people stocking the dispensary knew that they might well need not one but more likely several ampoules to treat a serious bite, and that its effectiveness expires after it has been stored for a couple of years), but it would probably be useless against the bite of a cobra or mamba. The first step in solving the snakebite mortality problem has got to be learning more about the snakes—a herpetologist's job. Dr. Parra tells me he and his colleagues are very glad to have me join their team.

Claude does his best in the hours that remain to make sure I will be okay in Brazzaville. He tries to persuade me to buy a cell phone, but that seems to me a ridiculous expense since I will be spending most of my time in the remote north where it wouldn't work. In retrospect I should probably have bought one. There are no land lines here and everyone communicates by cell phones charged up by calling cards. The trouble is that cell phone owners mostly use them for telling people they are supposed to meet that they will be late or that the meeting has been canceled, and since they do a lot of delaying and changing of plans here, I often, during my time in the city, find myself waiting for people who never arrive because they had no way to contact me. Though I can't receive a call, it is possible for me to make an outgoing call from one of the many little stands set up in the streets by entrepreneurs who charge for the use of their cell phone. It's a lot of bother, but if you are really desperate, and think you can yell loud enough into the phone to be heard over the passing traffic, it's an option.

The most useful person Claude introduces me to is Père Joseph of the Catholic Institute. If you come with a good recommendation, the institute will rent you a room for 7,000cfa a night. Basin in the room, shower and WC down the hall. Claude is leaving for Pointe Noire tomorrow morning. I will move to the Catholic Institute after he goes. It's been one whirlwind day in Brazzaville, and soon I'll be on my own.

Père Joseph welcomes me to the Catholic Institute the following morning, and upon hearing that I have not had breakfast, calls for coffee and baguettes and jam. He even makes a call to Jean, who comes to pick me up in a taxi. Taxis are how people who don't have their own cars get around. There's a flat rate of 700cfa for going anywhere in the city. Jean is my companion for the remainder of the week, and gradually, through his company, I get the hang of Brazzaville. Soon I negotiate taxis by myself and meet him at the lab each day at 9:00 a.m. Well, it's 9:00 a.m. in theory, but maddeningly, Jean is always late. Waiting an hour and a half is not unusual. On those rare days when the Internet is working I don't mind the delay so much, because I can occupy myself doing e-mail. Later, I wish I had been more understanding. Jean is trying to do all his own work while at the same time hosting me, but I am often short with him after a long wait. Then as the day unfolds I start to see why it takes so long to get anything done in this country. When Jean arrives at, say, 10:00, we wait half an hour until the director, Dr. Parra, arrives, and then pay him a "courtesy visit." How can poor Dr. Parra ever get anything done, I wonder, if every employee of the lab pays him a courtesy visit every day?

Eventually Jean and I set out on our errands. This means trekking all over Brazzaville, sometimes by taxi, sometimes on foot, to the various government offices from which I need permits. The director of the WCS base at Lac Télé has emphasized that even though I already have a permit from the DGRST and from two other offices, I must also have a research permit from one other government department in order to work within the reserve, so we start at that office on Tuesday. After hanging around in three waiting rooms, we are finally ushered into a large office where two officials, a man and a woman, sit down across from us on couches surrounding a coffee table. Their expressions are not welcoming or encouraging. I start to explain my project, but Jean jumps in, interrupting me. "Madame wants to catch examples of different kinds of amphibians and reptiles and preserve them in jars of formalin," he explains matter-of-factly, "so that when the forest is all destroyed, the little children will be able to look at the dead animals in the jars and learn about what used to be here, in their country."

I stifle a gasp of horror. This bleak and sinister vision of the future is so appalling that I push it out of my mind immediately. At least I try to. Is this really what Jean thinks my expedition is all about? I can only bear to think about the forest and its creatures as things which are threatened but which will be saved by the efforts of scientists. A future in which all the components of long-since-destroyed ecosystems exist only as dead curiosities in jars of formalin is too awful to contemplate.

But the two officials, who have been listening to Jean, just make photocopies of the papers I have obtained from other offices and tell us that my permit will be ready to pick up on Thursday. The director who has to sign it is out of town at the moment.

The working day ends at 3:00 p.m., which forces me and Jean to put off other errands for the following day. By that time I am hot, sweaty, dusty, and tired. Jean knows little restaurants all over the city where for 2,500cfa you can get a cheese omelet and a liter of beer, so we have a late lunch.

The cuisine is probably the thing I like least about the Congo. Staples of Congolese cooking are fish, manioc, and a vegetable that resembles grass cuttings. All the food, whether a fish stew or a side dish of "vegetables" has a salty, fishy flavor mixed into it. The flavor is hard to describe, but the smell of it stimulates my gag reflex. Manioc, a root vegetable, contains a nerve poison, which, by means of many steps and great effort, can be removed. Manioc is most often a foul-smelling, tasteless paste, wrapped in leaves to make it into rubbery lumps, which are then cut into chunks. It can also be made into *fou-fou*—manioc flour mixed with boiling water and formed by hand into lumps, which thankfully have no taste. As for the fish, it always seems to be mostly skin and bones, eyes and fins, which makes me squeamish. And finally, everything is cooked in immense amounts of oil. Fou-fou and manioc are served on the side, like bread, for wiping up the oily sauce. Since neither is in the least bit absorbent, all they do is get oily sauce from the bowl all over your chin. I can't understand how there can be so many overweight people in Brazzaville when the food is so horrible. I've found that often restaurants that otherwise serve only Congolese food will make an omelet, so I eat a lot of omelets.

The beer here is *Ngok* (Crocodile), and has a label with a crocodile on it. Since I am fond of crocodiles, I am constantly peeling labels off Ngok bottles and drying them out to save as souvenirs. Ngok comes in 1-liter bottles, and you don't throw away the cap after opening the bottle. You're going to need it for keeping the bubbles in and the flies out.

After lunch, Jean goes back to the lab to finish his day's work, and I go back to the Catholic Institute, exhausted. The Catholic Institute turns out to be much better than a hotel, not only because it is cheap but because the community provides congenial company. My first evening there I venture out into the main room and find Père Joseph and several of the brothers lounging in armchairs, drinking beer, and watching an exceptionally violent and sexually explicit French movie on TV. The beer comes from a minifridge available to everybody. There's an honor system: you help yourself and count up how many you've had and pay for them when you check out. I join the brothers for about 45 minutes and then announce that I'm going to bed. "You've got more sense than I have, my girl," Père Joseph calls after me cheerfully, eyes still glued to the set. Other visitors come and go; often in the evenings there are people sitting around talking and drinking beer. Everyone is here on some kind of mission, ranging from French church groups carrying out charitable works to people with projects as outlandish as mine.

My horrible dress is the only one I have, and it is getting smellier by the day. I had never anticipated spending so much time in Brazzaville. So far everyone has been very polite about my increasingly pungent body odor. I try to wash the dress in the shower at the Catholic Institute, but the only result is that the next morning it is wet as well as smelly.

🐲

One morning at the Public Health Lab, Jean calls me downstairs to the clinic. An old man, a peasant, is in the waiting room, and Jean wants me to hear his story and see what I think. The man tells me that he was bitten by a snake and that he is in pain and wants antivenom. Gradually I get the full story from him. The snakebite, it turns out, happened 4 years ago! The bite was on his right foot. There was some localized swelling and discoloration. "Localized" means effects from the venom just around the site of the bite wound, such as swelling and bleeding into the surrounding muscle. "Systemic" means effects from the venom that affect the whole body, such as nausea or paralysis. He took traditional medicine in the village and recovered. "What did the snake look like?" I ask out of curiosity. He tells me it was thin and brown and "20 feet long." Right. Anyway, 4 years later he has pain all up the back of his right thigh, which he attributes to the bite.

Antivenom is certainly not going to be of any use 4 years after a bite! It seems unlikely that there's any connection between the snakebite to his foot 4 years ago and the current pain in the back of his thigh. Maybe the people at the lab can give him painkillers or something. It's interesting to see my first real case, though, and helps bring Jean's numbers and statistics to life.

On Thursday we go to the government office to pick up that essential permit, but it turns out not to be ready. The director has not got around to signing it yet. We must come back tomorrow. But on Friday it is *still* not ready, and my flight to the north is first thing Monday morning. Fortunately, Saturday mornings are working days, so we hope for the best.

I am especially excited to be going to Lac Télé because the habitat is flooded forest, something I've never seen before. Lac Télé, the lake that gives the wildlife reserve its name, is famous as the home of Mokele-Mbembe, the African equivalent of the Loch Ness monster. I get used to being teased when I say that I am going to Lac Télé to collect reptiles: "Are you going to catch Mokele-Mbembe?"

"If I do I'm going to need an awful lot of formalin."

Buying chemicals is another thing that has to be done in Brazzaville, since I wouldn't have been allowed to carry them on the plane from Toronto. My friends at the Public Health Lab find someone who will sell me chloroform and 38 percent formalin at what seem to me exorbitant prices—20,000cfa for a liter of chloroform, and 30,000cfa per liter for the formalin, which I buy 2 liters of. The bottles are worryingly dusty-looking, with the labels peeling off, but apparently this salesman has a monopoly on the market. The other chemical I need is 90 percent ethanol (alcohol), but the Public Health Lab stocks that and can give it to me for free.

Saturday morning is our last chance to get the permit. Jean and I arrive at the office only to be told that all my paperwork is at another office in a building across town, so we get in a taxi and go there. The place appears to be deserted, so we have no choice but to go back to the office we came from. Once again the officials send us to the office across town. This time, by walking all around the building and banging on all the doors and shutters, we rouse a listless young woman, who looks at us without interest and seems not to have the energy to say hello. We ask her if the director is in, and as though with great effort, she makes a faint gesture with her head in the direction of a door which presumably leads to an inner office. Sure enough, in the inner office we have finally found the elusive director. "I can't sign this!" he says indignantly when we explain the reason for our visit. I can see the photocopies of all my other permits in the folder open in front of him. "This is not how one submits a request for a permit," he pushes the photocopies aside. "Permit requests are always submitted to me on a pink form, like these"; he opens a three-ring binder full of thin pink pages. I decide to try abject apology as a strategy.

"Oh dear!" I say, as though I had made some unforgivable mistake, "I'm terribly sorry. I had no idea that a special form was required.

When we made the permit request to the head office staff last Tuesday, they photocopied all my documents and said that the permit would be ready in 2 days. Unfortunately they never mentioned the pink form. If only I'd known! I hate to make your work more difficult by not presenting my request in the correct format. What can I do at this stage to set things right?" But he goes on and on about the format of the pink form to the point of absurdity. I try a different tack. "Look, I'm really sorry for the misunderstanding, but basically you and I want the same thing. We're both conservation biologists working to protect the animals of the Lac Télé Reserve. Surely it would be a better use of your valuable time to concentrate on preventing poachers from taking dwarf crocodiles out of the reserve illegally rather than preventing a conservation biologist from collecting some amphibians and reptiles legally."

The West African dwarf crocodile *(Osteolaemus tetraspis)* is a species terribly threatened by the bushmeat trade; the animals are killed in the forests of the north and then sold for their meat in the big cities. Although they are not the only species endangered for this reason, crocodiles are especially popular since, like other reptiles, they take a long time to die. This means they can be piled into a boat and carried down the Congo River to Brazzaville alive, which eliminates the need for refrigeration to prevent the meat from going bad in transit. Dwarf crocodiles are such tame and gentle creatures that they are easy prey for poachers. A common way of catching them is to set traps around the edges of forest ponds. A piece of rotting fish with a big size #8 hook concealed inside it is tied to a stake in the ground. The crocodile swallows the hook with the fish and then waits, tethered to the stake by the hook in its gullet, for the poachers to come and pick it up.

"But taking the dwarf crocodiles is prohibited!" the director objects.

"But it still goes on. The markets of Brazzaville and Pointe-Noire are full of them." I have the feeling this conversation is veering in a direction which is not going to help get me my permit. Jean is kicking me under the table. "It must be a terribly difficult problem for you to deal with."

"We do what we can, but the government only gives us a staff of 500 people, and 400 of those are administrators in Brazzaville, so that leaves only 100 ecoguards in the north. What can one ecoguard do against a group of poachers?" I let Jean take over. The kicking under the table is becoming quite painful, and in about 45 minutes he gets the man to promise to have the permit ready Monday morning. There will not be time for me to pick it up before my flight, but Jean can pick it up after I leave, scan it and e-mail it to Lac Télé, so that I will be able to start work right away.

The chaos of the Brazzaville airport is always an ordeal, but my departure for Impfondo, the next day, is absolutely the airport experience from hell. Jean is to pick me up at 7:00 a.m., and I know that for once he will be on time because Célestin, the Public Health Lab's chauffeur, is driving us to the airport, and I know Célestin will pick up Jean on time. At the airport, Célestin stays in the car to protect it, leaving me and Jean to deal with my cumbersome luggage. Jean flags down a porter, a young boy with a luggage cart, and they get my stuff piled onto the cart. But inside the airport the crowd is so dense that the ends of my box and my duffel bag, sticking out from the sides of the cart, are getting caught by peoples' legs and the porter has trouble getting our cart into the line of carts of baggage waiting to go through a door into the next stage. The line starts to move ahead, but our porter has disappeared. "But where did the little guy go?" demands Jean indignantly as the people behind us start to get restive. The little guy reappears just in time to push our cart farther ahead, into the doorway. But then when we should be moving forward into the next room he's gone again. One of the airport guards tells Jean to get the cart out of the way because it's preventing other people from getting by. "Who am I preventing from getting by?" Jean is shouting now. The porter reappears. He is trying to do two jobs at once to make more money. "Disappear like that one more time and you're fired!" yells Jean. Finally we are into the room and Jean has persuaded the baggage inspectors that there is nothing worth inspecting in my bags and box, but the crowd is pushing us apart. I'm carrying my toolbox in my hand as well as my pack on my back. Suddenly someone is telling me that I have to pay 20,000cfa for excess baggage. I hadn't expected this fee, and 20,000 happens to be exactly the amount in my billfold. I pay the fee, leaving my wallet empty. To get at the rest of my money I will have to rummage in my pack, for the big envelope that holds *all* my money—an impossibility since I am encumbered with the toolbox, in a crowd which is sweeping me along toward the x-ray scanner—and the x-ray scanner is the point that Jean can't go past. Jean is pushing his way toward me and shouting. I can't make out what he's saying but I think he wants me to pay the porter.

"How much?" I shout, but I can't hear his answer. "My money is all in my pack," I try to explain. "Would you mind paying him?" How much can it be, after all? But Jean either doesn't hear, or doesn't have the money on him to pay the kid. I find a handful of 100cfa coins in the pocket of my backpack, and try to hand them to Jean, but he shouts angrily, "Don't pay me, pay him!"

"How much?" I still can't hear what he's saying so I hand 500cfa to the porter, who looks at it disdainfully and hands it back. Not enough. So I hand him my whole handful of coins. Jean is yelling at me. I think he's saying it's too much, but at that point the crowd sweeps me into the x-ray scanner room and there's no going back.

Finally, I board the plane, escaping into quiet and comfort. The man who takes the seat beside me is Alain. We've exchanged names and addresses even before take-off. People always want to exchange addresses with no apparent intention of ever following up on it. It seems just to be good manners. And the Congolese think nothing of asking probing questions about one's age and marital status within moments of shaking hands for the first time, to the point that I have invented a fictional fiancé simply to avoid disapproval, incredulity, and unwanted advances.

I watch out the window as the brown and gray sprawl of Brazzaville gradually gives way to forest. From the air it looks remarkably like broccoli extending for miles and miles. We fly over uninterrupted forest for a good 45 minutes before starting our descent into Impfondo.

chapter 3

in
limbo

Impfondo is a dusty town centered on the asphalt road that passes through it. The sun beats down on a network of small, packed-dirt streets that spread out on either side. Its most notable feature is a sizable market, a warren of narrow, muddy alleyways between stalls selling everything from soap to spaghetti to dried caterpillars (a popular snack) to plastic sandals. My wealthy friends in Pointe Noire call these 1,500cfa sandals *souliers à jeter* (shoes to throw away). Here they are the shoes worn by everyone—everyone who has shoes that is.

Hugo Rainey, the director of WCS Lac Télé, is supposed to meet me at the airport. I quickly pick out the only other white person in the crowded terminal. He is about my age, tall, thin, and English, to judge by his accent when he greets me. He is accompanied by half a dozen men who work at the field station. I briefly describe my luggage, and they all push through the crowd to wait for it to be unloaded. Eventually we are outside the airport and the men pause from lifting my boxes into the back of the truck to politely introduce themselves and shake hands.

We stop for lunch at a restaurant on the outskirts of Impfondo—tables and chairs with a canopy above to provide shade. A girl perhaps 8 years old comes out. We are the only patrons. "What do you have?" asks Hugo.

"Poisson" (fish), she murmurs. We order the fish, and add a round of liter bottles of Ngok. The poisson, when it comes, is exactly as I expected: a bowl of fish broth with a bony chunk sitting in it, flesh and skin hanging from it for me to pick apart. It comes with the choice of bread (slices of baguette) or lumps of manioc, to soak up the broth, and I have no difficulty deciding on the former.

The men are tucking in, and I am pushing the food around on my plate without eating much of it, when a man pops his head into the restaurant and says something in a mixture of French and Lingala that I don't catch. The men explain excitedly. The man has a boa and wonders if we are interested. Am I ever! And he came in not even knowing there was a herpetologist in the group. What luck! I run after the man to his house, not far away. *Boa* is the name people here use for *Python sebae*, the African rock python. There are no true boas in Africa, but for some reason the name sticks. Generally, pythons are found in the Old World and lay eggs, while boas inhabit the New World and give birth to live young. (I have worked in parts of Central America where the locals have the confused notion that boa constrictors give birth to vipers!) But there are real boas in Madagascar, an exception.

In the Congo, the "boa" is the one species of snake that most people can recognize, and know is not venomous. The other 100 or so species native to the country are all thought to be indistinguishable and all believed to be venomous. The reason they recognize the "boa" is that they eat it. That is why I made a point on my collecting permit application of specifically saying I would not collect *Python sebae*. It is the only species of snake in the country with any legal protection, though it is one of the commonest, I find.

When we arrive at the man's house, the python turns out to be a juvenile caught in a fish trap, an elongated basket. The snake is cowering at the far end. The man starts to open the other end. It is tied tightly shut with vines, and he has some difficulty getting it undone. Clearly this animal has not been fed or watered in some time. I take over the job of opening the basket. With the basket open, I peer in just to make sure it really is just a python I'm dealing with, and then reach in and haul it out. It is a very tame specimen and makes no effort to bite.

There are a number of children hovering around at a cautious distance. Crouched on my knees, holding the snake, I try to persuade them to come and touch it, to be amazed that it is smooth and dry and not slimy like a fish. But the children are frightened. Finally, a little girl about 2 years old, too young to be afraid, approaches, and touches the snake. Seeing the little girl touching the snake shames all the older boys into proving that they are not scared. Soon the python and I are surrounded by a crowd of curious children, touching a snake for the first time in their lives. The older boys pinch the snake and then run away, so that I have to protest in Lingala, "Malembe!" (Gently!)

WCS makes a couple of trips a week to Impfondo, always with several errands to run. Next on the to-do list today is buying supplies at the market. Hugo says that I should plan for spending 3 weeks in the field in "terra firma," the nearest dry land to Lac Télé during the wet season, and 4 hours by boat from the field station. Since I will be leaving as soon as possible, I will buy provisions today. One of the WCS men specializes in the logistics of shopping at the market. I tell him I need enough provisions for two people (me and a guide) for 3 weeks. He scribbles calculations of numbers of cans of tomato paste, sardines, etc. needed and adds up their prices, and then disappears into the crowd. He knows the market well, and the merchants won't try to charge him *mondele* (white person) prices as they would me. Fearful of getting lost if I venture into the maze-like market, I stick close to the truck, taking it all in. I watch a man on a bicycle weaving along the main road, right hand on the handle bar, left hand holding a long fish by its mouth. Inevitably, the swinging fish eventually catches between the spokes of the front wheel and topples him over into the dust.

I start to imagine what this expedition will be like, and how I will get along with this guide for whom I am buying food and with whom I will be living and working so closely throughout my time in the field. I ask Hugo if guides are necessarily men, or whether I could hire a woman for a guide. Hugo says doubtfully that he has never heard of a female guide, and that although there's no good reason why a woman couldn't be a guide, it just doesn't seem to happen. The people here just don't socialize little girls to work in the forest as they do boys.

The man doing the shopping returns with my boxes of provisions and a handful of receipts, which he carefully counts out. Hugo adds a bag of chocolate lollipops to my stash, saying that they are good to have in the field. These lollipops turn out to be known to the local children as *bon-bons sifflets* (whistle candies) because when the candy has been sucked away the remaining stick works as a fairly loud whistle, guaranteed to drive parents to the brink of insanity. The expedition is finally coming together. Seeing all those cans of sardines really drives it home. I'm so excited!

There is a good asphalt road extending 80 kilometers from Impfondo west to Epena, where the WCS base is located, and north from Impfondo, following the Oubangui River, to the unremarkable village of Dongou. The road, I am told, was built by Brazilians in the 1980s. But why? How strange to build this excellent scrap of road in the middle of nowhere, when there isn't even a proper road joining Brazzaville and Pointe Noire. The WCS base is in the town of Epena, and surrounded by the Lac Télé Reserve, so that a large part of the road actually passes through the reserve. Scattered all along the edge of the road, from Impfondo all the way to Epena are villages. Every village we pass gives off a horrible smell. What can it be? Not latrines. Not garbage. Not something rotting. I can't place it. Some are Pygmy villages, most Bantu, apparently never a mixture. The WCS men are all Bantu and as we look out of the back of the truck at the villages and people we pass they point, as though drawing my attention to some rare and interesting animal. "Look," they say, "those are Pygmies."

I put my question about the possibility of a female guide to the men in the back of the truck. Absolutely not, they say. Women can't be guides. Women are naturally less courageous than men. Of course, this makes me furious. The issue keeps us arguing for the rest of the trip.

I soon learn that the back of the truck is the place to be. The cab has two bucket seats, which are considered suitable seating for three people. While the cab is the seat of honor, the back is not only more comfortable, but more fun—lively conversation in the local mix of French and Lingala, which I try my best to follow, and constant action. The only downside is that everyone we pass, driving through the villages, peers into the back of the truck and is intrigued by the novelty of a mondele they don't recognize, so I have to wave back to them, like the queen in a parade, all the way to Epena. A hefty woman wrapped in a dress of bright African cotton, and carrying an infant, climbs aboard at one village. She is the wife of one of the men in the back. We shake hands and

I open the bag of bon-bons sifflets to give one to the child. Two villages later she gets off, only to be replaced by two goats, tied around the ankles and bleating piteously—and so the show continues until we finally reach Epena.

The WCS compound is quite a big place. It has one house, which Hugo lives in, and many other buildings used for office space, storage, and so on. I had expected that there would be other researchers here but apparently I'm the only one at the moment. Hugo shows me where I will be staying for a couple of days while I get myself organized to head off into the reserve: a small clean room with a bed in a sort of annex to his house.

There is a routine to life at WCS, which I don't expect to be here long enough to get used to. Hugo's day is spent working in his office while his dog, Treacle, lies loyally across the doorway. The best part of Treacle's day is dusk, after the staff has gone home, when he and Hugo go for a walk together. Hugo is an ornithologist, and his idea of an enjoyable walk is a stroll before dark, along the asphalt road, with binoculars. He recognizes all the birds, and delights in sometimes seeing a species outside of its known range. But I soon discover that the best end-of-the-day walk for me is just after the end of Hugo's walk, in the first hour of darkness, when I wade in the marsh behind the compound. One species I can always count on seeing is a little brown treefrog that I can find easily just by following the sound of its call: "Tok-tok, tok-tok." I am not allowed to collect, but there is nothing to stop me trying out my new MP3 recorder on the tok-tok frog. The recorder works extremely well and I get an excellent recording of the call. It will be very useful if I can get recordings of frog calls to go with the specimens I collect, because some species can be identified for sure only by their call. It is hard to resist grabbing a few of the frogs off the reeds, but I comfort myself that it will be just as easy to do in a day or two when my permit comes.

We are out of cell phone range here, and e-mail works by satellite phone, so expensive that it has to be strictly rationed. Hugo's account gets checked once a day, and messages composed off-line are sent at the same time, so you can't respond immediately to a message. Monday, when we return from Impfondo, I am surprised and frustrated that the scan of my permit has not been sent by Jean. The following day there is still no message from Jean. Or the day after that. I have his phone number, but can't make a call from here. More days pass as I wait for the next WCS trip to Impfondo to try to reach Jean by phone. When I finally get through, Jean is delighted to hear from me. He tells me he misses me. He has been to the permit office every day this week and every day the officials give him some excuse for the permit's not being ready. He is going to see if Dr. Parra can put some pressure on them. The e-mail has been down all week at the Public Health Lab, which is why he hasn't been able to tell me what's going on. I tell him not to give up, *bon courage,* we'll get that permit.

So in Brazzaville Jean does battle with the permit office every day, while in Epena I fall into an empty routine centered on checking the e-mail, which might bring my permit. Epena is in savannah, not forest, so there is no shelter from the sun. Most of the day is so hot that being outside is almost intolerable, and I spend my time sitting in the shade on the steps to the house. The only creature at WCS doing less work than me is Treacle.

More days pass and still the permit doesn't come. As the days go by, Hugo is unperturbed. It'll come eventually, he assures me during a dog walk; it's just a matter of waiting a few more days. I think constantly of the part in Joseph Conrad's classic, *Heart of Darkness,* when the expedition up the Congo River is stalled for 3 months waiting for rivets to repair the boat. But those travelers didn't have an unchangeable return flight to Toronto looming ever closer on their horizon. All I need is a stupid signature!

Hugo lets me send an e-mail to Claude. "Come now, let's not have any despair!" Claude writes back, *"Courage!"* I feel a little bit better. I must pull myself together and not give up.

On several occasions a villager comes to me, having heard that I know a lot about snakes, to ask me what he should do if he gets bitten by one. In every village, it seems, there's somebody who has a concoction that he claims cures snakebite. The villagers have heard of antivenom, and, like the old man at the Public Health Lab in Brazzaville, view it as the mondele snakebite concoction—the same kind of thing as the village concoction, but better. "Madame," the villagers say, "what should I do if I am bitten by a snake?" I am not sure what to tell them. I don't for a moment believe that the traditional medicine practiced in the villages offers anything more than a potentially dangerous false sense of security. But thinking of Jean's statistics, which showed equal rates of mortality for victims who went to the hospital and for those who chose instead to take traditional medicine in the village, I am not inclined to push them to go to the hospital, because that would cost them a lot of money, and the hospital would not be equipped to treat snakebites.

My not very helpful compromise is to explain the failings of both options, but to add that if I were to be bitten by a snake I would opt for the hospital. I can teach them the correct first aid for snakebite, but, maddeningly, the last line in the instructions is always, "Transport the victim to the hospital." In the past, the recommended first-aid treatment for snakebite was a tourniquet. If the bite was to the hand, for example, you were to tie a tight cord around the upper arm, completely cutting off circulation. The failing of this approach is that it was tremendously painful, and the whole arm would die if it was cut off from its supply of blood for too long. The first-aid treatment now recommended is the pressure-bandage technique. The pressure-bandage technique for snakebite first aid was developed relatively recently in Australia. The principle it works by is that a snakebite is highly unlikely to inject venom directly into a blood vessel. The venom usually ends up in, say, muscle tissue, and is transported around the body mainly by the lymphatic system. The lymphatic system is a circulatory system without vessels, by which fluids, infection, and snake venom slowly ooze through the body. So by applying a pressure bandage you confine the venom to the bitten limb. Only when the victim is at the hospital with antivenom at hand, and the symptoms of envenomation are ready to be treated, is the pressure bandage removed, and the venom released into the rest of the body. Though I teach the villagers the pressure-bandage technique, I emphasize, "It is not a cure. It just slows down the action of the venom." What help is that to somebody bitten by a snake in northern Congo?

Of course there are complications and exceptions. For bites by snakes such as vipers, in which the venom does a lot of localized tissue damage (such as internal bleeding in the area surrounding the bite wound), applying a pressure bandage can actually worsen the tissue damage at the site of the bite by concentrating the venom there. But for anyone encountering a serious viper bite far from medical help, for example, it may be necessary to make a judgment call. Sacrifice a limb to save a life.

But the villagers seeking my advice don't want to hear all this. They want me to give them a pill or potion that they will have confidence in because it comes from a specialist on snakes. Surely a snake expert should, at the very least, be able to provide a snakebite cure.

More precious days are wasted. Eager for any way to pass the time, I submit to what I've come to think of as the *mbote* gauntlet—good manners dictate that I must greet every person I pass in the village of Epena, and I find it stressful because there are a lot of people and it's easy to cause offense by missing someone—and so I walk under the midday sun to the pharmacy in the Catholic Mission to buy a course of quinine to treat malaria (this is Hugo's suggestion: "Everyone here gets malaria eventually"). I am also glad of an excuse to go to the Catholic Mission because I have heard that the Père there makes *pierre noire* (black stone). All sorts of people offer potions and mixtures that they guarantee will cure any snakebite, but the one treatment universally believed in is pierre noire. This Père must be a very unusual Catholic priest, I reflect, and even if I'm not allowed to study the snakes themselves, nobody can object to my learning a bit of snake-related cultural anthropology.

There is a customer ahead of me at the Catholic Mission's pharmacy, so I wait on the front steps talking with Père Jude's cook. She tells me that although many villages have people who offer a snakebite cure, the one people have most confidence in is made by a man in the village of Boha, inside the reserve. Maybe I should seek out this man once I get into the reserve. I buy my course of quinine for 850cfa, and ask whether the Père is in. "Just round the back," I'm told. I go around behind the building and ask a boy in the yard full of wandering chickens and pigs where to find the Père. He leads me to an outbuilding, from which emerges a smiling, portly man, not over 40 by my estimate, wearing a loose, vibrantly colored tie-dyed shirt.

"I'm Katherine," I explain. "I'm a researcher staying at WCS. I study snakes, and I heard that you make pierre noire. I'm very interested and was hoping we could talk about it."

"Pierre noire, oh yes," he chuckles. "Pierre noire, of course, come on into the house." I'm not sure what I had expected, but Père Jude is not it. It's not only that he seems too young and modern and well educated to believe in a snakebite cure I associate with gullible villagers. What surprises me the most is his total openness and willingness to answer my questions. There is none of the secrecy about ingredients and methods that I expect of people who make money by selling useless snakebite cures. He happily sits me down in his living room and takes out a few pieces of pierre noire to show me. He laughs delightedly when I start scribbling in the back of my journal.

The first big surprise is that pierre noire is apparently not a stone at all. The piece in my hand looks like a slightly porous chunk of graphite. Père Jude has me touch it with my tongue to feel the suction it exerts. I let go with my hand and it stays attached to my tongue. When I put my hand back to remove it, it comes off easily, to my considerable relief. Père Jude explains in detail how it is made from a chunk of bone from the thigh of a cow. This chunk is boiled in water, with several water changes over several days, until all the oil has been removed from it. Then it is dried and becomes one big chunk of pierre noire. The difficulty lies in making pieces of the right size and shape for treating bites, because the substance is extremely hard to cut, but shatters easily.

To treat a snakebite, you slash open the site of the bite wound with a razor, and apply the piece of pierre noire, which adheres by suction. The pierre noire is left on the bite wound until it falls off naturally, in hours or days. Falling off indicates that all the venom has been sucked out. I don't for a moment believe this rubbish, and wonder briefly if Père Jude is having me on. But in spite of all his laughter he is apparently completely serious and hasn't the slightest doubt about the effectiveness of his cure. He tells me that he sells it to pharmacies in Brazzaville and other places, and that a piece sells for about 500cfa. I badly want a piece to keep. Would he sell me one? Père Jude laughs at the suggestion and picks out a piece of pierre noire that would be an inconvenient shape for use on a bite wound, and gives it to me. I thank him effusively. He laughs and tells me to come back whenever I like and that he quite often visits WCS and hopes to see me there.

Walking the mbote gauntlet back to WCS, the sun no longer quite so hot, I reflect that the idea of suction applied locally to a bite wound is intuitively appealing. But experimental evidence shows that it doesn't work. Venom, once injected, can't be sucked out. Suction applied may draw out some blood and plasma, and people may mistake plasma for venom, since they are both fairly viscous yellow liquids. As for slashing open a bite wound, that must *absolutely* not be done—it just adds a serious wound open to infection to the primary problem of the snakebite. The idea of treating snakebites with suction applied to the bite wound is not restricted to proponents of pierre noire. Pierre noire is really no different in concept from the little suction device included in U.S. Army snakebite kits until very recently. Even in the herpetological community some people still swear by a device commercially available, a sort of syringe with an open end big enough to cover a bite wound. Absorbed in thought, I overshoot WCS and get lost. I ask directions of an old man who is dragging a large palm frond along the road. What is he going to do with it, I ask? Make a broom, he tells me, and points me in the right direction.

The days are turning into weeks, and still my permit has not come. It is time to think of other options. In theory I could set up somewhere outside the borders of the reserve, but in similar habitat. The permits I already have would allow me to do that. People make it sound so simple. I would have no idea how to go about just "setting up" in the middle of nowhere. I had been counting all along on using WCS's infrastructure so that all I had to do was catch snakes. So I just hope even more desperately that the permit comes soon. Hugo has been incredibly patient and tolerant, letting me stay here for much longer than either of us ever imagined, but there must be a limit.

After 3 weeks, I really cannot afford to lose more time, and gradually resign myself to the idea of pitching camp outside the reserve, though I feel very uneasy about it. I have so little understanding of the details involved, and am unable to imagine what the set-up would be like. Nonetheless, I go along on the next expedition to Impfondo with camping outside the reserve in mind. I venture into the chaos of the market accompanied by the man who bought my provisions the day I arrived in Impfondo, in search, first of all, of a tarpaulin. We scour the market before finally finding just one for sale. My companion is holding the folded tarpaulin while bargaining over the price with the salesman, when a teenaged boy runs into the shop, and after a brief tug-of-war grabs the tarpaulin from them and runs away with it. It really does seem to be the only tarpaulin in the market, and we end up having to track down the boy, and buy it from him for far too much money. Shopping for mosquito nets and pots and pans is much less dramatic. It takes another trip to the market, on the next expedition, to find me a second tarpaulin.

I also take the opportunity to do something I've been longing to do at the market: get a good dress for Brazzaville—a bright cotton dress like the ones the urban Congolese women wear. In one shop I buy brightly patterned blue and yellow fabric. Then I take the fabric to a shack in which three old men are hard at work using foot-pedal sewing machines. I explain to them that I want a skirt and top. The skirt is to be flatteringly close fitting, but with a slit up the side so I can walk easily. The top must be sleeveless, with a square neckline, and with darts around the chest to give it some shape, and I would like a matching headscarf. When they tell me it will cost 8,000cfa to make the outfit, I think I must somehow have misunderstood since the amount seems so small for such skilled work. And they can even have it ready in 2 hours so that I can take it back with me today. They take a dozen or so careful measurements of me with a tape measure, and send me off to let them get on with it. When I go back to try the clothes on, a small crowd has assembled to watch me do it. They hand me the dress and escort me behind a curtain into a pitch-dark storage room. I trip over a sack of manioc flour, and call out to ask if there's a light switch. Everyone laughs at such a silly question. The dress is a perfect fit, beautifully tailored, and I am very pleased with it.

As usual, I sit in the back of the truck on the return journey. In the middle of a long stretch of road through the forest, I see two old women standing at the side of the road holding up enormous, elongate fishes. Somebody's wife who had joined us at the last village we passed wants to buy them, so we all shout, bang on the window at the back of the cab, and hang out of the truck sideways so as to be visible in the rear-view mirror. Eventually the driver notices and stops. The women approach carrying the three fishes. I immediately recognize them as African lungfishes, creatures I have read about but never seen before. The woman in the truck starts bargaining over the price. The driver, who can't bear to be left out of a good bargaining session, leans out the window of the cab, shouting "1,500 *maximum!* Who else do they think is going to buy them here in the middle of the forest?" I spend the rest of the trip watching fascinated as the lungfishes pull themselves around on the floor of the truck with their long, attenuated pectoral fins.

Back at WCS I immediately put the dress on to try it out. I am delighted with it, but it is 6:00 p.m. and the staff has all gone home, so there's nobody to show it off to except Hugo. He will have to do.

"That's actually, er, quite nice," he says, looking slightly surprised.

It has now been decided for sure that I will be setting up camp independently, outside the reserve. I have been gathering together all the equipment and supplies that I anticipate needing. Hugo is away on a trip when it all comes together, but Cepet, his second-in-command, is there to help.

Emmanuel is the expert to be consulted on camping outside the reserve. An elderly man, he is said to have been an exceptional guide in his youth, and to know the forest better than anyone. Unfortunately he doesn't speak French, so all the arrangements have to be made with somebody acting as a Lingala interpreter. My needs are explained to him. Emmanuel knows a suitable place near the village of Ganganya Brousse, where his daughter lives.

So on the way back from Impfondo we stop at Ganganya Brousse, and Emmanuel introduces us all to the Chief. Cepet and Emmanuel have a conversation with him in some combination of French and Lingala that I can't follow. I try to introduce myself to the villagers who have gathered around, but nobody seems to speak much French. Several half-naked children have gathered around to stare at me. One of them has a nasty-looking scab across her forehead. I wave and smile, "Mbote," but they just continue to stare.

The negotiations are finished. I will pay the Chief a fee of 15,000cfa to camp and collect near his village. I will hire a guide and cook from the village. I have stipulated that I want a campsite in the forest close enough to the village for the guide and cook to go home at night, but far enough from the village for some privacy, and near a source of water where the cook can fill buckets for washing and drinking. At a minimum I want a bucket of water to wash in every day. And I want to get away from that African village smell which I can never tolerate. What is it, anyway?

On the drive back to Epena, the driver is uncharacteristically quiet. Finally he breaks the silence to give his opinion that I would be better off living in the village for "security." He worries that if I am alone in the forest people may come and "do things" to me. "Do what?" I ask, but he just stares grimly at the road ahead. Oh well, I will sleep with my machete beside me if I have to. When we arrive at Epena, it feels like coming home. The French suddenly seems easier to understand, the children look healthier. The WCS compound is full of friendly, familiar faces. I realize that I am going to miss these people.

It is Friday and there is a lot to get organized if I am going to be dropped off at Ganganya Brousse tomorrow morning. Since Emmanuel doesn't speak French, the go-between is Ruffain, the boy who organizes the stores. I am all set with sketches to explain drift fences and pitfall traps to Emmanuel, but Emmanuel is hardly through the door when he notices that the fishnets are still in their plastic packages. Apparently they have to be prepared in some way that would be too time-consuming for us to do in the few days he has with me setting things up. So there is a minor panic as Emmanuel searches the village for someone willing to string the fishnets by 3:00 p.m. Fortunately he finds someone. In his absence I explain pitfall traps to Ruffain, but discover after 20 minutes of explanation that he is visualizing some kind of pit full of sharpened stakes, of a size suitable for capturing an elephant. Finally we get Emmanuel sitting down to join the discussion. He is determined that for the amount of work I need done I must have a cook as well as a guide. Doubtful that I'll get anywhere with an old guy like Emmanuel, especially with the language barrier, I return to my longstanding question: Could I get a guide who is a woman? Everybody has so far said no very firmly, and Emmanuel reacts to the question with such a show of disbelief that he clearly assumes there must be some flaw in Ruffain's Lingala translation. I sigh. Oh well, I tried. Now it's settled I must have both a cook and a guide.

Eventually Emmanuel decides that the cook must be paid 2,000cfa a day, and the guide also 2,000cfa a day. I start scrawling calculations in my notebook, but then it turns out that this does not include a *prime* (extra) of 1,000cfa every day for the guide if he is doing a satisfactory job. So essentially the guide gets 3,000cfa a day. It is explained to me that this incentive is necessary because I might choose to hire someone else if the guide is not good. But it apparently never crosses anyone's mind that the cook's work is important enough to be considered satisfactory or not.

I know that work stops here at 3:00 p.m. and I am rushing to get everything done by then. Just before 3:00 a toothless old man appears at the door of the house with an armload of unraveled fishnet. He has strung all three nets, all 150 meters of them, and I owe him 1,000cfa for each, which I give him. Next Ruffain, a step ahead of me, arrives at the door of the house with a wheelbarrow carrying the box containing all my provisions bought that first day in Impfondo, and hands over the keys to the two padlocks on the box.

By 3:15 the compound is deserted. I am left to contemplate my fate. I open a warm 1-liter bottle of Ngok. Without warning a wind picks up, and within minutes it is pouring rain. Suddenly, termites—great awkward, flapping, flying things—appear out of nowhere. First there are 6 and I swat them. They are not all that hard to catch. But soon there are more than 20 lurching around the room on big, filmy wings. I keep a hand firmly over the open beer bottle. Anyone who tries to crash land in that has had it, but otherwise I try without much success to ignore them. I hear a faint mew at the door—poor Tache, Hugo's cat, left out in the rain. I let her in and she immediately sets to work catching the termites. I see a little gecko on the wall, and instinctively get up to catch it. But it has a big termite in its mouth—valiant little soul—and I haven't the heart to disturb it. Although I know I have a busy day ahead of me, and I remind myself that this is the last mattress I will sleep on for some time, I lie awake until almost 4:00 a.m.

chapter 4

the
flooded
forest

On Saturday morning the villagers are ready for me at Ganganya
Brousse. On a second visit the place doesn't seem quite as squalid as I
remembered it. Not quite. I greet everyone with "Mbote," and a handshake, as I pass through the village. Some people have their hands wet
or dirty from whatever work they are in the middle of. Rather than be so
rude as not to shake hands, these people, as is the custom, politely extend the right arm, hand hanging down, offering the wrist to shake. I
hardly realize it when the person I am being reintroduced to is the
Chief, with whom we made arrangements on Thursday. Cepet, Ruffain,
and Emmanuel step aside out of earshot to discuss the wages of the
guide and cook with the Chief. I really hope this will work out. I told

Cepet what I could pay and I can't deal with anything more. All my calculations depend on exactly the rates we settled on yesterday if I am to have enough money for at least a month here. I'm also worrying about having the right denomination of bills to pay people. Small-denomination bills are very hard to come by, so it will be very inconvenient if the Chief bargains from 2,000cfa up to 2,200cfa, say, even though the difference is minimal. But bargaining is so culturally entrenched here that I fear the worst.

I am pleasantly surprised, however. The wages I offered are accepted, and without haggling for more, as I suspected he might, the Chief sticks to the agreed fee of 15,000cfa to camp on land he considers his. He even encourages me to pay just an initial instalment of 5,000cfa for now. Ruffain gets him to write me a receipt.

The next thing that happens is the most important, though I don't realize it at the time. "This is your cook," the Chief announces. A wizened little old woman with bright mischievous eyes grins at me. She looks as if she is going to be either a lot of trouble or a lot of fun. I introduce myself: "Katherine." She is "Florence."

"She speaks excellent French," the Chief assures me. "So does your guide. This is him over here." I look where he is pointing and just see a group of boys, but then one of them steps forward slightly, solemn and shy. "His name is Etienne." Can he possibly be as old as 16? "He will take good care of you in the forest." One last thing remains to be settled, but apparently the Chief has decided this along with everything else.

"I need a place that is in the forest . . ." I start explaining my requirements, but nobody is really listening to me.

"Yes, yes, there's a place juste à coté" (just over there), he says, waving his hand in the general direction of the other side of the road. I hope the site won't be too close to the village.

As many people as possible are piling into the truck and more are following on foot. We stop at the edge of the road, at no landmark that I can see, and my boxes and bits and pieces are unloaded. Ruffain, Cepet, and the rest from WCS are ready to leave. They each shake my hand and wish me luck. They seem to think I will need it. I bite my lip. I will miss their friendly, familiar faces. What have I gotten myself into?

Picking out a trail so faint that I'm inclined to doubt its existence, a procession is setting off into the forest. I see a single man carrying on his head a box that two of the men at WCS had trouble lifting into the truck. What I am carrying is not heavy, but is extremely awkward. Two buckets with dishes in them that keep tipping out, and two armloads of snake hooks, snake tongs, and a shovel, which all slide in different directions. I am lagging behind. Up ahead of me Florence yells back from a slightly raised bit of ground, "Madame Katherine, you need to run across this part as quickly as possible. There are ants." I like her already. People who praise my bravery with snakes don't know what a coward I am when it comes to ants.

I've never been fond of ants and the ones in central Africa win the prize as the worst I've ever seen. You're walking through the forest and gradually become aware of a rattling sound coming from nearby. A rattlesnake? Not on this continent. Look down and the forest floor as far as you can see is a moving carpet of large ants. Just as you begin to notice them on the ground you start to feel fierce biting in the depths of your underpants. There is only one thing to do: Run. Run and run until you have outrun the moving carpet and then strip naked (nobody will mind under the circumstances) and do your best to remove the ones that have got their pincers into you. Often if you pull on an ant the head and pincers will stay attached and clenched even after the body is pulled off.

We walk and walk and I start to think we will never get where we are going. To think that I was worried about being too close to the village. "Juste à coté" indeed! The shovel slides out of my hands for the fourth time, and when I turn to retrieve it it has already been picked up by the young man coming up close behind me. He smiles, and as we make our way, proceeds to pick up all the things that I drop. The march goes on. I am bumped and scraped, wet and muddy from puddles, scratched by vegetation, and bruised by the several logs I've fallen over. I don't know how long we've been walking. My arms are numb, fingers clamped white around the handles of the buckets, and my mind has drifted into such a self-protecting blank that I don't immediately notice that we've arrived.

The place is a clearing in the forest, an abandoned Pygmy camp. Four little domed payottes, huts made of thick, bent lianas are scattered around a space cleared of trees. They have fallen into disrepair but would once have been thickly covered with fresh leaves to waterproof them. Inside are the remains of platforms which must have served as beds, made from cut branches. One of the payottes clearly served as the kitchen because I see the inevitable smoked-fish rack.

The sight of the smoked-fish rack brings back a vivid memory of a taste that almost makes me gag just thinking about it. My first experience of smoked fish was near the beginning of my first Congo expedition, when I was camped in the forest with two Pygmies doubling as guides and cooks. I was new to the country, still unused to and uncomfortable with giving orders to servants. So when Bakembe and Dada asked me what I wanted them to cook for dinner, I said, "Oh, whatever you like. You choose." Their choice was fou-fou with smoked fish. The smoked fish start out as fish caught from the river, killed, and spread out on a rack above the fire, exactly like the rack I am looking at. The campfire is always burning, and the fish are above it. If you move camp, you just carry the fish with you and set up the rack over the new campfire. By this method, the fish get cooked in a manner of speaking (they shrivel up and turn black), but in the process of moving them, and perhaps depending on the size of the fish or its distance from the fire, flies lay eggs in the flesh, which grow into maggots, and some bits rot. But since the whole fish, cut into pieces from head to tail, is served after dark in a sauce composed largely of oil, you don't notice a rotting bit until you have a big mouthful. After that first experience with smoked fish I learned to give orders—orders for sardines and rice, or for corned beef and spaghetti.

I feel a jab of pain in my shoulder and turn to find the largest fly I have ever seen in my life, a tsetse fly, the vector of African sleeping sickness. I swat at it, and it drops satisfyingly to the ground. I hope there aren't going to be many more of them. The men have all gone back to the road to collect a second load, and I feel only slightly guilty leaving them to it and staying here with Florence. Florence has made a broom out of a bundle of sticks and is vigorously sweeping leaves and twigs from the campsite. She throws out the collapsing Pygmy furniture disdainfully. "So where is the water for filling buckets?" I ask her.

"Juste a coté," and she leads me some distance, both of us fighting our way through dense and prickly vegetation to a shallow, stagnant pond. She crouches down and fills a plastic mug with the murky water, which she proceeds to drink thirstily.

"You can drink it? Just like that?"

"Oh yes, our guts are used to it. Don't worry, I'll boil it for you."

"Well I envy you your guts." She hoots with laughter. I think we're going to get along.

The men soon arrive with the last load of equipment. The Chief has joined them. While he reclines on a log and I flutter around uselessly feeling I ought to be doing something, Etienne and Emmanuel are expertly hacking down branches with the machetes I bought, hammering pointed ends firmly into the ground, and lashing big branches to tree forks with vines. With the addition of the two tarpaulins an amazingly sturdy-looking edifice starts to take shape. One tarpaulin for the floor and walls, the other for the peaked roof. I notice that the tarpaulins have "United Nations Refugee Agency" printed on them, and wonder how they made their way to the Impfondo market. Florence has already got a fire going, and is unpacking the provisions box, looking at the contents appraisingly. Cans of tomato paste, sardines, cans of a dubious substance labeled "Pork luncheon meat" on one side of the can and something in Chinese on the other. Plastic bags of rice and an enormous supply of macaroni, coffee, sugar, Nido (powdered milk), and a few luxuries: chocolate bars, bon-bons sifflets, and, by me most coveted of all, Vache Qui Rit cheese.

"No salt?" Florence demands, in tones of disbelief. Shaking her head at such an extraordinary logistical oversight, she puts everything back in the box and sets off all the way back to the village. Some time later she returns with a little parcel wrapped in a leaf. Salt.

Meanwhile, the structure that we come to refer to as "the house" has taken shape. I didn't buy nearly enough rope, but it doesn't matter. The men are tying everything together with vines. I start dragging my equipment box—a plastic box of exactly the maximum size allowed by Air France, crammed with all my equipment—into what I suppose is the front of the house, and unpack the bottles of chemicals, setting up my laboratory. I warn everyone that the formalin and chloroform are deadly poisons, and the box is filled with dangerous things. They are all wide-eyed with fear and steer very clear of my "lab." Perfect. I am keeping all the money I have to last me for the rest of the expedition in an envelope in a box of other envelopes deeply buried among scientific supplies in the box.

Everything looks to me just about ready, but the men are still hacking branches into pieces. They are building something resembling a park bench outside the house, and another two in the payotte that has become the kitchen, entirely with branches lashed together with vines. One of the benches even has a back to it, to lean on. We call it the "sofa." Even Florence has borrowed a machete from someone and built a sizable table outside the kitchen using the same sticks and vines method.

All this is impressive, but I have to admit I'm looking forward to being left to myself in the camp. But that is not to be. "I can't leave you alone in the forest, Madame," says Etienne earnestly, and the matter is settled. I'm waiting at least for the crowd to leave, when the sky darkens and out of nowhere we are in the midst of a torrential tropical downpour. "Everyone into the house," I shout unnecessarily over the roar of the rain. At some point along the way I have started to relax, to give up any effort to control events and to adapt to whatever unfolds. These people are not the strangers I had feared. So much has happened today that it is hard to believe I have only known them since this morning. So here we all are, sitting together, waiting out the storm. "Does anyone here like whiskey?" I ask. I break out my precious bottle of J & B, a little luxury that I had planned to keep hidden and enjoy a nip from now and again when I was alone. Now I'd rather share it.

Waiting out the storm has turned into a party. The rain is beating down on the tarpaulin roof. The house is almost up to it but not quite. A small puddle appears in a corner. I find one of the kitchen rags and start to mop it up. Laurent, the man who walked behind me on the trail, takes over from me. The rain is coming down harder. Etienne is outside, soaked to the skin, digging an elaborate set of trenchworks with the shovel to divert the water around rather than into the house. Florence is outside too, and the fire, amazingly, is still going because she has *moved* it, log by log, to another payotte, which she has shored up with leaves to keep the rain out. Inside the house there are more and more puddles, and Laurent, by now completely drunk, is alternately refilling plastic mugs with J & B and trying to keep up with the puddles. But the rag is completely soaked and almost useless. Reluctantly, I relinquish my extra towel. As new puddles appear, boxes, equipment, and luggage get piled up in new ways in an effort to keep them dry. A log has been moved into the house for me and the Chief to sit on, and the Chief is getting through the bottle of Scotch almost single-handedly, but with help from everyone except Emmanuel. Emmanuel has found a relatively dry corner, where he lies curled up on the little plastic mesh bag that holds his few belongings, as though trying to blot out the chaos around him.

Gradually the rain starts to let up. Etienne comes in soaked, in jeans and souliers à jeter. It seems to be his only outfit. One of my pairs of cargo pants is a pair from Wal-Mart that's always been too big for me. "Etienne, I have a pair of trousers—boy's trousers—they might fit you and they're dry. Would you like to borrow them?"

"Yes." No sign of surprise or pleasure or gratitude. It is not the reaction I would have expected from polite, deferential Etienne, but much later I come to understand. During the whole time that I am camped here, nobody ever turns down an offer, and nobody ever says, "Thank you." Florence is similarly soaked and reacts just the same way as Etienne when I lend her a dry t-shirt and boxer shorts printed with lizards.

The rain has almost stopped but now it is dark. The Chief gets ready to leave. I have to lend him a flashlight, and he scrounges two tins of sardines from me. He announces that he will be joining us for breakfast tomorrow, and will then return in the evening, bringing a duck for dinner. And then stay, he says to me ominously, "to sleep with you. Vous comprenez?" Yes, I understand only too well.

"How nice," I reply enthusiastically, "we have two mosquito nets: one for the men and one for the women. You will be sharing with Etienne and Emmanuel."

The moment the Chief is gone, I scoop up a couple of plastic bags and set off into the night, announcing that I am going to look for frogs. I can hear them calling all around us, "Tok-tok, tok-tok," just like the ones I saw every night in the marsh at Epena. Some species of *Hyperolius* is my guess.

"Madame, I cannot let you go alone—please wait!" Etienne is struggling back into his wet jeans. I set off in the direction of the frog calls. It is pitch dark and all I can see is the narrow beam from my headlamp. I crawl along a slippery branch and drop down into thigh-deep water. I tear my way through a dense and prickly bush. The frog calls still sound just as far away. "Madame, come this way," Etienne calls to me, "you are going deeper into the forest. They will be easier to catch in the puddles along the trail, and I know a marsh." I am lured back. But Etienne and I spend the next 3 hours scouring every puddle and wading through the marsh, with frog calls all around us, and return with empty bags. I am soaked and have walked through ants. My clothes are full of them, viciously biting my skin. I rummage around in the house until I locate my pack and a dry change of clothes, but changing my clothes outside in the light rain in order to pick the ants off gets me wet all over again.

At the camp, everyone is getting ready for bed. The puddles have been mopped up as much as possible, and the mosquito nets have been hung with vines to keep them in place. I retrieve my one remaining towel from Florence, who is proposing to sleep on it. (There are limits!) Each of the two mosquito nets is designed for a twin bed, but Florence and I crawl under one and Etienne and Laurent under the other. Emmanuel prefers to brave the mosquitoes and sleep alone, outside the nets. Emmanuel is also isolated from the conversation going on under the nets, which, for my benefit, is in French and not Lingala.

I learn all sorts of interesting things about my new companions. Incredibly it turns out that Etienne, who looks so young, is 24. More amazing still, he has a wife and a 4-month-old baby. "So what are you doing here in the forest with me? Don't you miss your wife?"

"No, Madame, we are used to it. I am away whenever I find work, and I am glad to have the work. My wife and I don't mind." Other revelations: Laurent is Etienne's uncle. How old is Laurent? Thirty-three.

"Laurent is single," Florence says. They want to know if I am married and I produce my fictional fiancé, though I confess, to their disapproval, that I have no children. Of course I also pump them for information about any reptiles they know in the area.

"A snake that lives in the water, with red, black, and yellow rings, and deadly venomous?" I ask in disbelief. What can they possibly mean? I'm imagining some kind of Old World, aquatic, coral snake. "Rings or bands?" I wonder out loud, though either way I'd still be none the wiser. I explain that rings go all the way around the snake, but bands are just across the back and sides. They are not sure. But I'm sure of one thing: I long to catch that snake!

At last, out of sheer exhaustion, we drift into a tremendously uncomfortable sleep. At least Florence must be sleeping, if the loud snoring beside me is anything to go by. I am wearing all my warmest (though damp) clothes and am wrapped in a sheet, but even so the ground through the tarpaulin is cold when I wake at 3:00 a.m. to find my feet in a puddle. Flashlights are turned on, the wet rag and towel located, and we do our best to mop up this latest batch of puddles. Finally at 5:30 a.m., at the first sign of light, everyone gives up on the night and gets up. At least it isn't raining, and as we huddle around the still-burning fire, nursing plastic mugs of Florence's coffee—boiled in a pot and made more nourishing by the addition of vast quantities of sugar and Nido—the first glimmer of sunshine filters through the canopy of trees. Gradually we stop shivering and watch the beginnings of a beautiful day.

The first item on the agenda for the day is the house. Emmanuel has rethought its design and chosen a new site. He, Etienne, and Laurent set to work with more hacking down of branches and lashing with vines. Eventually the new house takes shape. It is smaller than the old one, to allow more of the roof tarpaulin to overhang the floor and walls tarpaulin, and one end is closed by an upward fold of the floor tarpaulin. It lacks the grandeur of the first attempt and I'm a bit disappointed, but they guarantee that this one will keep the rain out. We move everything inside it.

Florence has hauled a bucket of water as brown as strong tea up to the campsite for me to wash in. She clearly sees no sense in this bizarre mondele requirement, but it was in the job description. I start by washing my hair in it, encountering a large water spider during the rinsing process. I splash my face and shoulders with soap and water. There's not much left of the water now, no point in washing my feet, which will immediately get muddy again, and no way of washing the rest of me.

The men have finished the house and without waiting for instructions have started untangling the fishnets. I haven't had a good look around the area in daylight yet, but now I get to explore. Our camp is surrounded by a network of flooded forest. Florence's stagnant pond isn't a pond at all, it's the shallow edge of the finger of flooded forest extending closest to our camp. With the exception of the trail we came in by, we are entirely surrounded by tropical forest often waist-deep in water. I would say "as far as the eye can see," except that the eye can see only as far as the next watery opening between the trees. I have never seen any place remotely like it. Emmanuel has already decided on two good places for the nets. How he distinguishes between different locations in this endless assemblage of trees and water I can't understand. It all looks the same to me. All equally and spectacularly beautiful. This first day, with the rising sun starting to make the forest hot, I fall deeply in love with the flooded forest.

I wear cargo pants, jungle boots, and my backpack to set the nets. Everyone else wears whatever they have. Knee-deep and then waist-deep in the water, I find that flooded forest, although often referred to as swamp forest, is actually different from a swamp. The bottom is firm—no mud to sink into—which is a good thing, but it is also strewn with stray logs to trip over, and pitted with occasional depressions that you step into, suddenly finding yourself in up to your neck. In some places there are slippery logs near the surface that Etienne, barefoot, runs along. But in boots I inevitably end up slipping and falling completely underwater. My bare feet are not strongly callused like his, and I cut my feet to pieces if I try going barefoot. Better just to plod along the bottom, even if it is deep in places. Etienne always walks ahead of me, often saying, "You must walk around this way, Madame, there is a hole." It is a mystery to me how he can tell where the holes are until I learn that the forest is only seasonally flooded. Right now, in October, it is the height of the rainy season and the water is as deep as it gets. But in the dry season there is no water at all, and the whole forest floor is revealed.

We set the nets in the places chosen by Emmanuel. He and Etienne have tied one end of a net to a branch and are unraveling it lengthwise along a long, thigh-deep channel. Laurent is hovering in the slightly shallower background, hitching up his shorts in the futile hope of avoiding getting them wet. I am in the deeper water trying to get Etienne to explain to me what he is doing. It is easier for him just to get the job done, communicating in Lingala with Emmanuel, so what I learn I learn just from watching. The first net is set in a long line along the channel, looking like a long string along the surface, tied at each end. Hanging from the string, beneath the surface, is a mesh of threads. The mesh would stretch to a depth of about 3 feet if the bottom edge was weighted, but we haven't weighted it, so it hangs, and drifts a bit in places where there is a slight current.

I am not satisfied with the arrangement. Most of the string is hanging slightly below the surface. This may not matter for catching fish, but snakes tend to swim along the surface, and with the net as it is they will swim right over it without getting caught. The "water snakes" in this part of the world are not specialized in any way for life in the water except for their appetite for fish. But conveniently, the lateral undulations that snakes use to propel themselves on land adapt very well for swimming, and almost any snake can swim if thrown in the water. They generally swim along the surface with their heads held up, though the water snakes here are sufficiently aquatic that they will dive after a fish. In other parts of the world there are true water snakes—the sea snakes. Sea snakes, close relatives of cobras, have so many anatomical adaptations for life in the ocean that they can move on land only with considerable difficulty.

In any case, we will not be catching sea snakes here, so I explain the swimming on the surface problem in French to Etienne and he passes it on in Lingala to Emmanuel, who sets his mind to the problem. Eventually we cut sticks and use them to prop up the top edge of the net at regular intervals. Anything that tries to swim across the channel should get caught. We set up the other net the same way in a deeper channel farther away from the camp. Tomorrow will tell if what all the fishermen say about nets getting full of snakes is true.

It feels as if a whole day's work has been done and I'm astonished to look at my watch and find that it is only 8:30. I am hungry. We return to the camp to find Florence preparing in a large pot a curious concoction of rice, macaroni, spaghetti, sardines, and tomato paste. I'm baffled by how spaghetti and rice can be cooked together in the same pot, but eat the food without caring. I am left with a whole lot of day to organize.

"Etienne and I had no luck catching frogs last night in the rain, when they should have been there. When everyone's finished eating, let's go to that marsh near the road and see if we have better luck by day."

I issue a plastic bag to everyone and we set off along the trail, through mud and prickly plants, our progress punctuated by occasional mad dashes to avoid patches of ants. When we finally reach the marsh I can hear the frogs calling, "Tok-tok." I tell everyone to look on the reeds for a small brown frog. We all wade around in the swamp for an hour, surrounded by frog calls, but without anyone seeing a single frog— until Emmanuel makes a quick grab under water and comes up with a great big African bullfrog, *Hoplobatrachus occipitalis*. So much for my little brown frogs on the reeds. Wordlessly, he hands me the frog in a bag and announces (translation by Etienne) that he is going to the village for a visit, and disappears for the rest of the day. This seems fair enough. The rest of us brave the trail back to the camp.

I now have a specimen to fix, and everyone else is off-duty so far as I'm concerned. I start my new notebook by trying to take a GPS reading, but the forest canopy is too thick for the GPS unit to detect any satellites. So much for my hopes of using it to find my way around the flooded forest. The best I can do is to take a reading from the nearest place clear enough for it to detect satellites, and that means a walk back along the trail until it comes out of the forest. At a distance from the camp that I estimate to be approximately 3 kilometers and generally north, I get a reading accurate to 11 meters. It will have to do. When I return to the camp, Laurent is sleeping in the house, and Etienne is hovering around, occasionally turning to hack aimlessly at the underbrush surrounding the camp with a machete.

I set out a white snake bag as background and photograph the frog. The frog keeps hopping away as I'm trying to take the picture and Etienne, who always seems to be there suddenly just when you need another pair of hands, recaptures it. From my toolbox I take a tube of benzocaine gel and smear some on the frog's head. The sun is beating down on my "lab" corner of the tent, and with much regret I give up my sleeping sheet to hang across the open end. Shade for my work is more important than being slightly less uncomfortable at night. While waiting for the benzocaine to take effect, I fill out the first entry in my notebook and cut a tag from the roll of Smithsonian field tags, corresponding to the number in my notes. Since this is the first specimen of a species I get out all the fussy equipment needed for taking tissue samples. Samples of tissue are taken from freshly killed animals and preserved in 90 percent ethanol. That is done because the next step is to preserve the whole animal in formalin. DNA can be extracted from the tissues preserved in ethanol, but not from tissue fixed in formalin.

The tragedy of this is that the specimens in the vast herpetological collections of museums in the United States and Europe were all fixed in formalin when they were collected, before DNA extraction was an issue. Central African specimens are rare in museum collections, specimens that come with a tissue sample, an identification, and locality data even more so. I am here for the snakes, but on my return, many lab-based frog and lizard experts who don't themselves venture into the field, or who collect in other places, will be glad to have these tissues.

Once the frog is dead I take the tissue sample, snipping out a tiny fragment of liver through a small incision in the abdomen, and then tie the tag around its knee. I remember that I need to mix formalin. I carry with me 2 liters of formalin, which will go a long way since I use it at a concentration of 10 percent. I have no choice but to use flooded-forest water to dilute it, and the resulting solution, which should be transparent, is a worrying shade of medium brown. I hope it will do the job.

I am well into my work when, to my annoyance, the Chief arrives. He was probably too hung-over to join us for breakfast; he has not brought a duck as promised, and he has "forgotten" to return the borrowed flashlight. He requests whiskey, having apparently forgotten killing the bottle last night.But he is delighted to accept orange Gatorade as a substitute. First of all everyone is amazed to see *jus* (any sweet, nonalcoholic drink) made from powder. Here such drinks come as a concentrated syrup. That is the first of its magical properties. Then I try to explain that it is a special kind of jus, made with ingredients to replace sweat lost during hard work or exercise.

"It gives power," the Chief summarizes my explanation, nodding.

"Well, not exactly . . ." but I decide against an attempt at a more accurate explanation. What does it matter? The Chief's French, I've come to realize, is not very good, and I have no Lingala, so I do my best to keep to language as simple as possible. We have a photo shoot. The Chief wants a formal shot of the two of us shaking hands. Having learned from the sad loss of an excellent 35-millimeter Nikon, rusted to pieces from 3 weeks of exposure to the forest on my first trip to the Congo, I now carry a cheap little digital camera, which takes pretty good pictures and promises to be water resistant. It is also very simple to use. I teach Etienne in about 10 minutes, and from that moment on can scarcely prize it away from him. He especially loves checking the pictures on the "quick-view" screen after he has taken them. Anyway, gradually learning to hold the camera still and not put his finger over the lens while pressing the shutter, he gets a few reasonable shots of the official encounter.

With everyone together I try to clarify something that has been puzzling me. "So how long is Laurent staying with us?" There is an awkward silence. That is a matter that must be discussed with the Chief. Etienne, Florence, the Chief, and I retreat into the house, leaving poor Laurent pacing outside.

"But we made a clear agreement that I was hiring one guide. Did you think I would hire a second one by sort of not noticing?" I say, baffled. "I would love to keep Laurent, but it's not in the budget. If I hire Laurent I can't keep Etienne." (I think of Etienne madly digging trenches around the house in the rain, and I think of Laurent hanging back in the flooded forest, trying not to get his shorts wet.) This is eminently reasonable, and everyone accepts it, greatly relieved when (remembering Laurent smilingly picking up after me on our first way in to the camp) I assure them that I will pay Laurent 1,500cfa for each half day he's worked so far. Out of the tent I explain all this to Laurent, who accepts it very good naturedly, shaking my hand the conventional way, and then, more firmly, thumb to thumb, with an affectionate grin. He will always be a welcome visitor to the camp, I assure him, and if I ever need an extra person for anything, he is the first one I will think of.

Eventually the Chief leaves, having scrounged a few tablets of Tylenol from me for one of his (two) wives, who he says has a sore back, and having accepted a plastic bag because, he says, he thinks he can pick up some toads around the village (he probably just wants some brand new plastic bags, but perhaps I am unfairly misjudging his motives). He also promises to return the flashlight on his next visit. As he leaves he announces, to my dismay, that he intends to visit every day "for security."

I finish fixing my specimen, and spread it out on a plastic tray to harden, making sure that fingers and toes are neatly spread out. Examining the digits and webbings will be essential when it comes time to identify it. I put the tray in one of the abandoned payottes, to keep it dry if it rains and to keep the formalin fumes out of the house. Florence starts calling that payotte "the morgue." As I am setting the tray down on the remains of a Pygmy sleeping platform, I hear a rustling sound above my head. I look up to see a pretty little skink disappearing through the roof of leaves. I rush outside the payotte and see it sitting in the sun on the roof. I make a grab at it, but it is too quick for me, disappearing through the leaves to the inside of the payotte again. I rush back inside, and am of course too late. Soon it scampers off into the forest. I am furious with myself. How could I have been so clumsy? That lizard would have made a fine start to my collection. Just one more specimen, but of a species that I don't have yet. I try to comfort myself that it will come back. Skinks are creatures of habit and I will catch it another sunny afternoon on the roof of the payotte.

I tell Etienne about the lizard and teach him how to make and use a lizard noose. I bet he will be good at it once he gets the hang of it. First I send him to find a thin branch with a bit of flexibility to it. Then he looks on reluctantly as I take some thread from my sewing kit and tie a little sliding loop to the tip of the branch. Etienne is fidgeting. This is the kind of thing he should be teaching me, not the other way around. I show him how without going close to a basking lizard you can gently lower the loop around its neck, and then catch it with a quick upward jerk of the branch. I show him where I saw the lizard and tell him we must check that place whenever it is sunny, until we catch it. He nods without much show of interest. Perhaps he is just tired.

It is after dark and we are tucked in under our mosquito nets when Emmanuel returns from the village. He brings with him that awful African village smell. I trace it to a package wrapped in leaves, and ask what it is. Manioc. So there's the explanation. "Well find somewhere to keep it outside of the house. It smells terrible."

The mosquito nets are arranged with their length across the width of the house, side by side at the back of the house with the closed end. Etienne is in the back and Florence and I are in the outer one. Emmanuel immediately insists that the men must be in the outer one, so there is a great scramble of rearranging. The advantage of the back mosquito net is that you don't have people climbing through your stuff all the time, but the disadvantage is that you have no way to get out without climbing over (and waking) whoever is sleeping under the outer net. I will be glad when Emmanuel leaves tomorrow and it is just the three of us. I try to persuade Etienne to take advantage of Emmanuel's still being here for his last night tonight to spend the night in the village with his wife, but he won't hear of it. He seems quite offended at the suggestion that I could get along without him.

It's another uncomfortable night. I am wearing the warmest, driest clothes I have, but it is surprising how difficult it is to sleep without a cover, even though the cover that I gave up to make a curtain for my lab was only a thin sheet. Moreover, the new house has been built over several bumps in the ground—probably tree roots. To avoid lying on them I have to either curl up facing to the right, with Etienne's hot breath in my face, or stretch out on my back like a cadaver. Florence's snoring starts. I must eventually have fallen asleep because I wake at 5:30 to find everyone else up and about. I am still dressed from yesterday so I just crawl through the men's mosquito net and am almost out of the house when Etienne stops me.

"Madame Katherine, you must stay in the house. There are ants." Sure enough, the whole campsite, as far as I can see, is crawling with them. Etienne and Florence are rushing about with logs from the fire, bashing the smoldering end on the moving carpet. Amazingly, the ants have not come into the house. There is a little raised lip to the floor tarpaulin and mercifully that seems to keep them out. Emmanuel is sitting on the new bench in the kitchen with his feet up off the ground. I make a dash for the kitchen, and soon we are all perched on the benches drinking coffee. Gradually the ants dissipate a bit so that there are enough ant-free patches of ground that we can get around by darting from one to the next. There is a shout from the trail and we look up to see that Laurent has arrived. He has traps set up to catch forest mammals, and since our camp is on the way to the traps and he's not in a hurry he joins us for a mug of coffee and a piece of chocolate.

The first job of the day is the exciting one: checking the nets. Are they as effective as everyone says? Will we be lucky enough to get anything on the first day? In the water, Etienne rushes ahead of me, lifting the net as he goes. It makes sense for him to go ahead since he knows the terrain, but he's really doing it for the excitement of seeing what we've got—like opening a Christmas present. I follow closely, looking over his shoulder. Suddenly he stops dead. "Madame, a snake." Around us the casual banter in Lingala gives way to a tense silence. Over his shoulder I see a snake that must be over a meter long, gray with faint black bands. "Okay," I take over. "Let me deal with this." Etienne hands me the net and I tell him and Emmanuel to stand back out of the way. I don't need to say it more than once. For the first time I see something new in their eyes: Respect? Or is that wishful thinking on my part? I may not have a clue how to string a net or build a house or burn ants or walk through the flooded forest without tripping over things, but here is one thing I can do that they would be afraid to do. Of course it's probably more likely that they just think I'm crazy.

I approach the snake, lifting the net out of the water as I go. It must be either a harmless water snake of the genus *Grayia,* or the very dangerous water cobra, *Boulengerina annulata.* I will need a good look at the head to be sure. Out of my backpack I take a snake bag and a 12-inch hemostat. I am also carrying cumbersome 24-inch snake tongs, bought over the Internet from the United States and intended for working with rattlesnakes, which are rough skinned and soft bodied. The snake tangled in the net mid-body, with 8 inches or so of neck and head free, is solid and slippery. It is striking and hissing angrily, but I am close enough to tell that it is a harmless *Grayia*. Even so, this will be good practice for capturing a *Boulengerina* without getting bitten. I need to get a firm grip on the snake just behind the head, so it can't turn and bite while I untangle it from the net. I start with the 24-inch tongs. The salesman had tried hard to persuade me to buy the 48-inch model, but I'd used one of those before and found them terribly clumsy and difficult to manipulate, even on rattlesnakes. Here the 24-inch tongs soon turn out to be absolutely useless. I close them around the snake's neck and the snake simply glides through, as if nothing were holding it at all. I pass the tongs back to Etienne to get them out of the way, and find I have much more success with the hemostat. The problem with the hemostat is that at a length of 12 inches it doesn't leave much space between me and the snake. But when I clamp it down on the snake's neck, as close to the head as possible, it holds. I am able to get the snake in a behind-the-head hold with my left hand, untangling it from the net with my right. As soon as its body is free, it wraps itself around my left forearm. I put a white cotton snake bag over its head, and by feel transfer the left-hand head hold inside the bag to a right-hand head hold from the outside of the bag. I unwrap the body from my arm, stuff it in the bag before it can throw a coil around me again, and quickly tie the end of the bag closed. The tension that was gripping me vanishes. I turn to Etienne and Emmanuel and give them a reassuring smile. The show is over.

We find another snake further along. I am over the moon. Two snakes the first day! Maybe I have a chance at a decent collection after all. Returning triumphantly to the camp, we are all revived by enthusiasm. Suddenly the wet clothes and the uncomfortable nights don't seem important. The ants are now only in a few patches, which can be carefully avoided. We eat hearty bowls of Florence's rice-based concoction. I tell her we have to use up all that macaroni, so space out the rice a bit. This is another oddity I encounter here. Nobody ever saves anything special for enjoyment sometime in the future. Any treat is consumed immediately, and no matter what I tell her, I discover that Florence won't resort to macaroni until all the preferred rice is used up. I have complained about the bumps under the tarpaulin, and the men (even Laurent who isn't getting paid) partially disassemble the sleeping end of the house, and hack away the protruding roots with machetes. They get most but not, as I am to discover that night, all.

The final job of the day (though it isn't even 8:30 yet) is the construction of my drift fence and pitfall traps. Laurent disappears into the forest to check his traps, and Etienne and I, carrying shovel, wire mesh, and a bucket, follow Emmanuel as he leads us to the place he has chosen on dry land in the forest. I explain the design of the traps. The men are to dig holes the size of a bucket but with straight sides, so that the animals that I hope will fall in will not be able to climb out. The earth dug out of these holes must be scattered in the forest, not left nearby where it might arouse suspicion in our potential captures. There will be four holes in a line. Then the fence must be built along the line. This is to channel animals into the holes. Instead of passing between two holes, they will encounter the fence, and have to change direction. Whether they follow the fence left or right, it will lead them to a hole. The fence must be built tight against the ground so that nothing can crawl under it. Barely listening to my instructions they set to work, digging a hole and dumping the earth in the bucket, which one of them then carries off into the forest while the other starts on the next hole. I stand around feeling useless; surely I could carry away the buckets of earth. Would it be helpful if I unrolled the wire mesh and rolled it back in the other direction to straighten it? Finally Etienne says solemnly, and as politely as possible, "Madame Katherine, please go away and let us do our work."

Chastened, I leave them to it. I return a short time later with bon-

bons sifflets to sustain them (received without thanks and pocketed), but really to check on progress. The holes are good, except that they haven't measured the space between them, and the 10 meters of mesh will not be suffcient to make a long enough fence. Emmanuel ponders this only for a moment, and soon they are building a section of fence, every bit as solid as the wire mesh part, out of sticks, vines, and leaves, to fill the space between the two lengths of mesh.

They are both soaked with sweat and sucking on the bon-bons sif-flets. I praise the result effusively, but none of my compliments seem to get through to Emmanuel until I show him on the camera's quick-view screen how many pictures I have taken of his work. A rare smile spreads across his face, and the final picture is of Emmanuel standing proudly in front of the fence.

It is shortly after 10:00 a.m. That is the required day's work done, and it is Emmanuel's last day. I had paid him in advance, but he scrounges a couple of D batteries from me before he leaves—my last link with life at Epena.

I will depend on the occasional traffic along the road for communi-cation. A letter can be sent, free of charge, with the driver of one of the transport trucks that rumbles by twice a day between Impfondo and Epena. So if I need something I can send a message to WCS. The people there can send a message by return post, care of the Chief of Ganganya Brousse, telling me what day and time to wait for their truck by the side of the road.

neighbors,
nets,
and
nothing

With Emmanuel gone, Etienne and Florence and I settle into a routine. Life in the camp is not at all as I had imagined it would be, but I am happy. Two people could hardly be more different than Florence and Etienne but we make a very contented trio. Etienne tells us that he sees me as an older sister and Florence as a mother, which, though well meant, seems to please me more than it does Florence. One day Etienne returns from a rare visit to the village with four precious photographs of his wife and baby to show me. I recognize what an honor this is and I am touched. I say all the usual admiring things about the beauty of the baby and the wife. Noticing that the edges of the photos are already starting to curl from the humidity, I find Etienne a Ziploc sandwich bag from among my equipment, and show him how to open and close it so he can protect the pictures in it. The baby is a girl, called Patience. They chose the name, he explains, because she took a long time to come, even though they were trying, and as they fretted over the problem, people kept telling them *patience*.

We are always up at first light, with Florence complaining about how terribly cold it is as she boils water for the coffee. According to the thermometer in my toolbox it is 20°C (68°F). I try to explain to Florence what real cold is like—how cold it gets in my country, but I can't find any way to illustrate it. She's never encountered a refrigerator; she's never seen an ice cube . . . or anything else frozen for that matter. I can find no way to describe a cold January day in Toronto to her.

The insects are a discomfort that never lets up. It's either an ant day, a wasp day, or a fly day. On an ant day the whole surface of the campsite may be covered in an uninterrupted carpet of biting ants that run up your legs and get all through your clothing before you even realize you have stepped in a patch of them. The only escapes are the house, which they *usually* stay out of, and crouching on the benches with your feet off the ground. On an ant day you wish more than anything that it would be a fly day. On a fly day you long for a wasp day, and on a wasp day you think even the ants would be preferable. The "flies" are really sweat bees, tiny and black. They don't bite, but just swarm around you like a buzzing blanket. They crawl into anything moist—eyes, mouth, any open cuts—and swatting them just seems to attract more. These can be escaped by running faster than they can fly, but the moment you stop your entourage will catch up with you. The wasps have a different strategy. Usually one wasp alone takes it upon itself to drive you mad, swooping past your face, landing in your food, and buzzing in your ears. On our first wasp day a wasp lands on the brim of my morning coffee. I take a swipe at it and knock over the mug, tipping half a cup of hot coffee into my lap. I set the mug on the table while I wipe up some of the mess, and the wasp uses the opportunity to drown itself in the remaining half cup. Your best hope for escaping a wasp is that it will decide that the person sitting beside you is more attractive than you are. The mosquitoes are so dependable as to be hardly worth mentioning. They appear every day at dusk, without fail, just as Etienne and I are setting off on our evening search of ponds and trails.

The first hour of each day is spent companionably over the coffee and bars of chocolate, a luxury I stocked up on in the Impfondo market, after which the air has warmed up sufficiently that the prospect of getting into wet clothes to check the nets is bearable. Etienne and I always enter the water at the same place, progressing from boots soaked through to ankle-deep to thigh-deep to waist-deep water as we slosh our way to the beginning of the first net. Walking the length of the net, lifting it out of the water as we go, takes some time because of the fish. For every snake that finds its way into our nets, many, many fish get themselves caught. They all have to be removed from the net—left in place they would rot and create a terrible mess—so Etienne floats a plastic bucket along beside him, and is delighted to finish each morning with some fish. Florence smokes the fish on the rack above the fire, and she and Etienne sell them in the village.

Florence keeps busy while Etienne and I are in the water. We return to find washed wet clothes hung up to dry all over the camp and on protruding bits of the surrounding forest, the mosquito nets tied up out of the way, and Florence in the process of vigorously sweeping out the inside of the house with Etienne's t-shirt. Then comes a real meal. Florence's best, when she goes to the effort of using both pots, is rice with a sauce of garlic, onion and pork luncheon meat sautéed in far too much oil, and then mixed with tomato paste.

Florence is soon fed up with my requirement for a bucket of water carried to the camp to wash in. It's a nuisance and it's irrational, even I can see that. I watch her taking her daily bath just standing in the water a few discreet feet out of sight of the place where the dishes are washed, stripping naked and soaping herself up. I never really manage to get completely clean from my bucket. So one afternoon when Etienne is away from the camp, I ask her if there is a place where I could have a good wash—a real lathering up. She is delighted to find me a place. It is almost knee deep and leafy rather than muddy at the bottom, but to get to it I have to fight my way through several thickets of prickly plants, hang my clothing on overhanging vegetation (checking carefully for ants), and then slip on the muddy bank getting out of the water, so that I return from an admittedly pleasant wash muddy and scratched. So Florence, always more at home with a machete than a cooking pot, cuts a trail to this bathing spot which is to be just for me, and builds a small dock out of logs for climbing in and out and leaving the soap on. In a living arrangement in which I am never left alone, my bathing spot becomes the one place I can count on privacy; it's not a cold, deep Ontario lake, but the cool water of the forest is very refreshing after the hot stickiness of work during the day. My Ivory soap, brought from Canada in a plastic travel soap container, has turned to mush. One day on my way to the bath I see the dishwashing bar of soap, sitting on a leaf in the sun on Florence's table, invitingly dry and solid. I borrow it and then throw out the mushy Ivory soap and help myself to a bar of tough African soap from the provisions box.

Often we have visitors to the camp. I am surprised by several things. First of all this camp, which had seemed to me to be in the middle of nowhere, is apparently well known to everyone in the area. People will come to visit for no reason (well, maybe some of the more curious have come for a glimpse of the mondele woman who collects snakes), and then just *stay*, for hours on end without doing anything. I suppose most of them have nothing better to do, and that may also explain the huge distances people seem to think nothing of walking. At first, I feel compelled to play the hostess to these guests, but I soon learn to welcome them on arrival with a handshake and an mbote, and then go back to whatever I am doing and ignore them. This seems to be expected. When they are ready to leave they say so and we shake hands again as they set off back along the trail.

But many people come to my camp to scrounge. What appears to be a friendly visit turns out to be an attempt to get something from me. Scrounging attempts are exhausting, forcing me to fend off efforts to separate me from my belongings; disappointing, because each time someone who I thought was just being friendly turns out to want something from me; and isolating, because they make me feel not like a person surrounded by friends and acquaintances, but like a lone mondele in the midst of an endless stream of people who want something that I have. Sometimes, among all these people, I feel terribly lonely. I gradually learn not to be a generous pushover, and I build a strong emotional wall around myself against scroungers.

Some people ask me for things they think are so small I might not miss them: batteries, soap, canned food. Other people ask for bigger-ticket items "after [I] leave." People seem to have the notion that my need for, say, clothing, will disappear when I disappear from Ganganya. Within hours of my arrival at the camp everyone, it seems, is asking, "Madame, when you leave can I have X?"

The concept of "borrowing" turns out to be different here as well. Etienne and Florence both seem to have regarded the dry clothes I lent them the first night as for keeps. I get the boxer shorts with lizards on them back from Florence, explaining that they had been a present from a friend, and she is entirely understanding. The cargo pants are a much better fit on Etienne than they had been on me, so I just let him keep them. The towel I contributed for mopping up puddles that first night has served as doormat, mop, and trivet. Retrieving my flashlight from the Chief is a great coup.

Alone with Florence one afternoon, I sigh: "It's draining, Florence. Everybody wants something from me. Someone is always trying to get me to give away something that's mine. It never lets up."

"Well, it's because we're poor."

"I know. I understand why people do it, but it still wears me down. Think how lonely you would feel if you had to wonder if all your friends were only pretending to like you because they were hoping you'd give them something."

"Yes," says Florence firmly, "it wouldn't be right." We sit for a moment in silence. "Do you think *I* scrounge?" asks Florence.

"Well, you did once ask me what was going to happen to the buckets at the end of the project, but overall I think you've given me as much as I've given you. Remember how you brought one of your own sheets from home so that I could sleep more comfortably? And how you let me borrow that piece of plastic rope when the string for one of my fishnets wasn't long enough? And when you let me use your little mirror?" Florence beams. I have a hopeless cook but perhaps a friend.

One visitor is an elderly Pygmy woman, an unlikely friend of Florence. Friendships between Pygmies and Bantu are rare. I am sitting in the kitchen with them, eating a bowl of cold macaroni, while they have a conversation in Lingala. After the woman has left, Florence gleefully translates their conversation for me: "But I thought the mondele you were working for was a woman," begins the Pygmy woman.

"She *is* a woman."

"She doesn't look like it to me. She's wearing trousers, and I've seen her on the road. She walks with big steps like a man, and look, she's got practically no breasts . . ."

"What?" I interject indignantly.

"So I told her," Florence continues, "it's just that she's small and slight—and a mondele. You wouldn't expect her to have big tits."

I make a promise to myself that I will learn Lingala. I'm tired of being cut out of the conversation going on around me, and I certainly don't like the thought of people talking about me right in front of me with me totally unaware of it.

I am thinking one day of the Brazzaville graduate students whom I unfortunately couldn't afford to bring into the field with me to teach herpetological collecting techniques to because they required a stipend and a per diem on top of their airfare and any other expenses. It occurs to me that I have with me two intelligent people who would be even more useful to me if they knew how to prepare specimens. Would they be interested in learning a new skill? I ask Etienne and Florence if they would like me to teach them how to do what I do to preserve the animals we collect. They are both enthusiastic about the idea, though I can't imagine what possible use it will ever be to them once I'm gone. I warn them that some of the procedures are a bit complicated, but Florence says confidently, "Everything can be learned." I give them each a notebook, and start thinking about specimen preparation from the most basic level possible. I begin by filling a plastic mug with water and teaching them how to use a big 30-cc syringe. They practice, learning to draw water in and out without getting bubbles of air, and learning how to get rid of bubbles of air if they do get them. Etienne immediately starts laboriously writing every detail in his notebook. "I push the plunger of the syringe as far down as it will go. I put the tip of the syringe under the surface of the water. I slowly pull the plunger up, drawing water into the syringe. I turn the syringe upside down so that if there are air bubbles they are in the tip, which is pointing upward. I push the plunger slightly to push the air out . . ." I can see that at this rate several days of instruction are going to be needed. Then I add a needle to the syringe. They learn not to try to draw water into the syringe through the narrow needle, but to take the needle off by unscrewing it while they fill the syringe, then put the needle back on to use it to inject. They learn to manipulate the syringe using just one hand. Now for formalin. They are both terrified by the formalin, especially when, at my insistence and with great reluctance, they touch a frog I fixed the previous day and find that it appears to have turned to plastic. "That's what it will do to the tips of your fingers," I tell them. When the lesson is over, there is a mad rush for the water bucket to wash any trace of formalin off their hands. They wait only until I have washed my hands first before scrubbing their arms up to the elbows.

Florence soon drops out of these lessons. A cook's job seems to require constant attention to something or other, as opposed to the guide's job, which involves periods of hard work interspersed with free time. So Etienne ends up my only pupil. He picks it all up very quickly. Soon he knows how to euthanize a reptile with chloroform or an amphibian with benzocaine gel, how to inject a specimen with formalin—enough to prevent it from rotting inside, but not so much as to inflate it like a balloon—how to tie a museum tag onto a specimen using a reef knot ("right over left, left over right"), how to correctly position a frog for hardening, wrapped in formalin-saturated cheesecloth to keep it moist, and how to make a notebook entry. He even starts to get over his fear of formalin.

But I am starting to feel desperate about the lack of specimens. After all the effort that went into making this trip happen, how can I go home with a failed expedition to report? Three weeks wasted waiting for a permit, and now that I am finally in the forest I'm not catching anything. Nobody will ever fund me to come back. I insist on going out in the night when it has just rained, or is raining lightly, to search for frogs, wading in the marsh and the shallow forest puddles. Although Etienne wouldn't dream of letting me go out on these excursions alone, he is surprisingly reluctant. He shows little interest in and no aptitude for catching frogs, but I'm not having much luck either. It is maddening to me that I can hear the treefrogs I saw every night at Epena, where they would have been easy to catch, but for some reason I never see a single one here, though I can hear them calling. "Tok-tok, tok-tok."

"I can hear them singing, Madame," says Etienne in frustration.

"Singing? I think they're laughing at us," I say grimly.

Etienne, bored and impatient, cuts a way through the dense forest to allow me to crawl around turning over every log in sight, shining a flashlight into every hole in every fallen tree, for hours without turning up anything more exciting than a lot of large colonies of biting ants. One day I come across the overgrown crumbling foundations of a building that must once have housed the Brazilians who built the road in the 1980s. It looks very promising, but Etienne and I tear the whole thing to pieces without finding so much as a toad.

One afternoon two little girls emerge from the forest carrying a bucket with a lid. They are too shy to answer when I ask them what's in it, but when I cautiously open the lid it turns out to be a toad—a common species of toad, of the genus *Bufo,* but it is a specimen. I praise them lavishly for having caught it, and transfer it from their bucket to a plastic bag. I give them each a bon-bon sifflet and encourage them to tell all their friends. Do they know the difference between a frog and a toad, I ask? A shy nod. Fearing a deluge of common *Bufo*s, and not wanting to encourage children to interfere with snakes, I tell them that I especially want frogs.

With no specimens to spend my time fixing, I start obsessively recording statistics and calculations in my notebook. How many days? Four if you count the first days when we were setting up. How many specimens? Two snakes, Emmanuel's frog, and the girls' toad. Four days. Four specimens. Three species. I start adding a calculation each day to gauge exactly how disappointed the Smithsonian is going to feel by the collection I produce in exchange for its $2,000: $2,000 divided by the number of specimens equals how much each specimen is costing the Smithsonian. The result is not cheering. I try to explain the calculation to Etienne, but he doesn't quite get it. At this rate, I explain, the Smithsonian will be paying $500 for a toad.

"Five hundred dollars for a toad?" he repeats incredulously. "What will they pay for a snake?"

I already have blisters on my feet from the boots. This is serious because I still have to wear them every day, so the blisters, now burst, have no chance to heal. Any open sore in the tropics invites infection, especially in a place like this where nothing is ever dry. I know that only too well from experience. Putting on the boots every morning is agony, even with layers of Band-Aids covering my heels, but after I've walked for about 10 minutes they go numb and I forget about the pain. I dread to think what it will be like if I run out of Band-Aids. The only other footwear I have are my Tevas—sandals held on by strong cloth straps and Velcro. One of the straps goes across the heel, making it too painful to wear. Then the Velcro gets so muddy that it won't stick together anymore. So I walk barefoot, and the soles of my feet are soon cut and blistered.

Etienne takes to quickly checking the pitfall traps, which are near the camp, first thing in the morning, before I'm up. I can't understand why I'm not catching anything in my pitfall traps. Herpetologists working in Cameroon and Gabon report pitfall traps practically brimming over with small lizards and rare leaf-litter frogs. On my first expedition I had made pitfall traps by sinking plastic buckets into the ground. I caught a few toads, and even a small snake, but every time it rained and the water table rose the buckets floated up, so that their brims were well above the forest floor, which made them useless. And that was in the dry season in an area of forest that never floods. Imagine what the water table must be like here. So that's why I decided this time just on holes dug in the ground with straight vertical sides. No floating buckets.

I often wake to the sound of Etienne singing hymns in Lingala in a remarkably strong bass. Florence tells me that Etienne sings in church.

Etienne, it turns out, does more than sing in church. In fact he is so devout that he is single-handedly responsible for establishing a church in Ganganya Brousse. He has a little booklet of biblical quotations in Lingala (which he immediately stores in the Ziploc bag with the photos), but has never had an actual Bible.

On one of his visits, the Chief notices the state of my feet. What I need, he says, is a pair of what I still think of as souliers à jeter, which attach only at the toe and don't rub against the heel. He says he will try to get me a pair. I don't for a moment imagine that he will, but a couple of days later I am pleasantly surprised. Florence comes back from the village carrying a bottle of local whiskey, and a pair of souliers à jeter given to her by the Chief to deliver to me.

"Local whiskey" costs 1,000cfa per liter and is said to be made from corn. It's vile stuff, even watered down a bit, but it's alcohol. It vexes me greatly to realize that the Chief would probably have been just as happy with a bottle of local whiskey as he was with my expensive J & B.

On his next state visit I thank the Chief for the shoes and the whiskey, and am puzzled by his reaction: "Whiskey? Whiskey? There is whiskey here?" Florence, catching my eye, looks panic-stricken. In a hasty whisper she manages to convey to me that the whiskey is hers and was not part of the present from the Chief. Thank goodness his French isn't very good.

"Yes, whiskey," I say. "Florence's sister in the forest sells it." He seems to conclude that he had misunderstood what I had said, and Florence and I heave a sigh of relief.

Not even a week has gone by, but already all sorts of my things are starting to fall apart and run out. First of all my boots. I had for a long time longed for a pair of "jungle boots," boots developed by the U.S. Army for use in Vietnam, and now said to be worn mostly by mercenaries, but though I scoured the military surplus stores in Toronto, I couldn't find them in my size. So imagine my delight upon finding them for sale on the Internet in a size 4, for only $25! These, however, are clearly a cheap imitation of the real thing. All the eyelets come out of their holes the first time I lace them up, and after only a couple of days' use, the toe starts to separate from the sole on one of them. Laurent is delighted. Apparently he has a sideline as a cobbler. I can't imagine he gets much business in an area where everyone wears souliers à jeter. For 1,000cfa he will bring his tools and repair the boots on Thursday.

In the meantime one of the nose-pads on my glasses breaks. Its loss is a small thing but I can imagine the glasses rubbing on my face and it becoming quite painful over time. My doxycycline pills, big green capsules prescribed by the Toronto travel doctor against malaria, succumb to the damp of the forest, turning first to a wet paste, and then drying into a single, solid, useless lump. The remains of my hairbrush are held together with packing tape, and I dread losing it, since it would be impossible to find a replacement suitable for brushing Caucasian hair in this country. My ankles are swollen with mosquito bites, and my only relief from the itching is a product called After-bite, whose main ingredient is ammonia. I am getting through it fast and it will run out soon. I am not looking forward to that.

Laurent comes to repair my boots, as promised, assuring me that it won't matter that they are wet. He sets to work stitching the toe to the sole with a big needle and strong cord. It is hard work, pulling the stitches through the narrow inside of the toe. While Laurent is working on one boot, I notice Etienne, apparently not above a bit of scrounging, trying to fit his foot into the other one. "Etienne," I say firmly, "the answer is 'no.'" Everyone laughs. Laurent stitches the other boot as well, even though it has not come apart yet.

Just on the off chance, I ask him if he can do anything about my glasses, and show him where the nose-pad is broken. Then it occurs to me that I have a spare pair of glasses; the prescription for them is outdated, but the nose-pads are intact. Laurent examines both pairs of glasses. It's a job that really requires an eyeglass-repair kit with a tiny screwdriver. But Laurent takes the cheap penknife I gave Etienne, and grinds down the point of one of the blades on the machete sharpener, until the width is exactly right for the tiny screws holding the nose-pads on. He takes the nose-pads off the pair of glasses that has one nose-pad broken, and replaces both with the nose-pads from the other pair. That works perfectly. I am delighted. I pay him another 1,000cfa for repairing the glasses and, knowing that he'll spend it all on cigarettes, tease him, "Don't smoke it all at once."

Life in the camp is happy, but there is an undercurrent of anxiety about the lack of specimens. Etienne and I spend hours by day and night wading in forest ponds and in the marsh near the road in search of frogs, mornings checking the nets in the flooded forest, and the rest of the time turning over rocks and logs and scanning the vegetation along the edge of the forest, but with an inexplicable lack of success. The pitfall traps have still not caught a single thing. One wet afternoon, a little leaf-litter frog practically hops into my lab corner of the house. It is on the ground right at the edge of the tarpaulin. I grab it, but it is so slippery that it escapes my grasp. I grab again and miss, shouting at the same time for Etienne. The frog hops out of sight under the tarpaulin overhang along the side of the house. I am kicking myself for losing a specimen that almost hopped right into a collecting bag. Etienne, just as desperate, has taken half the house apart, and is turning over all the earth with his machete.

On one nocturnal frog-searching outing we have slightly more luck. In fact I manage to pick up a few big frogs like the one Emmanuel caught on the road on the way to the swamp. Etienne is pleased because all our plastic bags are used up so we have to turn back. During our night walks, he sees the advantage of my headlamp in keeping my hands free. Ingenious as ever, he manages to rig a headlamp for himself out of a flashlight and a scrap of string.

But it is checking the nets that soon becomes the favorite part of the day for both of us, partly because of the pleasure of walking in the flooded forest, but mainly because it's the one activity that fairly reliably produces specimens. After 2 days of catching no more snakes in the nets we set with Emmanuel, we move one of the nets to a place recommended by Etienne's grandmother. (How she could explain a location in the flooded forest is a mystery to me.) It is in deeper water, so that I have to take off my backpack and leave it on a nearby tuft of vegetation to keep it dry as I wade in water up to my chest, but it catches us a snake on the second day. Yet another *Grayia,* but at least a specimen.

Common as they are, I love the *Grayia.* Large, solid-bodied, gray, semiaquatic fish-eating snakes, they take me back to the first snakes of my childhood in southern Ontario: *Nerodia sipedon,* the northern water snake, also a large, solid-bodied, gray, semiaquatic fish-eating snake. I'm always being asked where my passion for amphibians and reptiles came from, and I'm not really able to explain it. Even my parents are no help, though they say with confidence that the interest predates kindergarten. I do remember the day I saw my first live snake, though. It happened the summer I was 5, while I was playing with my sister in a washed-up rubber tire at the edge of Lake Ontario. My sister was trying, without much success, to scoop water into the tire using a plastic colander. Without realizing it, she scooped up a juvenile water snake, and dumped it onto my legs. I screamed, and the little snake, equally startled, retreated hastily to the water. Our sensible babysitter scolded me for making such a ridiculous fuss—a big girl like me! To this day, and in spite of all the rarer and more glamorous snakes I have encountered in the course of my career, *Nerodia sipedon* remains my favorite of all the 3,000 species of snakes in the world. Most people dislike *Nerodia* because they bite when provoked and spray a foul-smelling foam, to discourage predators. But their underdog status just adds to my fondness for them. Here on the other side of the planet I have come across *Grayia ornata,* a snake that resembles *Nerodia* in many ways, but is only very, very distantly related to them. Their similarities are an example of convergence—acquiring the same characteristics independently of one another because they fill similar ecological niches.

As Etienne and I are checking the nets one morning, we hear a shout from the camp. Nicole, Etienne's wife, has come to visit. I am very pleased. It is high time I met this woman. Goodness knows what she imagines about me, the mondele woman whom her husband sleeps beside in the forest. I certainly want to be on good terms with Etienne's wife. And it will be good for Etienne to spend an hour or so with his wife and baby before we set out for the marsh. We finish the nets and return to the camp. Nicole, a large woman—late 20s, early 30s?—is seated on a bench in the kitchen, breastfeeding Patience, and chatting with Florence in Lingala.

I greet her warmly, adding that Etienne talks a lot about her. Her reaction is a blank stare. She doesn't even smile—total lack of expression. Strange. Perhaps she doesn't understand French. I admire the baby, and then get out my camera and take several family photographs to add to their collection. I show her the results on the quick-view screen but she shows no sign of interest. I go into the house to give Etienne and Nicole some privacy.

Then I start to wait for this visit to end. Nicole arrived at 7:20 a.m. She makes herself at home. She eats, she changes diapers, she chats with Florence and Etienne, and I notice her fingering one of the plastic buckets covetously. I glance outside the house and see Nicole, deep in Lingala conversation with Florence, simultaneously breastfeeding Patience and chopping an onion onto a manioc leaf with a machete. Florence, distracted by this congenial new companion, does no work. I have to tell her to cook a meal for me and Etienne, and the dishes stay dirty afterward. The inside of the house is also a mess until she clears a space in it for Nicole to sleep. I want to like her, I really do, but will she never leave? Etienne and I have work to do, and the way things have been going we don't have time to waste.

Florence needs to run an errand in the village and promises to be back by 1:00 p.m. I am finally saved from Nicole by the news that Etienne has to attend a meeting in the village at 1:00. It must be very important considering how difficult it is to persuade him to leave the camp for any reason. At 12:30 I point out that he must leave if he is to get to the village on time. He is very reluctant to go before Florence returns, and reveals that the Chief has forbidden me to be left alone in the forest. I insist. I point out that Florence will be back any minute. He will probably pass her on the trail, and he finally gives in, mercifully taking his family away with him.

But Florence does not return at 1:00. I am used to living alone, and feel wonderfully liberated after so many days of always being with other people. I brazenly strip off my wet clothes outside, rather than crouched furtively under the mosquito net, and wander around the camp picking out almost-dry clothes from those hanging up. I sing. First softly and in French, then louder, in English, and with increasing lack of inhibition.

And then I think.

I am getting desperate for specimens. I stand in the middle of the camp, gazing off into the dense tangle of forest that surrounds us. What am I doing wrong? Put me near the edge of an Ontario lake in the summer and I can usually turn up a *Nerodia* within a few minutes. Is it just because I know my home province better than this African forest?

There is one school of thought that says that the rainforests of the Old World are less biodiverse than those of the New World. I've always assumed this notion to be total nonsense, reflecting only the fact that the New World tropics have been much more extensively studied than central Africa. Now I wonder. I've worked in the neotropics after all, and have memories from Costa Rica of coming in after a night's collecting with bags of snakes and frogs. But this is a much harder place to work. This is no field station. The single most effective herpetological collecting method is not available to us: road cruising. Road cruising means driving slowly along a little-traveled road at dusk or just after, looking for snakes at the sides of the road, and often encountering frogs hopping across. We have a road, but no vehicle. Walking, we can never cover enough ground to make finding anything likely.

In Ontario, and temperate parts of the world in general, when you find snakes you often find lots of them. But all of the same species. In the tropics, where the biodiversity is greater, my first professor at Harvard once told me that he considered a snake a day a reasonable rate of success, and that even that took a lot of work. But, those daily snakes are likely all to be different species. So how on earth do the snakes of each species find each other? They must get together to mate, after all. Snakes can hear, see, and taste (or "smell"), and use these senses for different things. Although they lack ears, they feel the vibrations of sound through the ground and through air, warning them of approaching dangers (such as me). Vision is important for hunting and self-defense—anything that requires them to aim a strike. But their most developed sense, and the one they depend on for their social life, is chemical. Glands in their skin secrete pheromones—chemicals that convey information by taste or smell to others of their species. As they slither along they leave a pheromone trail that another snake can follow. Snakes flick their tongues in and out constantly as they taste their surroundings, and the forked shape of the tongue is especially effective at following trails. With two sensory points (the two tips of the fork), the snake can easily tell if it is veering too far to the right or too far to the left of the pheromone line.

I stand in the camp and ruminate for a long time. Finally I walk a few cautious paces into the forest, acutely aware of how easy it is to lose track of a trail or even a campsite as soon as my view of it is swallowed up by the trees behind me. I relax and listen to the forest sounds around me, the chirping of birds, the buzzing of insects, the distant crack of a large branch crashing down. The animals I am searching for are here, somewhere. The sense of living things interacting, humming all around me, is palpable. I find myself remembering a very different forest, one on the other side of the world. I spent my first summer of graduate school on the Micronesian island of Guam, studying brown tree snakes *(Boiga irregularis)*. Humans introduced brown tree snakes to Guam by unwittingly transporting them on ships arriving from the Solomon Islands, shortly after World War II. With no predators on the island, the snake population exploded, the snakes eating everything in sight, starting with all the island's birds, vulnerable to the impressive climbing abilities of this arboreal species. I once stood in the tropical forest of Guam just as I am standing here, and it gave me a creepy feeling. I eventually noticed that the forest was absolutely silent. No birds singing. Then I noticed that I was all tangled in cobwebs—the forest was shrouded with them. No birds to eat the spiders. I heard the occasional scuttle of a feral cat or pig, the forest's only surviving inhabitants. That's the image I carry in my mind of a trashed ecosystem.

But the situation here is very different. I look again at the dense forest and think of our fishnets. I bet I could spend 8 hours a day for a month sloshing through the flooded forest without ever seeing a single *Grayia*—they would be scared off by the noise of my splashing long before I got close to them, but with the fishnets we caught two the first day. The water must be full of them, and we've figured out how to extract them from it. Our two nets work. Why not add more nets and increase our odds? I will ask WCS to pick up some more for me in Impfondo.

If only we had something equally effective on land. The forest is impenetrable unless you hack your way through it with a machete, scaring off any animal long before you get close enough to see it, and I'm not having much success searching potential hiding places, in hard-to-get-at rotting logs tangled in vines. We might just get lucky walking trails, by day and by night, but the only trail is the one leading to the camp, and I'm inclined to think it is too well traveled by noisy people. Any animals that might have been nearby will have been scared off. Quietly walking trails is unlikely to yield much, but it just might provide a few interesting specimens from the deep forest. At least it's something we haven't tried yet.

I will get Etienne to cut a long transect trail into the forest near the camp, 5 kilometers long if possible. It will keep him busy for some time, doing the kind of tedious and exhausting work he enjoys; the new idea will renew our optimism, and we will have access—a way to move quietly through the forest without scaring everything for miles around, where I will have a hope of seeing and catching something before it disappears into the underbrush while I struggle with the thicket of prickly plants separating me from it. As leader of this expedition I am as responsible for morale in the camp as I am for producing a collection that I will not be ashamed to present to the Smithsonian Institution. Whether cutting trails works in the end or not, it is a new approach and a new source of hope. Etienne and Florence are not just in this for the pay packet. They will be happy only if our project is a success.

Soon I start to get tired of being on my own. I'm hungry and I want someone to come and cook me a meal—I must be getting used to having servants. Etienne takes his time in the village, assuming that I am safely in the care of Florence, and does not return until dusk. He is furious when he discovers that Florence is not back yet. He explains pompously that his authority is second only to that of the Chief and that Florence has to obey him. This is not the polite, deferential Etienne I know. This, I come to learn, is Etienne recently exposed to his wife, and filled with grievances. I haven't seen this side of him before, and I don't like it. It is getting dark and I don't think Florence has a flashlight with her. Etienne cleans the unwashed cooking pots and prepares dinner for the two of us. His cooking turns out to be a considerable improvement over Florence's.

Gradually as he cooks and we eat he calms down and reverts to character. He knows how desperately we need specimens, and tells me that while he was in the village some boys had found "the snake with two heads." They had offered it to Etienne, but he had rejected it because it was hacked to pieces. I explain to Etienne, in dismay, that DNA can be extracted even from a bad specimen, and that simply knowing the location that a specimen comes from has value, and he looks devastated. I wonder what "the snake with two heads" must be: either a typhlopid (a blind snake—small, harmless, and often found underground) or a legless lizard of the genus *Feylinia,* which looks very much like a typhlopid. I add the snake to my wish list. I assure Etienne, with more confidence than I feel, that if there is one there will be others. "After all," I point out, "we've still got a month left."

Florence returns early the following morning as Etienne is boiling water for coffee. She tells a rambling tale of an emergency in a neighbor's family, and then says she couldn't return to the camp after dark because she didn't have a flashlight. I can't bring myself to be stern— she already does far more work than was in her job description. I tell her that she is welcome to make overnight visits to the village from time to time, and doesn't need to make excuses. However, I must know when she will be back, and she must be back on the agreed time. It is only fair to Etienne, because I need to be able to coordinate their time off. Etienne and I set off to check the nets, and on our return find the camp completely restored to order, clothing washed, house swept and tidied, and a pot of food on the fire. All is forgiven and forgotten.

I explain the trail-cutting plan to Etienne and Florence. Etienne will cut a good trail, I tell them confidently, penetrating deep into the forest. After he finishes cutting it we will leave it for 3 days, so the animals of the forest will forget about the disturbance. Walking on this trail for any purpose other than collecting will be strictly forbidden. I look meaningfully at Florence and she puts on a serious expression and nods emphatically.

The next step will be to teach Etienne how to walk in the forest in a new way. The local habit when walking through the forest is to make as much noise as possible, presumably in the hope of scaring off dangerous animals. But since dangerous animals are exactly what I'm after, this will not do. Moving quietly will be crucial. If Etienne rushes ahead, shouting and hacking with the machete, the whole exercise will be a waste of time.

For the next few days, Etienne spends the afternoons happily wearing himself out cutting through vegetation in the forest. In the meantime, with help from Florence, I follow every lead, however improbable, in my desperate quest for specimens. How news travels around here I never do figure out. Florence tells me there is a family living deep in the forest (juste à coté!) that have found a dead snake and are saving it for me. I should go and get it as quickly as possible before it rots. I rush after her into the forest. There is definitely no trail, but Florence is confidently wielding the machete, clearing a way through the tangle of branches. I am slipping and tripping in the Chief's souliers à jeter, so I take them off and go barefoot, which is not a good decision. It takes us a good 45 minutes to arrive at the little clearing juste à coté, where a woman is sitting, vigorously grinding something in a wooden bowl, with a stick, on the doorstep of a little shack.

After the usual polite formalities, one of the several children who have appeared from inside the hut leads me to the snake. They wanted to make sure it didn't rot before I got there, the woman explains, proud of her initiative, so they smoked it on the fire with the fish. I look at the blackened carcass on the smoked-fish rack in despair. There is no way even to tell what species it was. If they find another one, I tell her, without much hope, don't do anything to it. Just get me as soon as possible. Or better still, I say, thinking of my cut-up feet, bring it to my camp. So as not to cut up my feet even more, we go back the long way, along the road. One of the children, a girl of about 11, leads us from the hut out to the road, cutting a trail for us with a machete. So much for girls not being brought up to work in the forest. I bet this one could be an excellent guide in a few years' time. By the time we reach the road, the midday sun, which we are protected from in the forest, is beating down on the asphalt, so when we finally arrive back at the camp my feet are burned as well as cut.

Morale is very low in our little camp. Etienne sounds half-hearted when he expresses optimism about the trail. "We will get lots of animals on the trail, Madame, I am sure of it."

"You know, I think we just might," I try to sound optimistic. Then the torrential rain begins again. Florence rushes around retrieving still-wet clothing from the washing line, bushes, roof of the house, and anywhere else clothes are left to dry. This time the rain doesn't let up. For 3 miserable days we put on wet clothes in the morning and sleep in wet clothes at night.

"This rain will get everything moving," says Florence confidently. "The fish are more active when it rains, and the snakes will chase the fish and get caught in the nets. You'll see." Going out in the heavy rain I am quickly blinded by the water on the lenses of my glasses. I keep hoping it will let up a bit, thinking the rain might have brought out frogs, but it doesn't. Florence gets soaked every morning bringing the morning coffee from the kitchen to drink in the shelter of the house, after which Etienne and I go and get soaked checking the nets. The water is deeper, which makes walking through the flooded forest even more difficult than usual, and in spite of all Florence's predictions we go 3 days without catching a single snake in the nets. As for the pitfall traps, checking them has become perfunctory. They have never caught anything.

I pay Etienne and Florence, realizing that a week has gone by since the day I arrived at Ganganya Brousse. And what have I got to show for it, I think miserably: 10 specimens. Tomorrow is Sunday. At least it has stopped raining. I insist that we check the nets early so that Etienne can go to church. I know how much that means to him. But he refuses to leave the camp until he remembers that this is his week to preach. Apparently, in the absence of a pastor the villagers take turns giving the sermon. Incredibly, even Laurent preaches—that would be something to see!

Two young men arrive at the camp on Sunday morning to accompany Etienne to church: Roger and Henri. We shake hands. "Roger is our photographer," announces Florence. Sure enough, Roger carries a cheap, battered 35-millimeter camera. Florence and Etienne want a picture of the three of us together. Florence and I sit on the bench and Etienne stands behind, resting a hand on each of our shoulders. I ask Roger to take a picture of us with my camera too, and show him how it works. He does it, but with strange reluctance. I soon find out why.

Once the picture has been taken, Roger informs me, a bit apologetically, that he has to charge me 500cfa for a photograph taken with his camera. This must be how Etienne got the treasured pictures of his baby. I pay Roger politely, but I am not pleased. I will have to speak to Etienne and Florence about putting me in positions where I am obliged to pay for something I haven't asked for. But now is not the time. As Etienne and his friends set off for church I offhandedly ask Etienne to ask God to send us some specimens. He earnestly promises me that he will do just that.

After they have left, I ask Florence, in mild frustration, why they got Roger to come and take the photo. "Lots of people visit the camp, and any one of them could have taken a picture of the three of us together using my camera," I point out.

"But we wanted one for ourselves."

"Of course—you know I'm going to send you all my best photos of us when I get back to Canada and can print them."

"You are?" It turns out that they had told Roger to take three pictures. He charges 500cfa for each one, and makes a bit of money in the village when people have something special (like a new baby) that they want to commemorate. Florence and Etienne had each paid Roger 500cfa of their own money for a picture of us together, leaving me to pay 500cfa for a copy for myself. I feel mean at having paid for the photo so grudgingly.

chapter 6

the
red
snake

Etienne doesn't come back until it is almost dark, but when he arrives he is triumphantly carrying a plastic bag containing two specimens of the lizard I missed on the roof of the payotte that first day. I am
ecstatic. Where did he catch them? "My wife caught them, Madame, in
the village this afternoon."

"Using the noose I gave you?"

"No, Madame, she just caught them with her hands." Yes, I notice
that they are missing their tails, but I'm in no position to be fussy. Lizards' tails break off easily if you handle them roughly. It's a defense
mechanism. The tail continues to writhe about for some time after it is

separated from the animal, and if the lizard is lucky, the resulting distraction will deter whatever predator is chasing it.

The next day Nicole herself appears bearing a bag with so many skinks in it that I can't count them, and another bag with several toads. Her face remains utterly devoid of expression as I kiss her on both cheeks. They're common species, but there are lots of them. My project is making a list of species present in the area, so I prefer getting representatives of as many species as possible, but I recognize the importance of collecting "series"—large numbers—of what appear to be the same species for studies at the level of populations, studies other people may carry out using the specimens I collect. Understanding the variation among individuals in a population is fundamental to understanding species.

I get WCS to pick up more fishnets and string at the Impfondo market, and Etienne and I set out 450 meters of net in the flooded forest around the area, with some places so deep we almost have to swim. We certainly catch more snakes, but all, to my disappointment, are large specimens of *Grayia ornata*. I had expected at a minimum juvenile pythons, hoped for water cobras, and dreamed of that mythical banded snake they'd told me about on the first night.

Then one morning, waist-deep in water, Etienne calls out in excitement, "Madame—the red and black snake!" It is not at all what I had imagined. In fact it basically looks like the *Grayia* we have been getting except that where it should be gray it is distinctly reddish. Could this be *Boulengerina*, the water cobra, at last? I don't know what the local color variation is. The head is tightly tangled in the net—tightly enough that I wouldn't have reliable control over the head with the hemostat, but not necessarily tight enough to prevent it from wriggling a few inches free at just the wrong moment. There's no way I can identify it without seeing the head. It could be another *Grayia*, just inexplicably red where every other specimen we've caught has been gray. It could be *Boulengerina*. It could be something else I've never heard of, which is

Etienne's opinion. "All right," I decide. Etienne has succeeded in sowing some doubts in my mind and transmitting his fear. "Mark the spot, then put a log on the net to sink it. We'll come back in 2 hours when the snake is drowned and take it out of the net."

I spend the next hour wild with excitement, and there's no way I can last the suspense of 2 hours. Etienne, by now used to the *Grayia,* is uncharacteristically nervous.

"Madame, when we take the snake out of the net will you take the head end?" Etienne asks anxiously.

"Of course."

When we return to remove the dead snake from the net, I am filled with anticipation. Imagine my disappointment when it turns out to be nothing more than another *Grayia,* albeit with unusual red coloring. But this is exactly the reason for collecting many *Grayia* rather than just one—we are learning what variation exists among the individuals in this small area. I tell Etienne that it is harmless and that it is another *Grayia.* Both of these facts he adamantly refuses to believe.

"No, Madame, this snake is venomous."

"Nonsense, look, I'll even open its mouth and show you. See? No fangs." But Etienne is not used to looking at snake teeth and this display does not impress him.

"No, Madame, this is a venomous snake. It is not the same as the others."

"I guarantee you it is not venomous. Look," I point out, getting irritated, "snakes are my specialty."

"We will ask the Chief," Etienne responds with finality.

"Ask the Chief?! What is the Chief supposed to know about snakes? I'll tell you what, Etienne, if we catch another snake like this one, a red one, if I let it bite me, then would you believe me that it is not venomous?"

"Yes, Madame," he grins, "then I would believe you."

Then there is the question of whether the red snake is another

Grayia ornata. Etienne is adamant that it is not. He insists that this must be another species. I would love it to be a new species of *Grayia*—even a new subspecies. I allow myself to fantasize about what I would name it.

Most people I meet seem to be under the impression that if you discover a new species you name it after yourself. Although you do get to choose the name, no scientists would ever do anything as crass as naming a new species after themselves. There are basically two types of names that you can use: You can name the species after somebody else, say as a mark of respect to your doctoral supervisor, whom you admire, or after an elderly expert who has written a lot about related species (for example, *Ptychadena perreti,* a frog named after the great African frog expert, Perret), or you can give it a "descriptive" name, one that adds some information about the biology of the species (for instance, *Bitis gabonica,* a giant viper, the first described specimen of which was collected in Gabon). Though the practice is less common nowadays, museum herpetologists of the past sometimes named new species after the collectors—people with no knowledge of herpetology. When I started learning about African reptiles, it did not escape my notice that there were a lot of species called *"jacksoni."* I've counted four so far: *Chamaeleo jacksoni,* Jackson's chameleon, the largest and most handsome of all chameleons; *Thrasops jacksoni,* a large black tree snake; *Aparallactus jacksoni,* a small snake with very interesting teeth, and some question as to the extent to which it might be venomous; and finally another lizard, *Adolfus jacksoni.* Perhaps if I make a name for myself in African herpetology people will one day imagine that all those *jacksoni*s are named after me. I did a bit of research to find out who this Jackson was. It turned out he was a British army officer with an amateur interest in natural history. In the late 1800s, wherever he was posted, he collected and donated the specimens to the British Museum, where the curator who identified them named each new species after Jackson in order to encourage him to bring in more.

But when I count the scales on my specimen, the standard routine for formally identifying snakes, every scale count confirms it as *Grayia ornata*. I won't be describing a new species after all. "Scale counting," the means by which herpetologists identify snakes, is more than a matter of counting scales. Look closely at the head of a snake and you'll see that it is covered with fairly large, smooth, interlocking scales. Now every scale on the head of a snake has a name: there are the supralabials along the upper lip, numbered starting with the one closest to the rostral scale, the scale at the tip of the snout; there are pre-orbital, post-orbital, sub-ocular, and supra-orbital scales in contact with the edges of the eyes; there is the nasal scale, usually divided in two with the nostril in between; then there are the loreal, the internasals, the prefrontals, the frontal, the parietals, the temporals, and so on—and then there are the scales on the body. Most of "scale counting" is actually detailed observation of the relative positions of the scales. Here's a typical example. It happens to be for *Grayia ornata:*

"The rostral is barely visible from above. The nasal is divided. The internasals are equal in length to the prefrontals. The loreal is greater in height than in length. The pre-ocular is almost equal in height to the diameter of the eye. The length of the frontal is equal to twice its width. The supra-ocular is slightly narrower than the frontal. The two post-oculars are approximately equal in size. The temporal formula is 2 + 2, or sometimes 2 + 3. There are 8 supralabials, occasionally 9, the fourth of which is in contact with the eye, and the seventh usually the largest, etc. . . ." (Translated from J.-P. Chippaux, *Les serpents Afrique occidentale et centrale,* Paris, IRD Editions, 2006, p. 92.)

I try to explain to Etienne that scale counts matter more than color, but he has never seen a washed-out, preserved snake in a museum collection, color leached away by years in preservative, and he does not know that scale counts are much less prone to individual variation than coloration. I point out that individual snakes might be either red or gray but still of the same species.

"Imagine if some zoologist caught you and me," I reason. "We are the same species, but we are very different colors. Much more different than the difference between these snakes." But nothing I say will convince him. So to humor him we take lots of pictures of the red *Grayia* beside a gray *Grayia,* and I process the specimen as though it were a new species, photographing it and taking a tissue sample.

One evening Etienne returns from a visit to the village with the news that he had passed the WCS truck on the road. He hands me a plastic bag, a gift from Hugo, who had found it on the road and carefully stopped to pick it up. It is dark and I am working by headlamp. The powerful stench from the bag as Etienne hands it to me tells me that whatever is in it has been on the road some time. Breathing through my mouth, I reach into the bag and pull out a small, very flat snake. There is no pattern visible to make it obviously identifiable. I squint at the scales and notice that they are missing in patches. At about the same moment I feel a tickling on my forearms and look down to see a swarm of ants, which had been picking at the carcass, abandoning it for me! I drop the snake and slap madly at the tiny ants. Okay, this snake is going in formalin NOW. I will try to identify it by scale counts by the light of day tomorrow, when the smell is no worse than formalin and the ants are drowned in it. I make what feels like a heroic effort to take a tissue sample before soaking the carcass in formalin.

The next day the morning light shows that the head scales, essential for identification, have been mostly nibbled away by ants. I'm able to determine the genus though: *Dasypeltis.* Snakes of this genus are famous for an anatomical adaptation which allows them to eat hard-shelled birds' eggs. One of the neck vertebrae has an unusually long process extending from its underside. As the snake swallows the egg, this structure neatly punctures it, and the pressure of swallowing collapses it completely. Even though I won't get a nice photo of this one, I have to concede that it is an interesting specimen in spite of its revolting condition.

Just as adding nets improves our odds with the water snakes, adding people allows us to cover more ground. The area has a highly efficient gossip mill, and as soon as it becomes known that I am camped in the forest and want frogs, lizards, and snakes, people for miles around pick up any specimen they come across in the course of the day and bring it to me in the hope that I will buy it. Buying specimens from locals is a standard and often very effective herpetological collecting technique. The most difficult problem I face in buying animals for small sums is the lack of coins and small-denomination bills. I've complained before about the lack of small change in the country, affecting everyone from villagers trying to buy and sell manioc for 100cfa to taxi drivers in Brazzaville needing to provide change for 700cfa rides. When I worked near a remote Pygmy village on my first trip to the Congo, nobody was interested in paper money. Everybody wanted *things*—ballpoint pens, cigarettes, balloons (for the children). But here in the Likouala region money is absolutely the only thing anyone wants. So obtaining small money is an ongoing problem.

A great variety of people come to sell me a fascinating range of animals. My heart leaps with excitement every time I see a stranger appearing at the camp bearing an ancient plastic bag, holes tied shut with vines, or a battered plastic bucket with a lid. Usually I have no success at getting them to tell me what the bag or bucket contains. Even with Etienne or Florence there to translate from Lingala, they usually don't know what the animal is called. So I open parcels not knowing whether I'm going to find a venomous snake or a treefrog.

Two little girls bring me a plastic bucket with a lid, and seem incapable of explaining its contents. I open the lid with reasonable caution, but evidently not cautiously enough. A frog leaps out of the bucket, over my shoulder, and vanishes into the forest before I can catch it. I make sure the second one doesn't escape, though. These frogs are *Ptychadena*, smooth, streamlined frogs with immensely long legs and capable of enormous leaps.

I soon get good at negotiating these purchases. In each case, the seller has no use for and doesn't want to keep the animal he or she is trying to sell, isn't going to find anyone else interested in buying it, and should therefore settle for a low price, but I want to encourage the individual seller to bring more, and to spread the word that I pay enough to make the trip to my camp worthwhile, so I want all the sellers to be reasonably satisfied with the price. Bargaining over prices is deeply ingrained in the culture of the whole country, so I have to get good at African bargaining.

The first thing I learn is to avoid displays of great enthusiasm and excitement. The people don't understand what criteria make one animal valuable and another not, so they are watching to see how I react. I learn, when faced with a bag containing three handsome frogs of a species I've never seen before, to appear to ponder before saying, "Well, this third one here is not in very good condition, but I think I can probably give you *something* for them." Then I have to be careful with the bargaining to consider what denominations of bills and coins I have on hand. I may start at 400cfa and let them bargain up to 500cfa; I can pay with a 500cfa bill, the difference in price is very small, and I would actually rather pay 500cfa than 400cfa since doing the latter means parting with four precious 100cfa coins.

I develop one excellent strategy, which seems to please everyone. Suppose I'm buying a snake from a fisherman. I offer him 1,000cfa. He tries for more. I tell him that I can't pay more than 1,000cfa today because I am waiting for my boss to bring me money (this also gets across, to the gossip mill, the idea that there is not a lot of money being kept in the camp). My boss is coming on Tuesday. If he can wait until after Tuesday, I say to the fisherman, I can give him 1,500cfa, or if he prefers I can give him 1,000cfa today. Then I take one of my paper envelopes, sealed shut by the damp of the forest and useless as an envelope, and use it to write out an IOU, which can be exchanged for 1,500cfa any time after Tuesday. The IOUs are very popular, and leave me time to get hold of the right small-denomination bills.

Many things surprise me. If a man offers me a frog to buy, and I offer him 500cfa, he will not be satisfied with the amount and will ask for more. Yet if I simply tell him that I don't want to buy the frog because I already have many of that species, he will release it and leave apparently perfectly contented.

Some people are aggressive and angry bargainers, some are gentle and accepting. Most people come one time only, but I have a couple of regulars. I learn that it is not polite to rush a business transaction (though I may immediately upon the seller's arrival transfer the animal to a more secure container). I do my best to be a good hostess, inviting sellers to sit down and join me in a plastic mug of local whiskey or Gatorade. Eventually we get down to business.

One afternoon a little boy comes with a frog in a plastic bag. It is a *Xenopus,* an African clawed frog, an aquatic frog of the same genus as the frog most commonly used in laboratories around the world. Frogs of the genus *Xenopus* are generally aquatic. (If you keep them as pets they should go in an aquarium, but in the wild they sometimes venture into the damp leaf litter of the forest floor.) *Xenopus* are built to float and swim and eat—large, webbed feet, hefty hips and thighs, tapering to a narrower front end with a wide mouth, and spindly little arms, used mostly for stuffing food into the mouth. But the frog the boy has brought is a different species from the lab frog, and the first one in my collection. *Xenopus laevis,* the lab frog, is so common that it can be cheaply bought in quantities over the Internet, but the species of *Xenopus* where I am working are different. I may never figure out exactly how different because many of the species can be distinguished only by the number of chromosomes. I split a chocolate bar with the boy and get him to explain where and when he caught the frog. Since it is the first in my collection, I give him 500cfa for it, and he goes away delighted.

People are bringing in so many specimens that I have less time for my own searching, and since I search in different places and at different times of day than the people who catch species that are common in the village during the day, I should be catching different species, even if in small numbers.

The same day that Nicole brings the skinks and toads, four boys arrive with a plastic bin full of the same lizards (most missing their tails from rough handling) and the toads that seem to be common in the village. I offer them 800cfa for the lot. They are incensed. Apparently they had made an elaborate calculation based on the 300cfa I paid the little girl who brought the first toad. They had reckoned on 300cfa for every animal multiplied by four since there were four boys. "Did you expect to become millionaires?" I ask them. I explain to them that large numbers are not what I'm after. The most valuable specimen is any species I don't already have. "That lady over there," I say pointing to Nicole, who after 7 hours is still showing no intention of leaving, "brought me far more of these same species just this morning, so I have lots of them."

"How much did she get?"

"She's a friend. Here, I'll give you each a plastic bag, and I promise you 500cfa for anything you can catch that I don't already have, even if there's only one of it." They take the 800cfa from me looking disgusted, and then try to pressure me into paying more by not leaving. The youngest one has a little ax and is going around the camp hacking at anything wooden. I tell him to stop it. "Why are you wasting your time here? If you want more money, go out and catch something to put in the bag." Eventually they give up and leave. I never see them again.

One evening an elderly fisherman arrives with a tattered old fishnet in a bag. There is a dead *Grayia* tangled in the net. I sigh. The last thing I need is more *Grayia*. Talking to the man, I find out that he has just one fishnet to support his family (this is it) set up in flooded forest several kilometers from here (he has walked from there). I explain to him that I have nine fishnets, and I have so many snakes of this species that I am considering starting to let them go. I really don't want any more. But he looks so sad and defeated that I can't bring myself to just send him all the way back home with his one tattered net. He turns out to be the grandfather of the little boy who brought the first *Xenopus*. He had reasoned that if I would pay 500cfa to a child for a little frog, a snake must be valuable. I feel so sorry for him that I end up buying a snake I don't want for the ridiculous price of 1,500cfa, enough money to buy two new nets. I ask him, without much hope, to spread the word that I'm not buying this kind of snake.

One morning, when Etienne and I are just back from the nets, a man arrives from the village in a great state of excitement. He and his companions had been building a brick wall, and had come across a snake, sheltering from the mid-morning sun in a pile of bricks. He has come all the way from the village, leaving his coworkers to keep an eye on the snake. It never ceases to amaze me the distances the people in this region think nothing of walking. But the whole experience seems to have overwhelmed him to the extent that he is completely incapable of giving me a rough estimate of the size of the snake, and I don't even attempt more complicated questions. So I arrive at the excited village bearing a meter-long snake hook, a pair of 24-inch snake tongs, and a 12-inch hemostat. I peer into a crack between the bricks where a loop of small snake is just visible, and immediately put down the first two tools. I get a grip with the hemostat and gently ease the snake out. *Lamprophis,* a house snake—same genus as my first snake ever in the Congo, but a different species: harmless and commonly found around human habitations. I recognize it at once. It is my lucky day. A few bricks later I uncover a second one. The audience of bricklayers is delighted by the show, but not so much that they forget to make sure they get paid.

My favorite collector by far is Fiti. Fiti is a cheerful young Pygmy in a porkpie hat who collects deep in the forest and brings more interesting animals than the common village species. Though an extraordinary animal catcher, he is not as worldly and materialistic as the Bantu villagers, and always accepts whatever I pay him with delight, never making any effort to bargain. As I get to know him I learn that every franc gets spent on local whiskey. One day I am running very short of small-denomination bills and coins. I try the IOU deal on Fiti and feel bad about it afterward. Even with both Florence and Etienne doing their best to explain, Fiti has trouble grasping the strange idea of getting paid a higher price if he is willing to wait a couple of days for it. I watch his face contort in an agony of indecision before he settles on the smaller sum right away. On seeing the real money handed to him, he seems reassured that he has made the right decision. Fiti brings species of frogs I've never seen before from deep in the forest. They are always alive and without so much as a scratch on them. I know he makes traps to catch them and try to get him to show me how he does it. He's perfectly willing to share his trade secret, but is unable to articulate it in a way that I can make any sense of, even with Florence acting as interpreter.

Last week I would not have thought it possible that I would ever complain of too many specimens, but with this flood coming in, I am kept busy in the camp just making sure that all the specimens get properly preserved. I am very glad that I trained Etienne in preserving specimens. He doesn't know how to do the tissue sampling, and when I try to teach him he doesn't take to it. He has trouble handling the tiny vials and no understanding of the need to maintain clean conditions in order to prevent contamination. There's also the issue of finding the tissue to fix; Etienne lacks a basic knowledge of anatomy, and is not able to recognize liver tissue, for example, and know where it is so as to make only a small hole getting at it, minimizing damage to the specimen. Despite these problems, the day that we have 30 skinks and a dozen toads, Etienne's help is a godsend, and after inspecting a few of his specimens I trust him to inject the right amount of formalin, to tie the tags properly, and to spread out the fingers and toes carefully for hardening. It is hard work because we don't have a table to work at (Florence's kitchen table, being made of sticks, is not smooth and stable enough), so we have to work on the ground, hunched over, which is hard on the back. But I underestimate Etienne. After fixing about 20 identical skinks he looks up at me and grins, "Madame Katherine, I *like* this kind of work."

The nights are always uncomfortable, but finally one night is so exceptionally awful that it brings the problem to a head. I am fed up with this business of Etienne and Florence going to bed at 6:00 p.m. if I don't drag Etienne out for night-time searching before he has time to settle in under the mosquito net. I spend 2 hours reading and writing, determinedly not caring if my flashlight is bothering them. The instant I turn off my flashlight, Florence starts snoring loudly directly in my ear. I must somehow have dropped off anyway, because I am woken by Etienne's arm landing affectionately across my buttocks. I'm sure he's fast asleep and doesn't mean anything by it except that he's forgotten he's not sleeping beside his wife. I remove the arm, waking him up in the process. That one root that bothers me the most never did get removed when the men tried to get rid of the rest. In fact there are two bumps from roots, and the only way to curl up in a position that avoids them leaves me with Etienne breathing right in my face. I opt for lying on the bumps and am so tired I drift off nonetheless. The sensation of somebody's fingers groping under my ribcage almost rouses me, but not quite, and I even manage to stay half-asleep later while someone is kicking my feet. I drift off into a wonderful dream. I am living in a luxurious palace, with soft couches and thick carpets, and filled with snakes of many different species. I have one in each hand and another one is right in front of me to pick up . . . and I am incensed to be woken by Florence shining a flashlight in my eyes. I am yelling at her for waking me up. She is protesting that I am lying diagonally and there is nowhere for her to sleep. I try to check the time, but when I press the nightlight button on my watch the whole LED display goes blank. Great. A broken watch. Etienne is awake too and shining a flashlight around. I straighten myself out and try to drop back into my dream, but they are yelling across me at each other in Lingala. "Silence!" I shout in French, "no more conversation!" There is maybe 10 seconds of silence before the racket begins again. Even now I am not entirely awake. "SHUT UP!" I roar in English. This time they stop talking and I go back to sleep.

But not for long. When I next wake, it is to the sound of Etienne, outside the tent, yelling at someone in Lingala. This time I am wide awake. Are there intruders in the camp? That could be serious. What can Etienne do alone against a group? I turn to Florence, lying beside me. She is awake, but doesn't seem especially perturbed.

"What's going on?" I ask her. "Are there people in the camp?"

"No."

"Well then, who is Etienne shouting at?"

"The owls."

"Owls?"

"It's a kind of bird that lives . . ."

"I know what an owl is! What is he saying to them?"

"He's telling them to go away."

"Why?"

I eventually pry out of Florence the explanation that Etienne, our great male protector against the dangers of the night, has a morbid fear of owls. He believes that they are sorcerers. No wonder he reacts as if I am punishing him every night when I insist on going out to look for frogs in the swamp.

The next morning is the tensest moment between us so far. Etienne is not singing. He is drooping on the bench outside the house. I greet him as I emerge, "Bonjour."

"Bonjour," he mumbles. Not even "Bonjour, Madame." Florence is grimly stoking the fire and boiling water for coffee. Etienne gulps his coffee and immediately starts putting on his wet jeans to check the nets. I tell him firmly that I will not be ready for at least an hour. He broods while I take my time over my coffee, recovering from the night, and then packing my backpack and changing into wet boots and cargo pants. But as we check the nets, as he fills his bucket with the fish caught in the net, and as the sun starts to warm us, the beauty of the flooded forest works its magic, and by the time we finish the last net, even though there have been no snakes today, he is happy and has forgotten any grudges.

On our return, Florence enquires about the catch, as always, and serves us bowls of macaroni, tomato paste, and pork luncheon meat.

"Madame Katherine," says Etienne, "bon appétit."

While we've been in the water, Florence has been thinking. "The way we are sleeping," she begins—it's a topic that has to be broached— "we're too crowded. Everyone gets in everyone else's way, and nobody sleeps well." She has a solution to propose. She is going to convert another of the useful Pygmy payottes into a little house just for her. She will make it comfortable and she will sleep in there by herself. "That way there will be space, and everyone can sleep as they like." A Pygmy payotte does not sound very comfortable to me, and I say so, but she is adamant. That day she builds a solid bedframe out of branches using one of the machetes; brings from her house in the village a thick layer of foam rubber as a mattress, a blanket, and a mosquito net; and then shores up the payotte with leaves, discarded plastic bags, and anything else she can find to make it waterproof. By the time she is finished I am quite envious of the result.

The new sleeping arrangement has several advantages. I now have a whole mosquito net to myself, which not only means more space to sleep, but also allows me to spread out my belongings in a messy way. It's like having my own bedroom. I had worried that having moved out of the house Florence would no longer think to sweep it out and maintain order, but I underestimated her. Every morning when Etienne and I return from the water, the mosquito nets are tied up out of the way, and she has tidied my room as much as is possible without impinging on my privacy by going through my things. The sheet and any dry clothing are folded, and my various bags and packs are neatly lined up against the back "wall." But the best result of sharing the house only with Etienne is that I am not excluded by Lingala conversation anymore. We are forced to communicate in French, and we often talk for hours, after returning from night work, through the mosquito nets, before falling asleep.

Etienne, always eager to learn, wants to learn English, and is determined to teach me Lingala. We spend hours lying side by side with our respective notebooks, under our respective mosquito nets, exchanging vocabulary. Somebody proposes a word in French, I give the English, which Etienne writes down, and he gives the Lingala, which I write down.

"Tortue."

"Turtle."

"Koba."

"Maison."

"House."

"Ndako," and so on.

One night I try an experiment:

"Merci" (thank you), I offer. Etienne is stumped. He can't think of the Lingala word. "S'il vous plaît" (please). He doesn't know that one either. I think how jarring and rude it always seems to me when the people around here don't say please and thank you when I expect it, and I realize that they don't mean to be rude. They're just translating into French from Lingala, where the expressions are apparently not much used. And it goes both ways. "Bon appétit," offers Etienne. Untranslatable. I have to explain that it's a politeness that we don't have in English. No wonder I always forget to say it when I come upon someone who's eating.

I pick up scraps of Lingala in other ways as well. The first word I ever learned in Lingala was on my first expedition: *nyoka*—snake. Overhearing Lingala conversation around the camp I keep hearing the word, and demanding to know what is being talked about. The conversation never seems to have anything to do with snakes. It is Florence who finally figures out that what I am mistaking for *nyoka* is *yoka,* the verb "to hear." Another word, which causes great hilarity, is *kati.* Every time I hear that word I perk up, because it sounds like the common mispronunciation of "Kate." When I think about it I realize Florence and Etienne can't possibly be talking about me since they know me only as Katherine. When I explain, and ask what "kati" means, they tell me "inside," as in *kati na ndako*—inside the house. This causes great amusement, and thereafter I am known irreverently by Etienne as "Madame Kati," and even less reverently by Florence simply as "Kati."

I still insist on dragging Etienne out on nocturnal frog searches. One evening as we set off there is a low hooting sound from the forest. "The owls are saying 'Good evening' to Etienne," says Florence mischievously. Our luck starts to turn. One night I fill a bag with *Xenopus,* the frog that the little boy brought the first specimen of. These frogs turn out in the end to be the commonest species of frog in the area, and in fact even more common during the day. The large numbers seem to encourage Etienne, but I prefer the nights when a whole evening's searching turns up just a couple of frogs in a forest pond that are of a species I can't identify.

Florence's cooking has deteriorated, something I would not have thought possible. I have discovered the secret of how she cooks pasta. She sautés the dry macaroni in an inch or so of oil, and then starts adding mugs of water to it until it is soft enough to eat. To this pot of macaroni she adds tomato paste and pork luncheon meat. To save herself work, she makes a pot of the stuff so big that we have to eat it cold for several days. It is Laurent who, picking at a cold dish of this concoction, comments, "I am eating the intestines of a duck." The comparison is so horribly apt that nobody wants to eat the macaroni any more. I put my foot down and refuse to buy any more rice until the macaroni is finished. So Florence and Etienne start bringing manioc from the village to eat. Etienne and Florence also eat some of the smoked fish from the nets (the rest they sell in the village). Florence, not wanting to have to prepare a separate meal for me, tries to persuade me to eat smoked fish and manioc too but I flatly refuse. Since she isn't going to have to eat it herself, Florence makes less and less effort in preparing my food. I threaten her teasingly. "If I go back to Canada skinny, my grandmother will be angry, and I'll tell her that it's all the fault of Florence!"

One morning Etienne and I come back from the water to find that Florence has left for a trip to the village, leaving nothing for me but a pot of cold, plain, leftover rice from the day before, burned and stuck to the bottom of the pot. I draw the line. I will not eat it and I will have a word with Florence when she returns. Etienne eats some of the smoked fish, but nothing could persuade me to resort to that.

It is that morning that three children arrive with a lizard in a bag. It is yet another *Trachylepis,* the common species that people from the village have been bringing in masses of. I feel sorry for them, but I have to get the message across that I am not buying this species any more. It is a nice specimen, alive and with the tail still attached. I sit the children down and ply them with bon-bons sifflets, but I explain firmly why I will not buy the lizard, and that it must be released. They nod resignedly and show little interest in watching it scamper off into the forest. Accustomed by now to these extended visits, I leave them to themselves and get back to work on my specimens. I am interrupted by Etienne. He wants to know if he may give the cold rice to the children. I feel terrible. They were probably ravenous, poor things, and there I had been giving them sweets when what they really wanted was just simple nourishment. They all sit together on a log and eat the rice out of the pot with their hands.

I get used to always being dirty. I have long since abandoned such affectations as tooth brushing and underarm deodorant. I decide I am definitely dirty when my last bra is muddy. Florence is always trying to get hold of my clothes to wash, but with so little sunlight and so much rain, clothes can hang for days without drying, and I would rather have dirty clothes than wet ones. She is persistent though. "Kati, do you have clothes to be washed? No?! What do you mean 'No!' All your trousers are caked with mud! And this?" She tugs at the sleeve of my fleece sweater, my only warm or long-sleeved piece of clothing. "Apparently it never gets washed? Put it all in that bucket over there."

Walking the trail has become part of our routine. With considerable difficulty I have taught Etienne to walk slowly and quietly, examining every leaf and branch before moving on. Looking at his souliers à jeter makes me cringe a bit, considering we are on a mission to find snakes, and I do my best to impress on him the importance of always looking at the ground before putting his foot down. This trail is nothing like the grand thoroughfare that gets called a "trail" at a field station or national park. The forest is impossible to walk through because you are immediately ensnared in the tangle of vegetation. By the time you struggle to be free of it, any animal in the area will be long gone. That is why everyone uses machetes when walking through the forest, but once again, this is a noisy and disruptive method not conducive to sneaking up on animals. The instructions I gave Etienne were to cut his way by machete in as straight a line as possible, about 2 hours into the forest. Dry land was what we wanted, but with so much of the forest flooded, some of our trail involves wading short distances through water. The idea was just to cut away enough tangled vegetation so that we could walk through the forest silently and without obstruction.

Etienne has made the trail exactly as I told him to, but what I hadn't counted on was that the trail would be virtually invisible—to me at least. The only way to tell which direction is part of the trail is that what appear to be tangled plants can be pushed apart by hand, without a machete. To Etienne the trail is apparently completely obvious. He stifles laughter when I try to mark the route with flagging tape—white plastic ribbon given to me by the Smithsonian for just this sort of purpose (I would have preferred orange). Even once I have marked the trail, I have great difficulty locating the next marker. And I had discovered on the first day that my GPS doesn't work in the forest. I had hoped to search the forest by night as well as by day, but the combination of my hopeless sense of direction and Etienne's terror of owls makes that impossible. I try to walk ahead, to be the first person to come across any animal on our transect, but I often have to turn to Etienne to point me in the right direction (yes, I know it's almost a straight line, but a straight line through the Congo forest is a very different thing from a straight Toronto street).

On most days, the walk yields nothing, though often I see a tail disappearing into the underbrush, or a frog leaping off into the dense forest. We get so few specimens on the trail that it is terribly frustrating to lose one. We walk the trail for several days without catching a thing. Etienne, who doesn't like this slow quiet walking, is soon doing the trails as perfunctorily as the useless pitfall traps. Although I have forbidden him to use a machete, I have relented and at least let him carry it. I think he views it almost as an extension of his arm, and I know how I hate to be separated from my snake hook. But hard-working, capable, and thoughtful Etienne occasionally shows an ugly side to his character, and after several days on the trail he is starting to get sulky and impatient. Sometimes I find myself putting as much effort into keeping him under control as into searching. The trail uses up a lot of time, but walking in the forest is such a pleasure that I don't mind. Etienne clearly views this collecting method as a great failure, but among the few things we do find on the trail are two species of frog that we get nowhere else. I consider the trail well worth the effort. I think the few *Trachylepis* skinks that I am quick enough to catch may be a different species from the ones we are getting in enormous numbers from the village. Possibly the toads *(Bufo)* also are a different species from the village specimens. I also get three small snakes, over the course of many, many days, all, I think, different species, and all so small that I will need to wait until I have access to a microscope to identify them.

One day Etienne starts to complain of feeling sick. His French isn't quite up to describing symptoms, so I don't know if there's anything in my first-aid kit that might help him. I try to take his temperature, but clearly he has never had his temperature taken before, because when I tell him to put the end of the thermometer under his tongue, I can see that he is holding his jaws as wide open as possible inside his closed mouth to prevent the thermometer from touching the underside of his tongue. I try to explain to him how to do it correctly, but he doesn't get it. I feel his forehead and it is not hot. The following day we check the nets, but he is quieter than usual, and as soon as we return to camp he asks for permission to go to the village to buy medicine.

Night falls and there is still no sign of Etienne. Laurent is hanging around, so he stays the night, sleeping in Etienne's place. I am really worried. Something must be very wrong to keep Etienne from the camp like this. I have the awful thought that perhaps he has malaria, and Laurent, fond of him as I am, would be a poor replacement.

He is still not back the next morning. The atmosphere in the camp is very different with Etienne away. We're all worried about him. I wake up and climb over Laurent, who, unaccustomed to the hard, bumpy ground, sits up crying, "Lord Jesus!" I go and check the pitfall traps, which Etienne would have done before I was awake if he'd been here. Today is Sunday, and Laurent's turn to preach.

I leaf through my notebook and can't help noticing that it was last Sunday afternoon after a week with almost no specimens that the deluge of specimens started. Of course it corresponds with adding nets and with locals starting to bring things in, but I can't explain how frogs have suddenly become easier to find at night. I wonder if Etienne noticed that our luck turned within hours of his praying to God for more specimens. I think he must have, but he's never mentioned it to me. Laurent leaves, promising to bring back news of Etienne from the village. With Laurent gone to church, Florence and I manage to check the nets together.

Etienne returns in the afternoon, with a diagnosis of *Ascaris* worms. I remember them from my undergraduate parasitology class. That's what comes of eating smoked fish. I feel vindicated in my refusal to eat anything not out of a can. But am I right about the fish? Now that I think about it, I think I'm right in remembering that *Ascaris* are intestinal worms, often a foot long, that can get dangerous if they migrate from the intestines into the lungs, but they're contracted from ingesting the eggs from human feces, not from fish. But what they call *Ascaris* here may not actually be *Ascaris*. I was initially very impressed by the way French often uses scientific names as common names. For example, the word for a rattlesnake is *crotale*, from the genus name, *Crotalus*. The little skinks we see around here, of the genus *Mabuya* (recently changed by lizard taxonomy specialists to *Trachylepis*), the villagers call *mabuyas*. But they use the same name for all other lizards as well. So who knows what kind of worms Etienne has. I'm still convinced that the smoked fish are to blame.

Etienne sits off by himself on a log, singing hymns in Lingala and banging out a rhythm on an overturned bucket, rather than socializing with me and Florence. I don't think he's still feeling sick; I think he is upset because Florence and I managed to check the nets without him.

Finally, one morning as we are checking the nets, it happens. Etienne is walking through the water ahead of me lifting up the net as he goes. He stops. "Madame, a snake." By this time we are both jaded by all the *Grayia* we've been catching in the nets, but this is different. "It is the red snake again." I push my way around him. Indeed, it is another of the red and black banded snakes that we had argued about. And it is alive, head and neck clear of the net and striking viciously as I approach.

"Etienne, do you still believe that this snake is venomous?"

"Yes, Madame, I know it is venomous."

"Do you remember when we caught the last one how we decided we would settle this disagreement?" It takes a moment, but he remembers. "All right then. Are you watching?" I start to extend my left hand toward the snake.

"NO! Madame, no! Please listen to me. STOP! I promise to believe you!" The snake clamps its jaws down on the ball of my thumb. I make no attempt to pull away. When it lets go its teeth have left a ring of little pinpricks which are bleeding slightly.

"Well, come on then," I say impatiently, "let's check the rest of the nets."

Etienne is quiet for the rest of the day, watching me anxiously. The next morning he is back to normal. We never discuss the red snake again.

chapter 7

a
bottle
of
snakes

Etienne and I are on our way back from the swamp one night, along the trail that leads from the road to the camp. Etienne is always greatly relieved when the work in the swamp is over, and rushes back to the camp making as much noise as possible. I am trying to break him of this habit, since my idea of the return from the swamp is that it is the last chance of the evening to catch something. Anyway, this night I am prevailing and he is fairly restrained. Suddenly we both stop. Something is moving in the undergrowth beside the trail, something too big to be any kind of reptile. I put my hand over my headlamp, letting out just the narrowest beam of light. I signal to Etienne to do the same and to wait. Just when I think he isn't going to tolerate another moment of waiting, we hear the rustling again, and an animal emerges onto the trail just in front of us. It is about the size of a cat, but with a small head, arched back, and a short, tapering tail. "Porc-épic!" (porcupine!), whispers Etienne with excitement.

The next morning we do the perfunctory check of the useless pitfall traps. When we return to the trail, Etienne sets off in the opposite direction from the camp. I am about to ask where he is headed, but he doesn't go far. He stops at the place where we saw the porc-épic, and sets to work, for once explaining as he goes. Apparently porc-épic is good to eat, which explains why Etienne was so interested in it. Then I look on, fascinated, as he digs a shallow hole, strips a slender sapling of branches and bends it over so that the tip touches the ground, carves a strong, straight, short stick with his machete, and fastens it all together with vines. He camouflages the stick and the hole with a few leaves, then turns to see that I'm still watching. He grabs another stick. "This is the porc-épic," he explains, demonstrating. He moves the porc-épic stick so that it steps on the leaves, and with a sudden SNAP. The sapling springs back up and the stick carved with the machete slams down on what would have been the porc-épic. I am astonished. He grins. This must be what Laurent's bushmeat traps in the forest are like. We return to the camp and get ready to check the nets. From that day on, checking the porc-épic trap becomes part of Etienne's early morning check of the pitfall traps. He is excited about it for the first few days, but then it seems as if it is just like the pitfalls, an ingeniously designed trap that the animals just don't seem to cooperate by getting caught in.

It is a hot day and an ant day. In the afternoon I go for a cold dip in my bathing spot. I am pleasantly cool when I get dressed and join Florence and Etienne, where they have spread out a tattered grass mat on a rare ant-free patch of ground at the far end of the camp. Florence notices that I have goose bumps on my arms. I mention casually that goose bumps are something that we have because we came from a hairy ancestor—even hairier than a mondele. If we had a lot of hair on our skin, then the tiny muscles that make goose bumps would make the hair stand on end, which would keep us warmer. We've lost the hair, over many generations, but we've kept the little muscles. I talk about evolution, about how the great apes are our closest relatives. "Of course," says Florence, "anyone can see that. And we all come from fishes to begin with." I don't seem to be telling them anything new. Here in the remote Likouala, it appears, Darwin has made more of an impression than in many parts of the world that would consider themselves more "civilized." They don't seem to understand my surprise.

In the United States, there are many people, I tell them, who don't believe that we evolved from the same ancestor as gorillas and chimpanzees. They think that human beings are something special and different from all the other animals. "But that's ridiculous," says Florence, surprised. "Of course the apes are our nearest relatives. Why on earth would they not believe that?"

"Often," I start, fearing that I may be treading on dangerous ground with Etienne here, "they are people who are very religious, and read the Bible as if everything that happens in it were literally true." I am finding it difficult to explain this in a clear and simple way, but I needn't have worried.

"Of course: the first page of the Bible," Florence nods her head knowledgeably. I go on to tell them about efforts by some groups in the United States to prevent children from being taught about evolution in school. But I have lost my audience. They may think what I'm telling them about is a bit strange, but they don't see why I'm making such a big deal out of it. After all, what is surprising about Americans doing things that are strange?

"Katherine," Laurent asks one day, sitting beside me on the "sofa," "when you leave can I have your machete?" I am disappointed by the request. I had thought Laurent was beyond all that "Madame, when you leave" stuff. I have promised one of my two machetes to Etienne. The other one I want to keep. Machetes are easy to come by here, but I don't know where I would look for a machete for sale in Toronto. If I found one I doubt if it would be cheap. Here a machete costs 2,500cfa at the Impfondo market. I tell Laurent I'm keeping my machete, but to my annoyance, he continues to pester me periodically about it.

I continue Etienne's training in specimen preparation. He soon grows to love the big syringe of formalin and its needle. I never do manage to teach him to take tissue samples, but I do start him on a bit of anatomy. When I catch a snake, one of the things I record in my notes is whether it is a male or a female. I teach Etienne how to determine this using a probe. A male snake, I explain, has two penises, both forked. He keeps them folded up inside out, out of the way, inside the base of the tail, in long pouches. Only during mating does he stick one out (they only use one at a time) through his cloaca (the single opening that serves as the end of the digestive and urogenital tracts), and insert it into the cloaca of the female. Hemipenes, as these double penises are called, often have a very elaborate structure of spikes and grooves. The patterns of these spikes and grooves are very specific to particular species of snake. Some herpetologists have spent entire careers studying hemipenes.

My probe kit is a little leather case containing short metal rods of different thicknesses (for probing different sizes of snake). To sex a snake you slide the probe into the cloaca and feel for the long pouch that houses the hemipene. In a male, the probe slides easily quite far into the base of the tail. In a female there is no opening to find. Often you can tell the sex of a snake even before probing, just by looking, since males tend to have longer tails and a thickening at the base of the tail. Etienne soon becomes adept at probing, and especially enjoys laying bets on the sex of the snake before using the probe.

"Etienne," I suddenly ask one afternoon as we are injecting formalin into a batch of frogs, "do you understand *why* we're doing this work? What the point of it all is?"

"Yes, Madame Kati, we are preparing the frogs so that they won't rot, and you will be able to take them back to Canada."

"No, I mean the whole reason for me coming here, and for us catching snakes in the forest, and taking notes, and, yes, taking them away with me in the end?" I start the long and circuitous explanation of the connection between injecting frogs with formalin, and protecting this bit of forest—this forest where Etienne has lived his whole life and which he knows so well. I explain what an ecosystem is, why it is useful for animals and plants to have scientific names, why so much attention should be paid to frogs and snakes, which aren't even good to eat . . . I soon give up. To Etienne this project is simply a set of tasks, many of them interesting, to be carried out as well as possible. The ultimate objective is earning money to support his family. My explanation sounds complicated even to me as I am speaking. But surely I am doing something good? Will the flooded forest really be any better off for my having been here?

One evening another elderly fisherman arrives carrying a big bag. I greet him and shake his hand and ask what's in the bag. He hands me the whole thing, wordlessly. It is an ancient plastic mesh shopping bag, holes in it tied closed by bits of string, and it smells very strongly of rotting fish. I open the bag gingerly to find an entire net, filled with fish in varying degrees of decay, and a live juvenile rock python tangled in the net with them. I manage to get the python disentangled from the net without cutting any of the threads, which pleases the fisherman. Then I explain to him that my permit does not allow me to collect "boas," so I can't buy the animal from him. But I would like to take a photo of it, and I'll give him 500cfa for that. He seems to find this more than reasonable. "I'm not allowed to keep it," I tell him, "but I don't think you want it back" (vigorous shake of the head). "Here's what I suggest: I've got 450 meters of fishnet set up in the water around here. If I release the snake it will immediately get caught in one of my nets. So I suggest that I keep it here alive, until my work is finished. When the nets are taken down I will let it go." We still have a week and a half to go, but a python can last, quite contentedly, much longer than that in a snake bag kept in the shade. This snake will be a sort of pet. Maybe if I handle her enough she will become docile, like most baby pythons. "We need a name for the python," I tell Etienne and Florence later. "She's a girl."

"Ariane," says Florence without a moment's hesitation. So Ariane she becomes. She never does become tame, and far from being the harmless, docile ambassador of snakes to the local children that I had hoped she would be, she makes a great display of hissing and biting me every time I take her out of the bag.

I had hoped that she would become tame enough that I could get a picture, to use as an illustration in my guidebook to snakes, of Florence holding Ariane, showing her perhaps to the brave little girl from the shack in the forest who led us back to the camp cutting a trail with a machete. But Florence is not enthusiastic. "I'll do it if she's dead, but if she behaves like that"—Ariane lunges at my nose—"I will throw her away into the forest," she says, demonstrating with a wide sweep of the hand.

One morning Etienne wakes me up with an excited shout from outside the house. I find my glasses and crawl out to find him beaming from ear to ear, holding up a large, furry body in one hand. "I caught the porc-épic!" His trap had finally worked.

On our return from the nets one morning, we find Fiti visiting, accompanied by his three children. The biggest of the children shyly hands me a frog in a plastic bag. We are long since out of Gatorade, but I give all the children bon-bons sifflets, which they immediately unwrap, dropping the wrappers on the ground. Florence pours Fiti a mug of whiskey. He lets each of the children have a sip, but they all wrinkle their faces in disgust at the strong taste. I take out Ariane to amuse them, but she still strikes at me viciously and the children scatter in terror, so I put her back in the bag, and coax them back to the bench. I notice the youngest staring at my tattoo, a European adder *(Vipera berus)* on my ankle. I catch her eye and she grins. I invite the children to touch the tattoo, but whether it's the image of the snake or the strange pale skin, they seem to find it almost as frightening as Ariane. They finish the bon-bons sifflets and say goodbye, whistling on the "sifflets" as they disappear into the forest.

There is no such thing as garbage here, and I often miss the privacy of the garbage chute in my apartment building in Toronto. Unless I surreptitiously burn it in the fire, anything I discard in the designated "garbage bag" in the house will be subject to scrutiny by Florence and Etienne. Often their ingenuity impresses me. I find Florence using a discarded prescription pill bottle as a wallet, and I peel the label with my name, address, and so on off it before giving it back to her. "Souliers à jeter" (shoes to throw away) are never thrown away here. When the plastic strap on Florence's breaks and they really are unwearable, Etienne cuts them into slices and uses them as floats for the nets. I start consulting them before throwing things out. When the trousers of my $9 Canadian Tire rainsuit tear almost into two pieces, Florence is pleased to accept them to add to the waterproofing on the roof of her payotte. As for the package the suit came in, a little mesh bag with a Velcro closure which is torn, Etienne is glad to have it to keep his soap in. I rather wish I'd thought of it first. It allows the soap to dry and is much more effective than my plastic travel soap container.

Their own "garbage" doesn't get confined to a designated bag. Wrappers from chocolate bars and bon-bons sifflets are carelessly dropped on the ground, not only by visitors to the camp, but by Etienne and Florence as well. It is true that Florence is constantly sweeping the camp clear of debris, but this just means that we end up with a ring of litter around the campsite. It drives me crazy. This beautiful spot, and within days of our arrival we have started turning it into a garbage dump. Empty sardine and pork luncheon meat cans, Florence throws over her shoulder toward the edge of the campsite. The cans, at least, don't stay, because whenever there are children in the camp they gather up all the empty cans and take them away with them. "What do they use them for?" I ask Florence, puzzled.

"As toys. They pretend that they're pots and pans."

Organic waste is another matter. I am disgusted to discover a pile of fish guts, discarded by Florence, floating in a puddle beside the house. When I draw it to her attention, she points out another floating pile of fish guts, farther out in the deep water of the flooded forest. Little fish are eating it, she says. It's true—you can see them nibbling around the edges. "Well, this puddle is landlocked. There are no fishes. So get rid of it and find somewhere farther away from the house to throw it."

That very night, checking to make sure that the fish guts have been removed, I catch a frog in that puddle. It is a large one, and, unable to see it clearly in the dark, I think it will probably turn out to be another African bullfrog (Hoplobatrachus), like the one caught by Emmanuel the first day. I put it in a plastic bag to deal with the next day. But the morning light shows it to be a remarkable-looking frog. Not only can I not identify it, I can't guess the genus or even the family to which it belongs. It is a large, roundish frog with bulgy eyes and a bright, pale line down the middle of its back. A distinctive-looking frog, and unmistakable, I am sure, if you knew what you were looking for. I photograph it alive, against a white snake bag for contrast, and then euthanize it, being sure to take a tissue sample, carefully, before fixing it.

Central African frogs are notoriously hard to identify. There are many, many frustrating species of what I call LBFs (little brown frogs). After my first expedition I did my best to identify all the LBFs I had collected, and my efforts are all now being accurately corrected by a graduate student and central African frog expert in my old lab at Harvard. He always sends me very tactful e-mails ("Dear Kate, I have taken the liberty of reassigning the *Leptopelis rufus* from your 1997 collection to *Cryptothylax greshoffii*"). But this frog is no LBF. This is something that anyone who knows anything at all about African frogs should be able to identify at a glance—I'm sure of it. Or is it something new? I start to feel the impatience and excitement of getting my collection shipped to the Smithsonian, unpacking, and finding out what I've got.

The Chief visits only occasionally now, and has more or less given up scrounging. I have forbidden Florence to serve him anything besides coffee, and she and Etienne and I agree to keep the contents of our provisions box a secret among ourselves. One day, sitting gloomily over a plastic mug of coffee, beside me on one of the benches, the Chief asks me, by way of making conversation, whether there are monkeys in Canada. I tell him that there are not, but, by way of making up for this failing, try to explain bears. I have no success describing a bear in any way that makes sense to him, so I move on to porcupines, which impress him considerably. "They are five times as big as your porc-épic here, covered in long, barbed spines, and they eat the paint off houses that are made of wood."

I am always pleased to see Fiti appearing out of the forest. "Monsieur Fiti! What have you got for me this time?" This time, with a proud smile, he presents me with a plastic mineral water bottle stopped up with leaves, and containing, to my great delight, several tiny snakes in different colors. Now when I deal with snakes, I generally determine if the animal is venomous or not by a process of elimination. The beautiful, little emerald-green snake in the bottle I scrutinize to make sure it's not a mamba. A really tiny all-black snake that appears to be dead is probably a juvenile house snake, though I doubt if I'll ever be sure of the species even once I get it under a microscope. The last snake in the bottle is too small for me to see its head scales closely, but it's a little black snake with a bit of yellow on it. I can't think of any little black and yellow leaf-litter snake that is venomous.

Now putting a snake into a bottle is a whole lot easier than taking one out. I start shaking the bottle, trying to shake the snakes out into the palm of my hand. "Madame!" Etienne exclaims anxiously, "The black and yellow one is venomous!"

"No, it isn't"; I don't feel the slightest worry. "People here think that all snakes are venomous, but it's just not true," I tell him. "There are approximately 100 species of snake in the Congo and only 30 of those are venomous." I've got the black and yellow snake's head near the mouth of the bottle and get hold of it with thumb and forefinger, easing it out.

"Madame, the black and yellow snake is not like the others! I know that snake is venomous! We see it in the village sometimes—Don't touch it! Please!" The little snake is behaving very calmly considering it's just been forced through the mouth of a bottle. I look at it more closely as it slithers through my fingers. Something about the face is faintly familiar. Although the snake is too small for me to distinguish head scales without a microscope, the face has that foreshortened look of snakes in the cobra family. I notice that the yellow bands on its underbelly extend only along the front third of the snake. Suddenly I have a picture in my mind of a big snake, reared up, showing the front third of its underbelly. A big snake that like this little one has yellow lips. A snake that's big and angry and standing up with its neck spread in a hood. Recognition hits me. This is really an inexcusable mistake. The snake in my hand is one of the most obvious species to identify. Now that I've realized what it is, I can't imagine how I could have thought it was anything else. Most people underestimate juvenile snakes. Their venom is often more potent than that of an adult.

"Etienne, pass me a snake bag please," I say, my voice level, my fingers immobile, "quickly." "Easy does it," I tell the snake, "no sudden moves." Etienne seems to take forever to find a snake bag. I take it from him and gently let the little snake drop into it.

"I tell you, Madame, the yellow and black snake is venomous!"

"Yes, Etienne," I admit, wiping my sweat from my forehead, "this time you are right. That snake is a baby forest cobra."

chapter 8

a
day
of
monsters

A mamba! Shit!

When Nicole turned up this morning carrying a large, plastic jug, this is not what I expected to find inside. But with the cap unscrewed I can just make out a thick coil of green body with smooth scales. I hastily screw the cap back on. Held up to the light, the white plastic is slightly translucent. I shake the jug from side to side, and estimate that the snake is a good meter and a half long.

This is going to be tricky work. I really don't want an audience, but I've got one: Patience, being held by Nicole, whom I can hardly banish since it was she who brought the snake, and Laurent, who has his dog with him, a creature who has never in his life obeyed an order, and of course Etienne and Florence. But the audience is now waiting for the show, and I haven't a hope of getting rid of anyone.

"Leave it alone!" I yell at Laurent, who is fiddling with the jug. When I look a moment later, he has unscrewed the cap and has his eye to the hole. "Shut the lid!" I shout in alarm. He grins rakishly. "Shut the lid!" He shuts it, but takes his time, and smiles at me. "Did you not understand what I said?" I demand. "I don't want to be responsible for some imbecile who gets himself bitten in the eye by a mamba!"

I eventually resign myself to doing everything I have to do in front of the audience. As I've said before, putting a snake in a bottle is a whole lot easier than taking one out. I soak a piece of cheesecloth in chloroform and drop it into the jug with the snake. Then I watch it closely. I want the snake groggy enough that I can safely remove it, but still with enough life in it that I can get a few good pictures. I carefully monitor the snake as the chloroform takes effect, shaking the jug and holding it up to the light, to check whether the snake still has some muscle tone or is completely limp, and I do my best to get the audience under control. "Nicole, please take Patience and go and sit on that log at the far end of the camp. Laurent—behind the house—no, not the payotte, the tarpaulin house!" Laurent does as he is told, but his friendly dog comes running up to lick my face. "And get the dog under control!" Etienne and Florence have disappeared. They don't need to be told what to do.

I am nervous. What I have to do is dangerous, and it is distracting to be watched and to worry constantly that somebody is going to get in the way. The snake is limp, and I want to take it out of the jug soon so that it will still wake up a bit when it gets some fresh air in its lungs, and I can get some good pictures. I'm going to have to be handling the snake, trying to keep it where I want it by using my snake hook, while trying simultaneously to get good photos of it. And then of course I have to get it back in the jug before it becomes really lively. I shake the jug again to make sure the snake still has no muscle tone. I unscrew the cap and set to work gently shaking the jug on its side, in an effort to get a hold of a coil with the hemostat. Finally I have dragged the whole limp snake out of the jug. All around me the audience is watching, wide-eyed. Then I see the snake's face. I look again. And again, at that unmistakable sunken-eyed head. It's not a mamba after all, but *Psammophis,* a large, relatively harmless, semivenomous green tree snake! Embarrassed, I convey this news to the audience. (This is one reason I don't like having audiences for this kind of job.) I am an idiot, I reflect. This isn't the first time this trip that I've reached that conclusion, but at least this time I have mistaken something harmless for something venomous, not the other way around. There is still a gasp from the audience as I pick up the limp snake, and sit with it until it starts to come round. When it does, I take a series of pictures of it before returning it to the plastic jug and the chloroform. By this time everyone else has long since lost interest. *Psammophis* is actually a much more interesting snake, scientifically, than a mamba. Mambas have already been quite well studied, but there is still disagreement on how many species of *Psammophis* actually exist.

Although it is the wrong time of day for it, I order coffee. I wait until we are all sitting around blowing on it to cool it off, to ask how on earth Nicole caught the snake. Nicole can't or won't speak to me, so all my questions go through Etienne as intermediary. The snake, he explains, had been eating a rat in the house. While it had the rat in its mouth she picked it up by the neck. Most impressive. It is still not clear to me how there comes to be no rat in the jug and what looks like a minor machete wound on the snake's right side, but communication with Nicole is too awkward for me ever to get the whole story. It occurs to me, not for the first time, to be suspicious of all these specimens ostensibly caught by this vapid woman. I'm undoubtedly being cheated in some way. But does it really matter? She is a useful source of specimens wherever she's getting them from. I might as well go along with the charade. But I feel a wave of loneliness all the same.

"Nicole," I make the token gesture of addressing her directly, "you are a brave woman, and an impressive animal catcher. Because you are Etienne's wife I feel that you are not in the same category as the strangers who come to the camp to sell animals. I could pay you the way I do them, bargaining over each specimen, but an alternative possibility is putting you on salary. I pay you 3,000cfa per week, and you catch whatever you can. Whether you catch a lot or a little, you still get 3,000cfa. What do you think?"

"She says she doesn't think anything," Etienne translates. I sigh. I can believe it.

"Okay, Nicole, I'm going to give you 4,000cfa for everything you've brought me so far. It's not a permanent solution, but it takes care of everything up till now. Does that sound reasonable?"

"She says, 'What about the plastic jug?'" says Etienne. "That stuff you put in it was a deadly poison wasn't it?" Hmm, slightly less passive. The chloroform. It will have completely vaporized by now, but I did tell them it was a deadly chemical.

"How much does a jug like that sell for at the Impfondo market?"

"2,500cfa."

"Okay, I'll pay for a replacement and add that to the 4,000cfa," I sigh with frustration.

Nicole has a habit, even beyond the local custom, of spectacularly overstaying her welcome. I hate having her in the camp. She eats and sleeps during the day, breastfeeds and changes diapers, and generally makes herself at home. I am miserable while she is in the camp. Florence chats with Nicole and does no work unless I give her a specific order; Etienne slacks off to spend time with his family and becomes a different person from the polite, respectful Etienne I have grown so used to. When I try to get him to come out to get some work done, he either pretends not to hear or behaves in a sullen and disagreeable manner, making minimal effort to search for animals. In spite of all my efforts to be friendly and hospitable, Nicole verges on open rudeness toward me. What does she have against me, I wonder? After all, I'm employing her husband and thus supporting her family. Would it be different if I were a man? Is that the issue?

The problem comes to a head when one day she doesn't leave at all. I see her that night, sleeping under Etienne's mosquito net, next to mine. The next day I wake up to a great fuss going on outside. The news of the morning is that during the night the fish Etienne caught setting baited hooks yesterday evening all jumped out of the bucket and were carried away by the ants (just in case you thought I was exaggerating about the ants). It is time to set some limits. I would have done it before now, but I didn't want Nicole to stop bringing in specimens. I ask Etienne when Nicole is leaving. It had better be soon. He gets angry and defensive and says that Nicole is here so that he can go fishing at night and catch fish so that she can eat. "But *she's* not doing the fishing," I point out. "She must sleep in the village. Is that clear? And *you* have a job to do." Etienne reluctantly promises me that she will leave in the afternoon.

I become anxious as the hours go by and Nicole shows no sign of getting ready to leave. It is late afternoon and the sky is threatening rain. I can just see a rainstorm starting and then Nicole having to stay overnight again because it is dark. She needs to leave now. I accost Etienne. "Okay, time to escort Nicole back to the village." He tries to ignore me. Nicole, Patience, Etienne, and Florence are sitting on a grass mat at the far end of the camp from me. I tell them flat out that it is time for Nicole to leave *now*, before it starts to rain or gets dark. Nicole is doing something complicated with Florence's hair, which obviously can't be interrupted until the last two rows are finished, so I tell Etienne to start gathering up her things from around the camp, washed diapers hanging out to dry and so on. But when I see him next he is lying in the house with Patience. As soon as the hairdressing is finished, I get Nicole to gather things up. She angrily pulls down damp clothing and diapers from the bushes and logs where they have been hung to dry, followed by Florence who is telling her that the things should be properly folded up. She is finally packed. Showing unusual initiative, Nicole murmurs something to Etienne. "She says that you're a bitch," he translates miserably, "and that she's never coming back." Well at least the last bit is good news.

Nicole and Etienne set off for the village at last. "What did I do wrong?" I ask Florence. "What could I have done differently? I didn't like having to kick her out like that, but if I hadn't she would never have left. I want Etienne to spend time with his family, but having them move in here is not the answer."

"No," says Florence loyally, "the forest is no place for a baby."

Another afternoon, three small boys arrive in the camp, carrying a mineral-water bottle plugged with leaves. I peer inside. A scorpion. The boys are predictably disappointed when I tell them I am not collecting scorpions. The boy with the bottle is about to throw it over his shoulder into the forest, when I stop him. No. The scorpion must be released. Just unplug the bottle and leave it somewhere and the scorpion will make its way out. But not near the camp, please. I give the boys a crash course in zoology. The scorpion is the cousin of the spider. I am looking for amphibians and reptiles. That means frogs, lizards, and snakes. I hasten to add that I do not want any more toads or lizards from the village. They look miserable and confused, poor things. Have they heard the frog in all the marshes and ponds, I ask, the frog that goes, "Tok-tok, tok-tok"? Yes! They nod their heads emphatically. Do they think they could catch a few? More emphatic nods.

"That frog is something I want. Here is a special plastic bag. If you bring it back to me with some tok-tok frogs in it, I will give you a reward. Now look, it is almost dark and you'd better go home."

In spite of her promise, 2 days later Nicole is back. She even tries to do away with the politeness of shaking my hand and greeting me as she arrives in my camp, as though hoping to slip in unnoticed. Leaving is something Nicole never initiates herself, so eventually I always have to order her to leave. When I do that there is a scene, and Etienne is sulky and disagreeable for the rest of the day. Eventually I figure out that the best solution is to order her to leave as soon as she arrives, before she even has a chance to sit down. There is a scene, and Etienne is sulky and disagreeable for the rest of the day, but why tolerate her for 6 hours before kicking her out, when I'm going to have to deal with an angry Etienne either way whether I do it after 6 hours or 3 minutes?

When we're all together that evening, including Laurent, who is visiting, I bring up the problem of Nicole. "Etienne, I've been saying all along that I want you to spend time with your family, but having Nicole move in here is just not on. I have an alternative to propose." Etienne is still sitting with his head hanging down in resentment. "We've got 12 days left, Etienne. Choose 4 nights that you would like to spend in the village with your family, and I will pay Laurent to sleep here those nights in your place." Then Etienne gets upset over the suggestion that I could get along without him—that he could be replaced. "It's only to sleep!" I point out. "Anyone can sleep. You would come back the next morning and we would check the nets as usual." Of course this arrangement isn't only up to Etienne. "Laurent, would you be prepared to take on that job? I'll pay you 500cfa just to spend the night in Etienne's place."

"1,000cfa," he bargains.

"1,000cfa? Ridiculous. I offer to pay you 500cfa to spend the night sleeping beside a beautiful woman and you ask for *more*? You should be paying me!" He laughs good-naturedly.

"But truly, to stay awake for a whole night—that's a lot to ask."

"You don't have to stay awake. All you have to do is sleep where Etienne would have slept. But you do have to be sober." He puts on his most serious expression (entirely unconvincing) and nods vigorously. Etienne asks awkwardly if the 500cfa for Laurent would come out of his pay. I tell him no. Anything to get rid of Nicole.

By this time my control of my camp is starting to slip. Etienne is still terribly reluctant to leave the camp, to let Laurent take his place. He starts to be unreliable about when he's going to be where. And what I hadn't counted on is that contact with his wife seems to be what turns polite, hard-working Etienne into sulky, insubordinate Etienne. Etienne is sullen and angry more and more, and our work is suffering from his moods.

A day that turns out to be one of the most memorable of my herpe-tological career begins badly. Etienne has had an overnight in the vil-lage. He should have been back by 6:00 a.m. at the latest to check the nets, but he doesn't turn up until 7:30, and, to my great annoyance, he is accompanied by Nicole and Patience. The whole point of sending him home to the village for the night was to avoid having them come here.

As we set out into the water, Etienne is still in the resentful mood he always seems to bring back from any time spent with Nicole. I tell him that we're going to start releasing any more *Grayia* we find in the nets, and he talks back sulkily, saying that we'll be wasting our time since *Grayia* are all we ever get in the nets. But the flooded forest is irresist-ible, and soon we are both happy checking the nets, the morning sun filtering through the canopy of trees. When we come across the first *Grayia,* we go through the now-familiar routine. I go in and immobilize the head, and then Etienne comes and helps me ease the body out of the net. But this time I'm not putting the snake in a snake bag. "What are you doing with it?" Etienne asks nervously.

"Letting it go, just as I told you."

"Right here in the water?"

"Of course in the water. What's the problem?"

"Well I'm *in* the water and I'm scared."

"How about if I walk over there and let it go far away from you?" He agrees, with some misgivings. I walk 10 meters away from where he is standing, and drop the snake into the dark brown water.

"Which way did it go?"

"That way," I point confidently away from where he is standing, as though there were any way to know in that almost-opaque water.

Only a few minutes later, Etienne is walking ahead with a plastic bucket for putting the fish in, when I notice, even from behind him, that the net ahead of us is moving. "What is it?" Etienne goes to lift the net, but it is heavy. Has it snagged a log? And then we see the head. A head above water of the biggest snake we've seen so far. I push past Etienne and have no difficulty whatsoever in recognizing *Boulengerina,* the water cobra. "This one is a water cobra!" I tell Etienne. "You stand well back," I add unnecessarily. The animal is enormous: 2 meters long when we eventually measure it. Right now I have a practical problem on my hands. I have in front of me a 2-meter-long cobra, tangled in a net with its head and neck free. I somehow have to get the snake from here to a sealed container back at the camp, where I can lightly chloroform it before taking pictures. The snake is so heavy that it takes all my strength to keep the net lifted above the surface. Calculating that he's still well outside of striking range, I get Etienne to hold the net up. "I'm going to get hold of its head," I tell him. "Once I have a good grip would you feel okay about untangling the body?"

"Yes, Madame Kati." This from a man who a few minutes earlier was frightened by the idea of a harmless *Grayia* swimming around his legs.

I have no snake bag big enough for this animal. My 12-inch hemostat won't open wide enough to get around the neck unless I use both hands. There are very few rules to the art of collecting venomous snakes. Every situation is different. Each one presents a new set of challenges and with a few sometimes-useful tools on hand the rest is improvisation. With considerable difficulty I get control of the head. "Okay, Etienne, are you ready?"

"Yes, Madame," he answers bravely.

"Right. None of my snake bags is big enough to fit this snake in," I explain, "so I'm going to try to put it inside my backpack, loose, to take it back to the camp. We're going to start by getting it out of the net. I'll hold the head while you untangle the body. Then I need you to unzip the backpack, take all the stuff out of it, and put everything into one of the snake bags."

In this serious and frightening situation, Etienne does what he would never do under any other circumstances: he cuts the net. Cutting a net is always a fisherman's very last resort, leaving big holes that make the net much less effective, but as I grip the water cobra by the neck, a job that requires both my hands, he slices through the network of threads with the machete. After a considerable struggle, I have the water cobra zipped up inside my backpack. I put the pack back on and decide that we will go straight back to camp with it, and check the rest of the nets later. Wading through the forest with my pack on my back, I wonder how long it takes a water cobra to undo a zipper.

We return to the camp shouting with wild excitement to Florence. She needs no persuasion to agree to wait until the snake's had a bit of chloroform before having a look at it. I put my whole backpack inside a white plastic garbage bag. I soak a piece of cheesecloth in chloroform. Then I open the zipper on my pack just enough to push the chloroform cloth inside using the hemostat. I tie the plastic bag shut and wait.

"Is Nicole going to go back to the village by herself, or are you going to accompany her?" I ask Etienne, annoyed. With very ill grace the pair of them set off down the trail toward the road.

Etienne has been gone about an hour and I am just finishing taking pictures of the water cobra when Florence shouts, "Kati, a snake!" This is not a convenient time for what will probably turn out to be just another *Grayia*. Three men are waiting outside the house. "Is the snake in the water or on land?" I ask.

"On land, in the forest, Madame, juste à coté."

"Is it big or small?"

"Big, Madame!" Probably a python, I think, jaded.

"Is it a boa?"

"No, Madame, another kind of snake. It is very big and deadly venomous. You need to come quickly. We left one man there, but it might get away." Get away from what, I wonder? Luckily my backpack is no longer occupied by the *Boulengerina,* so I grab snake hook and backpack. I could use Etienne now.

"Florence! I may need your help getting this snake in the forest. Can you come quickly?" We rush off into the forest after the men. As is so often true in these cases, I have absolutely no idea what situation I'm going to be presented with. "Juste à coté" this time means only about half an hour into the forest.

A fourth man has been waiting, keeping an eye on the snake. It is the largest forest cobra I have ever seen. When we measure it later it comes to 2.5 meters. I am in awe. This is almost certainly the only 2.5-meter-long forest cobra I will encounter in my whole career. It is absolutely magnificent. The men are bushmeat hunters, who make traps in the forest, like the one Etienne made to catch the porc-épic. They are ingenious contraptions that snap shut and hold fast, constructed out of sticks and vines. But cobras are *not* what they want to find caught in their traps. This cobra is pinned to the ground, mid-body, by a 6-inch-long piece of wood, part of a trap that has snapped shut on it. It looks as though it has broken the cobra's spine. But the front meter of cobra in front of the trap is struggling frantically, angry, terrified, and in pain, striking fiercely at anything that approaches. I take in the scene. I wonder how firmly that trap is going to continue to hold? What a day! I've never before had the problem of not having a big enough snake bag, and now it's happening for the second time in one day!

I don't think this cobra will even fit into my backpack like the *Boulengerina*. Hoping that the trap will hold, I decide to wait. A snake injured that badly is not going keep striking indefinitely. At first I worry that I have underestimated it, but soon it weakens. I am able to easily pin the head with my snake hook, and safely get hold of it behind the head. I tell the man nearest that it is now safe to open the trap.

I've got a behind-the-head grip on a 2.5-meter-long cobra, and no container to put it into, and I'm a half-hour walk through dense forest from my camp. There is nothing to do but carry the snake by hand all the way back. Ahead of us Florence is helping one of the men to cut a way through the forest with a machete. I think as we walk about what to do with the snake on arrival at the camp. By the time we get there I have a plan. "Florence, we need to use my box, the box with all my supplies, to put the snake in. Can you go into the house and just empty the box? Dump everything out of it onto the floor. I'll sort it out later. And bring the box and its lid out here as quickly as possible." Soon we have the big cobra in the box. My knuckles are numb from maintaining a grip on it for such a long time. I offer the men coffee, and Florence prepares it. I give them 1,000cfa each before they leave, but the excitement of having shared this once-in-a-lifetime experience seems to matter more to them than the money. We shake hands proudly over a dangerous job well carried off.

Florence and I marvel at the two enormous snakes. Once they are both photographed and euthanized, Florence takes pictures of me holding them up high to show their size. Even holding them as high as I can reach there is a big coil of forest cobra on the ground. I feel sorry that Etienne is missing this. I try to wait for him to return so that at least he can have his picture taken with them. But dusk is approaching and I have to go ahead with fixing them. I am just starting on the water cobra when he arrives. He is still sulking, but can't entirely resist my invitation to come and help with the snakes. He works without saying a word except when I ask him to read off the measurements. Injecting these two giants uses up nearly all the formalin, to my alarm. As soon as the snakes are coiled and wrapped (in toilet paper; we long ago ran out of cheesecloth), he gets up and walks away without a backward glance, leaving me to tidy up and put everything away. I am increasingly fed up with him, but don't confront him, hoping he'll snap out of it on his own. He continues to sulk the rest of the evening. I tell him that tomorrow morning we are going to take down all the nets. That will take longer than usual, and he should be ready for an early start.

Finding him still in a bad mood the following morning makes me angry too. I should have put a stop to this kind of behavior long ago. This will be our last time checking the nets in the flooded forest and it should be special. I try to impress this on him by getting Laurent to take a picture of us setting out to do the nets for the last time. Even so Etienne remains cross for a while, once not warning me of a hole, so I suddenly plunge in, backpack and all. But gradually something of the occasion gets through to him. "This was our lucky net," he says wistfully, as we take down net #6. We are on the very last net when he is untangling a fish, and so I go around him to go ahead to untie the far end. I am just reaching the end of the last net when I notice two tiny frogs perched on the string of the net, in amplexus, the mating embrace of frogs, the male with his arms wrapped tightly around the waist of the larger female, waiting for her to lay her eggs so that he can fertilize them. They seem blissfully unaware of my presence. They look like *Xenopus* except that they are covered in a rough, bumpy skin. I scoop them and some water into a plastic bag. They are the only frogs of this kind that I have seen in all the time we've been here. I'm going to leave them in the plastic bag until they lay their eggs before I fix them. Then I will return the eggs to the place where I found the frogs. It looks to me like a place where frog eggs will immediately become fish food, but it is the place chosen by the parents. I am eager to get my collection to the Smithsonian Institution, and see what these two little frogs turn out to be.

chapter 9

time
to
go

Taking down the nets is much less time-consuming than I had expected. I hadn't realized that all the work of untangling them and removing leaves and twigs is done on land. It will be something for
Etienne to work on over the next few days. But when we return with the
nets, Etienne informs me sullenly that he's going off to look for worms
for fishing. He doesn't say when he will be back, but when I put my foot
down he sulkily agrees to 1:00 p.m.

The camp is actually a much more agreeable place once he is gone,
and there is no sign of him at 1:00. Florence has disappeared too—to
the village I suppose. It is a beautiful, quiet afternoon. Today is a wasp
day, but the insects aren't bothering me too much inside the house

working in my lab. Laurent appears at the entrance and hands me a little frog in a plastic bag. It is an LBF of a species I don't have yet. I start worrying about whether I have a 500cfa note to give him, but with some embarrassment he makes it clear that he is not after money. "It's for you," he smiles. I am really touched. This is the first time since I came here that anyone has given me a present.

I get Laurent to help me with one important task that I had been waiting until the nets were removed to do: releasing the snakes. In addition to Ariane, I have three *Grayia* in snake bags. Taking them out of the nets and just letting them go was something I had eventually decided was a bad idea, since as long as the nets were up they just swam into them again, so I put them in snake bags, but have been keeping them alive. Laurent and I carry the bags to the place where Etienne and I enter the water every day, and as I let each one slither off into the freedom of the flooded forest, Laurent snaps a picture of me tipping each snake out of the bag. Releasing Ariane, even though she bites my hand before gliding away into the water, is the first of the many goodbyes of the remainder of my time in the Congo, and makes me a bit sad.

Florence is the first to return, and immediately retreats into her payotte and starts snoring. At dusk Etienne is still not back. Laurent wanders off, ostensibly also to search for worms. By this time Florence has woken up and emerged from her payotte. "We seem to be on our own," I tell her. On her own Florence is very agreeable company. We drink local whiskey and chat companionably. I even break out the last two precious little silver-wrapped wedges of Vache Qui Rit cheese. After what we've been living on I think it is the most delicious thing I've ever tasted, and it has to be eaten all in one bite because it is soft from the heat of the forest. There is a moment of reverent silence as we both revel in flavor and texture, mouths full. "I like it because it's salty," says Florence dreamily.

"I like it because it's creamy."

Florence points out to me something she is worried about. A thick, heavy-looking log, about 3 meters long, is hanging vertically above her payotte, its tip less than a meter above the center of the roof. It is a dead log, and all it seems to be hanging by is a tangle of vines, high up in the canopy. It really does look poised to drop, dagger-like, right into the middle of Florence's bed. Far above the payotte, it is out of reach. Apparently Etienne and Laurent had put their minds to the problem of removing it, but given up the task as impossible. So Florence and I decide to have a go at it on our own. Florence cuts a long, light branch and makes a loop of liana around one end. She tries to reach the tip of the log with the loop. "Here, let me try. I'm a bit taller." I take the branch from her and after a few tries get the loop just barely around the tip of the log. As soon as I pull it sideways, to try to make it swing, the tip comes out of the loop. I do this many times, extending the loop as far along the log as I can, with Florence holding me firmly around the middle, so I can lean as far as possible over the payotte. I don't want to stop now, because probably all we've done is to loosen it, making it even more likely to fall. Florence cuts a longer branch and makes a bigger loop, and for the better part of an hour we swing the log in an increasingly wide arc, trying to separate it from the vines it is tangled in. Finally all at once it is free. I pull it to the side as far as I can so that it won't fall on the payotte, and just as it lands, Florence pulls me out of the way so that it just barely misses me as it crashes to the ground. We are both shaken. The log turns out to be surprisingly heavy. Florence drags it away from the payotte, and with the machete starts chopping it into pieces for the fire. It occurs to me that even if the men never come back, there is really no work that has to be done that Florence and I couldn't perfectly well do together if we had to.

The next morning, I wake at 5:15 a.m. Laurent and Florence are up, but there is still no sign of Etienne, who left in such a bad mood yesterday morning, promising to be back by 1:00 p.m. We do not have long to wait. The first thing I notice is the jarring and alien sound of blaring recorded Congolese pop music approaching. Soon, the noise emerges from the forest into the camp, accompanied by Etienne, carrying a portable tape deck, and by Nicole with her baby on her back.

I immediately order the music turned off. It is. I then proceed to accost Nicole, who is setting herself up on the "sofa," before she has a chance to spread herself out and start breastfeeding and changing diapers, and generally making herself at home, that she has to leave. I tell her that I have things to discuss with Etienne and that it will not be the same if she is here. Silence. Does she understand? Slight nod.

Etienne, this morning, is the Etienne I don't like. Grinning and laughing, and showing off to the crowd. "Etienne, we have things to discuss. No, not here." I turn and set off down the trail toward the place where we always enter the water to check the nets, and he follows. Separate him from his Lingala audience, and give him a bit of suspense.

I walk a long way, until we reach a suitable log. I sit down and pat the space beside me. He sits. I break the silence. "What the hell is going on?"

"What do you mean?"

I sigh, afraid I may get nowhere with him. "Well to start with, you're almost an entire day late coming back from your visit to the village, with no explanation."

He says something vague and unconvincing about having to take care of his family because the roof blew off the house. The conversation that follows is entirely circuitous and futile. Etienne continues to sulk without explanation. All he will say is that for him the project is over and all he wants is to sign the papers (papers?) and for me to replace him with Laurent. That is all he wants; then he will go home. I have to admit that the prospect of genial Laurent for company has its attractions, and his lazy ineptitude wouldn't matter now that there isn't much work left to do. If that's really what Etienne wants, then Laurent needs to be part of the conversation. Etienne calls out to Laurent, who is in the camp, and he comes and joins us on the log. I explain the situation to him and offer him the job. But he turns to Etienne, his eyes sad. "Baby

". . ." he addresses his nephew, and sets off in Lingala. He is clearly attempting to talk him out of quitting, so I leave them to it.

I return to the camp, where I am pleased to find Nicole gone, and Florence desperate for gossip. "He's still sulking," I tell her, "he's young."

"He's a grown man with a wife and a baby," she replies indignantly, "he's got no business behaving like a child!"

Etienne and Laurent are coming back to the camp, but Etienne's features are still set in a determined frown. To my amazement it is still only 6:30 a.m., after all this drama. I will not be prevented from getting on with my day. I go and have my bath in the flooded forest, then set to work preparing the bags of frogs collected yesterday, absorbed in the task and not paying attention to the Lingala conversation, in increasingly raised voices, all around me.

Suddenly Florence is yelling furiously at me. "It's not right that we have to work like this and it was all decided by the Chief without asking our opinion!"

"It's not right that we have to sleep without a mattress on the cold ground," Etienne chimes in.

"Do I sleep any better?"

"But it was decided without our opinion."

"You mean the wages? That was decided before I came, in consultation with Emmanuel." I was going to elaborate and say that Emmanuel had not expected that they would be *living* in the forest—that was the Chief's idea, but there's no interrupting Florence.

"Emmanuel? Emmanuel! If Emmanuel ever comes to the village again to visit his daughter. . ."

"But it wasn't Emmanuel who—"

"He'd better not come here!" I give up and decide to let Emmanuel hang out to dry.

"What a day I'm having," I tease them. "I start the day with Etienne so angry he says he wants to quit; now Florence is furious with me too.

I bet in another 2 hours Laurent will think of some grievance as well, right Laurent?"

We laugh and the tension eases. They are resentful and angry, but I think they are still basically fond of me and don't really want to direct their anger at me.

I go back to my frogs, saying to let me know if any rational discussion is taking place. When I finish with the specimens I find that they are all sitting around drinking local whiskey out of the plastic mugs. One mug has been set aside for me, with a plate over it to keep the insects out.

"Excellent idea!" I say, meaning it. "Now we can all get drunk and have a real fight. Etienne will probably hit me!" I punch him lightly on the arm and he almost smiles. Slowly Etienne comes round. Time and booze are much more effective than rational conversation.

I'm holding things together, but only just, and I don't know how long I can keep it up. It is time to get out of here. I am wasting more and more time and mental energy trying to keep Etienne under control. I will not tolerate his sulking. I realize that I have been planning activities around his moods rather than around what will get us the most specimens. He's managed to transmit his sense of grievance to Florence, who is suddenly full of complaints, even if they bear no relation to his. At this point things are hanging in a delicate balance. We're supposed to be here until next Wednesday—6 more days—but I dread the situation getting ugly before then. It's already got to the point where I wouldn't feel comfortable leaving Etienne and Florence together in the camp in my absence. Etienne's moodiness has settled into almost constant sullenness, and Florence seems to be highly suggestible. I just don't trust them anymore.

I write a letter to Hugo, explaining my fears: right now things are under control, but barely. If I stay here much longer I think I may end up with a mutiny on my hands. I ask him to please pick me up on the next expedition to Impfondo. I can have all my gear out by the side of the road whenever he says. I want to be sure to get the letter to WCS on this afternoon's transport truck. The trouble with the transport truck is that the two trucks thunder by twice a day in each direction, but not on any fixed schedule, so you just have to wait by the side of the road, sometimes for hours. Etienne has gone to the village for a visit and is not back yet. Florence is inside her payotte. I ask her to take my letter to the road and wait for the transport truck. Instead of the expected "Oui, Madame," she shouts from inside the payotte that she has a bit of a headache and is feeling dizzy. This small act of insubordination is so out of character that I am almost frightened. Am I overreacting?

I set off toward the road by myself. It is raining lightly and I am wearing the surviving top half of my Canadian Tire rain suit, bandanna on my head, cargo pants rolled up to the knees, and the souliers à jeter the Chief gave me. As soon as I walk through the first mud puddle the souliers become so slippery that when I try to make a dash through a patch of ants, I slip and fall into them face first. But as I finally reach the road I am due for some luck. After waiting only about 5 minutes the asphalt starts to vibrate, and then I hear the roar of the approaching truck. It is an enormous vehicle. The tops of the wheels are up to my chest. The inside is so crammed with people, goats, chickens, and luggage that men are hanging off the sides. I step out into the road and hold out my arm with the letter in my hand. The truck takes about 50 meters to stop, and I have to run after it, with considerable difficulty in my slippery, muddy souliers. All the people hanging off the sides are shouting something I can't make out and waving me toward the cab. Yes, I know letters get given to the driver. What is all the fuss about? The bottom of the door of the cab is about at a level with my shoulder. As I arrive beside it, it swings open. A neatly dressed white man with round glasses peers down at me, muddy, soaked, scratched, and bleeding.

"Kate Jackson, I presume."

The man turns out to be Mitch Eaton, of the WCS New York office, a name from the distant past. When I was preparing for my 1997 expedition I corresponded with him for a while, for advice. I have never met him in person, and I have had no contact with him since 1997. Apparently as the truck approached me, he asked the driver who I was. "Some Canadian who's collecting snakes." That was enough. I quickly explain the situation to Mitch and he is concerned. He understands how dependent I am on the goodwill of the people working for me and how much I am at the mercy of an angry guide. Mitch wants me to get into the truck to Epena right away, but I can't abandon my guide, my cook, and all my belongings in the forest with no explanation. The people in the truck are getting impatient. I thrust the letter to Hugo into Mitch's hand and hope for the best.

Another night goes by. By my estimate, the earliest WCS could pick me up would be Saturday. Today is Friday and I intend to get everything done today that I want done before my departure. As always, we start the day over coffee at dawn. I have told Florence and Etienne about the possibility of ending the project early. There are plenty of practical reasons so I don't need to touch on the more delicate subject of deteriorating relations, which is what really scares me. I've got lots of specimens, enough to make a nice collection for the Smithsonian, so the objective has been accomplished, and I am running out of scientific supplies. The cheesecloth is long since used up and I am making do with toilet paper, which is a reasonable substitute for wrapping small frogs, but disintegrates when I try to wrap big snakes in it. I am almost out of formalin, and do not have enough to preserve another large snake should I get one. I'm even running low on plastic bags, and have been rinsing and reusing the big ones, which are in shortest supply, repairing holes in them with packing tape when necessary. Etienne and I have long since started releasing the *Grayia* from the nets, and finally have taken the nets down.

There are three jobs that must get done today: (1) taking down the drift fence and filling in the pitfall traps, (2) collecting all the little scraps of garbage strewn around the periphery of the camp and burning them, and finally (3) going into the water for one last time to take pictures of the flooded forest.

Disassembling the drift fence and pitfall traps takes only minutes. While Etienne and I are doing it, Florence builds a big bonfire for the garbage, and it looks as if it will be a beautiful day, a good day for burning. I had worried I might have difficulty getting them to pick up the detritus, since they don't seem to have any sense of littering being a bad thing, or of the beauty of the forest having been marred by our presence, but Etienne sets to work doing an efficient and thorough job of picking up even the smallest scraps of chocolate wrapper to throw on the fire, and very soon every vestige of a month's littering has disappeared. The flooded forest works its usual magic and Etienne and I are relatively happy together taking turns with the camera, seeking out particularly spectacular views and photographing them. Once again a day's work is finished by 9:00 a.m. I go to enjoy a final cooling dip in my bath, but the dock has fallen apart, leaving the banks slippery with mud, and Florence has done the laundry there, leaving a laundry soap wrapper floating in a soapy slick across the surface.

Then at noon, the Chief arrives with news and all hell breaks loose. The WCS truck passed this morning on its way to Impfondo. It stopped at Ganganya and somebody told the Chief to tell me that if I could get all my equipment to the road in time, it would pick me up on its way back to Epena, between 3:00 and 5:00 p.m.

I am very glad that I have calculated how much I will owe everyone and made sure I have the right denomination bills. I unstick some of the envelopes and furtively count money into pay packets under my mosquito net at the back of the house, while Etienne and Laurent shout at me to get out so that they can take down the tarpaulins. Florence, close to tears, is shouting angrily that this is not right, this is no way to say goodbye. Laurent, annoyingly, asks me again for my machete and once again I tell him I need to keep it, but relent and tell him I'll give him 2,500cfa to buy a new one. But this compromise doesn't seem to satisfy him. Florence and Etienne are scrabbling through the provisions, dividing up the canned food and batteries. They are at it so fiercely that I don't dare intervene. I hand out the pay packets and everyone immediately tears them open to count the contents. The Chief accepts the remaining 10,000cfa that I owe him for the fee.

"Where is my machete sharpener?" I demand. They search the boxes, but nobody can find it. "I must have my machete sharpener. Did one of you take it home and forget to bring it back?" Nobody admits to it. I am sure one of them has taken it, thinking I would not miss it, but it is the machete sharpener that Laurent made a wooden handle for, and I would like, in my future fieldwork, anywhere in the world, to have a machete sharpener that was special to me because it was a reminder of Laurent. Whatever else has happened here, I realize that I consider him a friend.

The inevitable result of this wild rush is that we are all sitting at the edge of the road with all the equipment by 1:30—a whole hour and a half before the earliest possible arrival of the WCS truck. The sun is beating down, and the sweat bees are relentless. We pile everything in a tiny patch of shade from a lone small tree. I try to make myself comfortable in various ways, with little success. I lie on a palm frond and try to write in my journal, restraining myself from making any effort to combat the sweat bees, knowing what an exercise in futility that would be. Florence goes off to the village to get something to eat. I send Etienne back to the campsite to search for my machete sharpener, but of course he returns empty-handed. He asks if he too can go to the village to get something to eat, and I send him on his way. Finally I end up sitting next to Laurent, the only one left, on the provisions box. We don't find much to say, and Laurent to my irritation asks me yet again for my machete. There is no reason for Laurent to stay here among the sweat bees, but he does. "I'm going to miss you," he finally blurts out. It suddenly dawns on me why Laurent, who I had thought was above scrounging, asked me for my machete, and why he was dissatisfied with 2,500cfa to buy a new one as an alternative. He wanted *my* machete, just as I wanted the sharpener with his handle on it. But my machete is by now buried deep in some box and it is too late.

I am hot and the sweat bees are swarming me, trying to crawl into my eyes and mouth. I long for my cool bathing spot in the forest, and start eyeing the marsh across the road. At 2:30 I can resist it no longer, and set off across the road. But the water turns out to be shallow and tepid and muddy, and I have to use my t-shirt for a towel.

Five o'clock goes by, darkness starts to fall, and WCS has still not arrived. At some point Laurent wanders off down the road, and when the WCS truck finally pulls up at 6:00 he is not there. Only Cepet, and of course the driver, are in the truck. Etienne and the driver load all my boxes into the back. Florence is still distressed by the sudden and unseemly nature of this departure. We awkwardly shake hands. Usually when I move and say goodbye to people I have become close to, it's not really a total goodbye. We exchange e-mail addresses; we invite each other to visit. But this is a parting from people I will never see again. It is hard to know what to say.

Minutes later I am squashed comfortably between familiar Cepet and the driver, in the front seat of the truck, Ganganya Brousse quickly disappearing behind us as we drive past all the little villages that dot the road to Epena. It is after dark when we pull into the WCS compound. I climb down from the truck and look around for Hugo. The light is on in his house but he is not out yet. There is some kind of fuss going on at the front of the truck. Apparently the driver has locked the keys inside, and Cepet is trying to figure out if they have a spare set somewhere. Not my problem. I start unloading my stuff without help, and dragging it up to the house. Will I be staying in the same place as last time? Finally Hugo appears on the doorstep. He looks me up and down. "You're quite dirty, aren't you?" he says by way of greeting. "I suppose I had better get in some beer."

red
tape
revisited

Hugo tells me to go and get washed up and that I'm staying in the same place as last time. Mitch is inside the house trying to say hello, but Hugo is planted firmly in the doorway to make sure I don't track mud indoors. "I'm too dirty to come into the house," I shout to Mitch through the screen door. Then I fill buckets from the well and have a really good wash.

Mitch is leaving tomorrow morning for the field and the evening spent with him and Hugo is one of great luxury after the forest. The cook has left us some food, but Hugo and Mitch, both accomplished cooks, are supplementing it with omelets and bread pudding. They send me off to arrange more beer. I give three empty 1-liter bottles and

3,000cfa to the night guard, who goes and fetches full bottles in the village. When I return to the house the omelets are perfect, and the bread pudding is filling and comforting. Mitch has me serve myself first, as the most recently returned from the field.

The next morning I get down to business. There is an e-mail from Claude telling me to come out of the forest *immediately,* and get myself to Brazzaville. This is a preliminary expedition, he says, and making political connections is at least as important as catching snakes. Hugo is saying more or less the same thing. There's no point in my hanging around here at Epena. I'd be better off using the time in Brazzaville to make sure that I get the export permit I need if I am going to take my specimens to the Smithsonian. I send an e-mail to Claude asking him to try to get in touch with Père Joseph to see if he can reserve a room for me at such short notice.

One thing I want to get done before going on to Brazzaville is completely emptying and repacking my big plastic box of equipment, supplies, and specimens. When I open the lid I am in for two unpleasant surprises. The first is that the bottle of ethanol, given to me by the Public Health Lab with a lid that never quite fitted, has tipped over and completely emptied itself all over the rest of the contents of the box. Fortunately I don't need it any more since I am not going to be fixing any more tissue samples, and since it was in such a high concentration, the ethanol has completely vaporized. Nothing it spilled on is even damp.

The other surprise is more serious. I sniff suspiciously at the plastic-wrapped specimens. Am I just smelling formalin, or do I detect a faint odor of rotting flesh? I take everything out of the box, and something is definitely rotting. To my dismay, I trace the smell to the 2.5-meter long forest cobra. We'd injected masses of formalin into it, but apparently not enough. I take it outside onto the front step and unwrap it. The stench makes me gag. An area of skin halfway along the body is puffed up with decomposition. I inject more formalin around the bit that has rotted. That will prevent it from rotting any further, but it won't do anything about the smell from the decomposition that has already taken place. Mitch steps out of the house and stops dead as the smell hits him. I explain about part of the cobra having rotted, and he comments mildly that the smell is "pretty ripe." I get as much formalin as possible into the cobra and then start wrapping it in many layers of plastic bags, each sealed with packing tape. The smell of rotting flesh is overwhelming, and spreading outward from where I am working. This is right on the doorstep to Hugo's house, and he is not going to be pleased, on returning from his office, to discover that his doorstep and possibly by now his living room as well smell like a mass grave.

I wrap the cobra in so many layers of plastic that I begin to think the smell must be coming from somewhere else. Just the smell picked up by other plastic things in the box before I rewrapped it? Is it on my hands? Am I imagining it? I wash my hands 10 times and I can still smell the cobra on them. I notice a sticky mark on the step where the cobra had been unwrapped, and wonder if that is the source of the smell. I scrub the whole step with soap, and rinse it with several buckets of water. And then Hugo arrives. I cringe as he comes within range of the stench. "Why is it so wet here?" he asks.

"I cleaned it," I tell him nervously, wondering why he hasn't said anything about the smell. He steps past me, into the house, looking puzzled. Later, I ask him to come and sniff the box to see if he can detect any odor besides formalin. He sniffs carefully, the full length of the box, but assures me that he doesn't smell anything. Hugo, I realize, must have no sense of smell. Thank goodness for that. I pack everything back into the box neatly, reflecting that it's just as well that I'm returning to Brazzaville soon, where I will be able to put the cobra in a freezer.

"The zoologist!" Père Joseph greets me the following afternoon. "You are here sooner than we had expected. Don't worry, we will figure out something." I get the taxi driver to help unload my luggage. Frère Jacques takes one end of my equipment box and I the other, and we carry it up the stairs and inside. There is somebody leaving today, but he hasn't left yet. I will get his room when he does. "Sit down and have a beer," they tell me, "the room will be ready eventually." I regale them with stories of 2-meter-long water cobras and waist-deep water until Père Joseph makes me stop because he says he's going to have nightmares. They are only slightly less wary of my box when I assure them that the snakes in it are all dead.

Once I've moved into my room, I ask for permission to store the rotting cobra in their freezer. Père Joseph shudders but allows it. Opening the lid of the box to take the cobra out releases a tremendous stench of rotting flesh in the small confines of my room. Père Joseph must have smelled it in the hallway, because he knocks on my door and asks, peering over my shoulder, if that is the smell of the formalin. The room smells as if I have been storing a corpse under the bed for a week. I tell him "yes," not knowing if that answer will reassure him or worry him. "Well . . ." he says, standing in the doorway, unsure what to do about the situation, "well . . . shut the door!" I'm pretty sure that the smell is only from the cobra, but that all the other plastic in the box has picked up the smell. In any case, the smell gradually dissipates once I close the lid.

The next morning finds me at the DGRST, in the office of the formidable Dr. Tathy, sweating into the brightly patterned African cotton of my Impfondo dress. A plastic bag of pickled toads lies on the desk between us. "I can't sign this!" bellows Dr. Tathy, brandishing my letter requesting an export permit. "It is missing important information— 'tissue samples?' How big are they? What kind of container are they in? It is entirely unclear . . . and what is *this*," he gestures at the Ziploc bag on his desk, "are all the 'specimens' in bags like this? Where is the formalin that you mention? And why are they wrapped in cloth? I want to see this collection—all of it—here in my office to be inspected!" My heart sinks at the idea of unwrapping over a hundred preserved animals, all carefully swaddled in layers of formalin-soaked cheesecloth, plastic bags, and packing tape. I would have no way of repackaging them. But I assure Dr. Tathy that they are all like the bag of toads in front of him, and at the prospect of a hundred such things unwrapped and dribbling preservative over the stacks of papers on his desk, he relents, but only to launch an attack on another front. "Why are all these things being taken to the United States and not kept here in the Congo?" I sigh, kicking myself for having suggested the idea of starting a national natural history collection as something for the country to consider some day, on my first courtesy visit 2 months ago.

"But where could I leave them?" I point out. "There is no institution here with the facilities to take care of them. Surely it is better that the specimens go to the Smithsonian, where they will be well looked after. It's a public collection, so they will be available on loan to scientists all over the world." He remains unimpressed. "With the report that I submit," I tried another tack, "I will include a CD with a photograph of every species I collected."

"A virtual collection," he nods, with grudging approval. But he is not finished with me. "This office granted you permission to collect amphibians and reptiles in this country for the next 3 years," he reminds me. "In the proposal you submitted you clearly indicated that your work here would include training Congolese graduate students—taking them with you into the field and teaching them how to do what you do. You have not done this." He is right. I had said that, and organizing and funding students was one of the many things that didn't work out on this trip.

"But you see the permit is for 3 years," I try not to sound as desperate as I feel. "This time was only a preliminary expedition. Now that I know people at the university it will be possible to recruit students to take with me on a future expedition."

"If you come back here, you had better." It is his final shot. I hope it isn't too obvious that I am trembling. After a silence that seems very long, his shoulders relax. From the top of one of the stacks of papers he produces a two-page document, and hands it to me. It is headed "AUTORISATION D'EXPORTATION," and ends with an official rubber stamp, already signed by Monsieur le Délégué Générale himself. Dr. Tathy had intended to give it to me all along.

The next stop is the Public Health Lab. Dr. Parra and the biomedical director greet me with surprise and affection, and are delighted by my African dress. They are fascinated by the pictures I show them on the quick-view screen of the camera, and try without success to set up something to allow them to be projected onto a big screen. But sadly Jean is away for the whole week at a conference in Cameroon. I will be gone by the time he comes back.

My next appointment of the morning is the best: Dr Pangou at the Biodiversity Study Group. Genial Dr. Pangou is delighted to see me back from the forest. He has me come around and sit next to him on his side of the desk so that I can show him my pictures on the camera's quick-view screen. Dr. Pangou ends up being the only person ever to look at all four memory cards full of pictures without reaching a saturation point and making me stop. I give him my species list, and he promises to have an export permit ready the following day. One bureaucratic oddity that I've noticed in this country is that there seem to be three different offices that all believe themselves to be solely responsible for the issuing of export permits, and none of them seems to be aware of the existence of the others. Dr. Parra at the Public Health Lab also offers to write me an export permit—make that four.

The best thing that comes out of the visit to Dr. Pangou is that he introduces me to Victor Mamonekene, whose lab is in the next room. Victor is an instructor at the university, and an ichthyologist. I am delighted to find that he has the beginnings of a museum collection of fishes in his lab. The specimen jars still have peeling jam and mayonnaise labels on them. Victor gets jars wherever he can. He has buckets of fishes still waiting for jars. The specimens are stored in formalin, which is really noxious to work with, rather than ethanol, which is more expensive. Some of the jars are not quite topped up, and here and there there is a fish tail sticking out of the preservative and drying out. But the shelves are labeled neatly and knowledgeably with scientific names. It's a museum collection at absolutely its most basic, but two young women are busily taking measurements of the fins of a tray of preserved fishes, with calipers. If somebody can get Victor some more jars and chemicals, this is a place where I would be very happy to leave half of my catch on each expedition, laying the first bricks in the foundation of a national natural history collection.

Victor produces a few preserved snakes. He tells me he picked them up in the little forested area outside his office. I can't identify them to the species level at a glance. One of them is clearly a *Grayia,* but not *ornata.* Another one is some kind of aparallactine, an interesting group, probably close relatives of atractaspidids ("back-stabbing snakes")—smallish smooth snakes with small heads, found only in Africa; they can move their two long fangs independently of each other, even sticking a fang out sideways without even parting the lips, for a backward stab into the thumb of any herpetologist foolish enough to grasp them behind the head. There are also what appear to be half a dozen tiny typhlopids (blind snakes), but I will need a microscope to be sure. Typhlopids are harmless burrowing snakes, with a blunt head and tail which make it hard to tell one end from the other. This is what I think the boys in the Likouala meant by "the snake with two heads." I am surprised when Victor presses the snakes on me. A true scientist, he cares less about keeping his specimens than he does about finding out what they are, and he understands that I will be able to identify them properly when I get them to the United States. I take the snakes and leave, wishing I'd met Victor sooner. We will certainly be staying in touch.

My timing has turned out to be just about perfect. I now have an export permit from every office that could possibly issue one, and just a few days before my flight home. It is time to return to Pointe Noire.

At the Catholic Institute, people get up early, and everyone is up as I set off to catch the first flight of the day to Pointe Noire. I remember the cobra in the freezer just in time. "Take good care of her," Père Joseph tells the taxi driver, shutting the door for me.

I feel like an experienced pro as I negotiate the chaotic Brazzaville airport on my own with all my luggage, for the flight to Pointe Noire. The one source of confusion is that apparently all the flights to different places are scheduled to depart at 9:00 a.m., and the announcement system is hard to make out, so the waiting room is a bit hectic, but my flight is on time and only takes an hour.

"Entrez," Claude calls from inside when I knock nervously on his office door. He is finishing something at the computer and has his back to me, a cigarette burning in the ashtray. He swings around in his chair to give me his full attention. "So," he looks me up and down appraisingly, "you have returned from the forest. Did you eat while you were there? You certainly haven't grown any bigger."

Claude invites me to dinner at his house that night so that I can tell him the whole story. He asks me for my ticket for tomorrow's flight, and takes it through to the secretary's office to have her reconfirm it. As he steps into the room he stops dead, as though hit by a wall. "What the *hell* is that? It smells like a rotting corpse in here!" It's true that my equipment box is in the corner, but I can't detect a smell. If Hugo's sense of smell was entirely lacking, it seems that Claude's is as sensitive as a bloodhound's. I explain about the cobra, and he rounds up two men to carry the box over to the lab building for me, directing them to a room at the back, shouting, "And open the windows!"

Sitting in Claude's living room that evening, I show him some of my photos on the quick-view screen of my camera. He shakes his head despairingly. "One does not conduct a scientific expedition by living under a tarpaulin with villagers in the middle of the forest for 5 weeks, and coming back weighing 40 kilos!" He exaggerates. I tell him more about the expedition, and about that official in Brazzaville, who wasted 3 weeks of my time by not signing the permit. I am still mystified by it. I describe my one meeting with the man. "You told him he should be spending his time on the dwarf crocodile problem?" Claude asks, aghast. "Just like a woman to say exactly what is on her mind without thinking of the consequences!"

Finally he drives me back to my hotel. I leave tomorrow, and we won't get to talk much again. At least this one isn't a permanent goodbye, as so many others on this trip have been. My flight the next day is not until 10:00 p.m. I have completely repacked my box, and I think Claude is greatly exaggerating about the smell. A man called Roland, who has a special pass to get him past airport security, is to take care of checking my luggage and accompanying me to the gate.

Luggage for the 10:00 p.m. flight to Paris can be checked in early at the Air France office in the afternoon. The place is packed when Roland and I arrive at 4:00 p.m. To my dismay the officials are opening every bag and going through the entire contents. Mine will be difficult to explain. Sure enough, my box of specimens generates a lot of questions. I confidently present my stack of export permits. Is there any further official paper I could possibly have? In answering the questions I'm trying to figure out whether they're going to give me trouble for possibly carrying endangered species, or for carrying dangerous chemicals (formalin-soaked and ethanol-preserved specimens), but it seems they are afraid of some kind of biohazard. Ridiculous. Everything is in preservative. But the documentation seems not to reassure them—rather the reverse. The DGRST permit mentions tissue samples preserved for DNA extraction. "Is it true that this box contains DNA?" They think I'm carrying some kind of contagious disease.

I tell them that of course the box contains DNA. Its whole outer surface is covered with the DNA of the baggage handlers. "A molecule is not a microbe!" I am speaking more loudly than is probably wise. Roland gets me to sit down out of the way and leave it to him. The end result is that my box is "conditionally" checked in. Roland says not to worry. They don't want to give people a hard time at the last minute, when the plane is boarding. He's pretty sure it will be okay.

But "pretty sure" leaves a lot of leeway for anxiety. Finally at 9:00 p.m. Claude drives me and Roland to the airport. The atmosphere in the car is tense. I am desperately hoping everything will be okay. I don't know what I'm going to face in the terminal. "Bon courage," says Claude, as I awkwardly shake his hand. And then he is gone and Roland and I are left to negotiate the airport.

The news is the worst it could possibly be. The officials have an e-mail from Paris confirming that nothing containing DNA may be carried on a passenger plane. That's it. There is absolutely no question of my specimens being allowed on board. I can yell a lesson in introductory biology at the airport officials if I want, but they are just ignorant people blindly following stupid instructions from stupid people in Paris. I can't do a thing about it except tell Roland to take the box and give it to Claude.

A lot has gone wrong on this trip, it is true, but being separated at the last minute from my precious specimens, obtained with such difficulty, suddenly pushes me past some limit. The tears well up inside me and pour down my cheeks. I pass the box to Roland, my eyes red and my nose full of mucus. Roland leaves. He will give the box to

Claude. I am now bawling uninhibitedly, barely noticing the x-ray scanner that I pass through and the inspection of my toolbox through the curtain of tears. I find my seat on the plane, and continue to cry, my face pressed against the window. If anyone notices, nobody says anything. It is too dark to see much outside. The glass is wet as the lights of Pointe Noire disappear beneath us.

chapter 11

planning
my
return

"That's what fieldwork in these countries is like," says George, the kind senior curator of herpetology at the Smithsonian, when I return from the Congo. "There's nothing you could have done differently that would have avoided the problems." The immediate problem, of course, is that my collection is stranded in Pointe Noire. But when I talk of shipping the collection to the United States, George is not optimistic. "We had to ship a collection from Cameroon once, and what with air freight and broker's fees and so on it came to a couple of thousand dollars." Clearly he is not going to pay $2,000 to get my collection shipped.

But I am immensely lucky in having my box left in the care of Claude. Before my plane has even landed in Toronto, Claude has already figured out a way to get the specimens to the Smithsonian. He is sure they can be shipped by DHL courier, and he has already researched the exact cost of shipping packages of different weights. We are looking at shipping prices in the low hundreds of dollars, and the Smithsonian manages to scrape together the funds to pay for up to $300 in shipping expenses. Since my box contains some equipment as well as the specimens, Claude proposes leaving the equipment behind, to pick up on my next visit, in order to make the package lighter. (My machete that Laurent wanted so badly is now languishing in Pointe Noire.) I suggest doing some triage of the specimens. Most of the weight of the specimens is the big snakes, and I am not in doubt as to their identification, so I could put together a species list even without the specimens. Then there are the species which I have large numbers of. "Don't send all the skinks and toads," I tell Claude, "just send me a couple of each."

So poor Claude, so sensitive to the smells of the formalin and of the rotting bits of some of the larger specimens that hadn't been completely preserved, has to unwrap everything and sort it all out by the tag numbers I've sent him, complaining unremittingly throughout the process. He eventually sends me a list of tag numbers of specimens to be included in the package, for my approval, and is just about ready to kill me when I say that actually I want *all* the *Xenopus* sent as well. The reason I want all the *Xenopus* is that, having found that pair of small bumpy frogs that I almost mistook for *Xenopus,* so close to the end, I want to make absolutely sure that I didn't catch any of them earlier and mistake them for *Xenopus*. To Claude, an entomologist, all small frogs look the same, so he has to go through everything again and identify the *Xenopus* by the tag numbers I've sent. George suggests that I owe Claude at a minimum several bottles of good French wine, and Claude is in complete agreement.

Finally the package is sent. It ends up weighing only 5 kilograms, so there is enough extra space to add the *Boulengerina*, the water cobra that I went through so much to obtain, as well as my snake bags and my hemostat. George is certain that the package will get held up by customs in New York, but, as I track its progress on the DHL website, it travels from Pointe Noire to Douala to Amsterdam to Brussels to New York to Maryland (where it briefly goes astray in the wrong truck) to Washington, D.C. And the final bill is $180.

When I arrive back in Toronto in late November, everyone assumes I must be suffering from the shock of the temperature change. But the hardest thing to adapt to is breaking myself of the habit of making friendly eye contact and saying "hello" (or rather "mbote") to every stranger I pass in the street. After a week I am able to stop myself at the friendly eye contact stage, and the Torontonians just take me for a harmless lunatic.

The most annoying question you can ask a herpetologist returning from the field, as she steps off the plane in Toronto, is: "How many new species did you discover?" The general public doesn't understand that new species are usually collected in the field, but "discovered" in the museum, and what a laborious process it is. As a student I had always imagined that a new species was discovered when a herpetologist saw something unfamiliar slither across the trail, and said confidently, "Ah, a new species!" The reality is usually much more mundane. A new species may be "discovered" by a scientist painstakingly studying a particular species in a museum collection. Two jars of specimens collected decades ago, in two different locations, are taken off the shelf. The researcher notices that all the snakes in one jar have 6 supralabial scales and more than 170 ventral scales, while all the snakes in the other jar have only 4 supralabial scales and fewer than 130 ventral scales. The two jars, labeled with the same name, are therefore found actually to represent two different species, so one jarful of snakes has to be labeled a new species. A photograph is taken of a shriveled, preserved specimen, and a detailed description of the animal is written up for publication in a scientific journal: "Description of a new species of . . ." Whoever the collector was, all those years ago, probably never guessed that the snakes would one day be described as a new species. To be fair, collectors often come across an animal in the field that they can't identify, and suspect may be a new species. But it takes a long time excavating through the literature and examining other museum specimens to be able to confidently rule out the possibility that it actually is a known species that is just rare and difficult to identify.

The second most annoying question you can ask that herpetologist, who has collected tissue samples for DNA extraction as well as whole specimens, is: "Oh, so are you going to use the DNA to identify what species it is?" In fact the answer is quite the reverse. Molecular biology has not progressed to the point of being able to identify species of Congolese amphibians and reptiles from their DNA. In fact one important reason for having a "voucher" specimen, the whole formalin-fixed animal that the tissue came from, is so that by studying the anatomy of the whole specimen, the species that the DNA comes from can be identified.

In February I make my way from Toronto to the Smithsonian's National Museum of Natural History to try to identify my specimens. I need to do the identifying at a big museum not only for the sake of having previously collected specimens for comparison, but also for access to a specialized herpetological library, in which all the literature I need to refer to—old, published in obscure journals, and in French—is available.

I am warmly welcomed at the Smithsonian, where nothing seems to have changed since my days as an intern. When I arrive in the Division of Amphibians and Reptiles, I find a desk set up with a dissecting microscope, plastic trays, cheesecloth, tools for counting scales, and my collection, which I haven't seen since wrapping it up in the forest, carefully rinsed and stored in glass jars of ethanol. So I set to work. It is a busy week. George is an early riser, arriving at the museum around 6:30 a.m. every day. If I'm not already at work when he arrives, he teases me for the rest of the day, addressing me as "slug-a-bed."

As I set to work identifying specimens, I am reminded of how much I enjoy museum work: The calm and concentration of scale counting, the excitement of taking a jar off a shelf to see if my tentative identification could be correct, and the satisfaction of figuring out for sure what species a specimen is. The familiar musty smell of the collection, the companionship of the people around me, all on their own scale-counting quests—even the familiar shriveling of the skin on my fingers from long hours handling ethanol-preserved specimens. It all brings back memories of happy times spent in museum collections. The only thing better is fieldwork.

I am initially baffled by a very thin, small, jet-black snake which I have no recollection of having collected. I check my field notes and find, matching up its tag number, that I had described it as "emerald green." Scale counts, laborious under a microscope with such a small specimen, confirm it to be *Hapsidophrys smaragdina*, a green, diurnal tree snake. It is surprising how different museum specimens, subjected to formalin and ethanol, may look from the live animal.

I had collected many geckos of what appeared to be the same common species, but when Claude sends me just three "representatives" I find that one of them is an entirely different species from the other two, and previously recorded from only two locations, both in west Africa. This is a reminder to me of the importance of collecting series of specimens, and makes me realize how much more I can learn from a specimen in a museum setting than I can under field conditions.

Thinking that they might be interested in hearing about how their specimens were obtained, I give an informal travelogue to the staff of the Herpetology Department, showing pictures of my camp and of checking nets in the flooded forest—even pictures of a bowl of Florence's food and a view of my tarpaulin "house." At the end of the talk, the general consensus among these men, who do fieldwork all over the world—Burma, South America, even Cameroon—is that the Congo sounds like a fascinating place, but I can have it all to myself, they tease me. You couldn't pay them to go there.

Though I don't think I've collected any new species, some interesting discoveries come out of my expedition. To begin with, my list of identified specimens represents the first sampling of the amphibians and reptiles of the flooded forest of the Likouala. Now there is at least a partial list. Many species that I collected were not previously known to exist in the Congo as a whole, presumably just because nobody had looked for them. At first I publish a "range extension" note in the journal *Herpetological Review* for each species not previously known from the Congo. But eventually I realize that almost half my collection qualifies for such a note, so I stop submitting each one and save them all up to mention together in some future publication. A specialist in frogs of the pipid family (the family that includes *Xenopus*) is delighted to receive my photo of the pair of small bumpy frogs that I collected the day we took the nets down, which he tells me are *Hymenochirus curtipes*. Indeed, without his assistance I can only imagine how long it would have taken me to figure out the identity of that strange creature. Mine is the first report of the species since its initial description in 1924 from a specimen collected in what was then the Belgian Congo (now the DRC). I put this information on my website and am soon contacted by a man in Düsseldorf, an engineer by profession but a pipid frog fanatic at heart, who draws my attention to a scattering of later mentions of *H. curtipes*, all from the DRC.

The big round frog with a line down the middle of its back that I found in a puddle beside the house the night that I told Florence not to throw the fish guts there, turns out to be *Aubria masako*, described in 1989 by a frog expert in Paris. She had described the species on the basis of a few preserved specimens collected long ago in what is now the DRC, and is thrilled to see, for the first time, a picture of *her* frog alive. Though known, many of the species in my collection are very rare. Online databases of amphibians and reptiles are pleased to have the first photographs available on the Internet of several species.

And then there are all the tissue samples, which for most of the species I collected are the first available in the world. I don't do any molecular biology myself, but as soon as word gets around that I am back, many people contact me to see if by any chance I have tissues from a Congo population of whatever species they are studying. These are scientists who are trying to reconstruct the evolutionary history of various kinds of animals by studying DNA and RNA sequences, and they want samples from populations in as many locations as possible.

So those are some of the "Results" of my expedition. But, looking back on it, I see so many things that went wrong. There are so many things I wish I had done differently. Surely if I did it again I could get it all right. The conclusion that I arrive at is this: I need to go back to the Congo. I plan a return expedition for October.

A lot happens in the intervening year. Now I have many contacts in the Congo. Communicating with Claude, as well as with Victor, Jean, Hugo, and Dr. Parra, I realize what a huge difference the Internet must have made to scientists in Africa. I am greatly frustrated to find that it is virtually impossible to send even a letter to the Congo by regular mail. I so often see things available cheaply in Toronto shops that would make a big difference to Congolese villagers, if only I could find a way to get them there. Claude's bottles of wine will have to wait to travel in my luggage on my next trip to the Congo. The only way to send anything that can't be sent by Internet seems to be DHL courier, prohibitively expensive for most things, but reliable at getting things at least to the big cities of Pointe Noire and Brazzaville.

As March approaches, I write up a report of my findings to send to all the offices in the Congo that would want a report. Claude goes over it several times, not just improving my French, but heading me off from making terrible political mistakes in the content. I end up with eight copies of my official *Rapport*, each accompanied by a CD. These I put into individual addressed envelopes to make up a single, expensive, DHL shipment to Pointe Noire. Claude will see that they are distributed within the country. I take advantage of the package to include another envelope, addressed to Père Jude at his post office box at the Catholic Institute. Inside it, with a cover letter, is an envelope addressed to the Chief of Ganganya Brousse, and nested inside that, like Russian dolls, are envelopes of printed photographs addressed to Florence, Etienne, and Laurent. I don't expect ever to know whether they reach their destination.

I suppose my decision to try to learn Lingala was an indication of my commitment to central Africa. French is the official language of the Congo, and all one hears spoken in the major cities, but in the small villages in the northern half of the country—the part covered by the forest of the Congo River drainage basin—Lingala is the first, and often only, language people learn. Congolese in the north often mix Lingala into their French, thereby rendering the French utterly incomprehensible.

On my recent expedition I had made a point of hiring a guide and a cook who both spoke good French, but I often felt lonely, isolated from the apparently hilarious stories told around the campfire, when everyone relaxed and reverted to Lingala, and, more seriously, I was totally dependent on my cook and guide to translate for the many people I needed to communicate with who spoke no French. None of the Pygmies I met on that expedition spoke French, and I started to suspect that there was an inverse correlation between facility with the French language and competence working in the forest and knowing how to find animals. I could get better guides if I was willing to hire ones who didn't necessarily speak much French.

So back in Toronto I start looking for instruction materials. Surely someone must sell "teach-yourself-Lingala" software, I think at first—or at least a book. But Google repeatedly comes up blank. I finally track down on amazon.fr an out-of-print paperback called *Parlons Lingala: Toloba Lingala* (Let's Speak Lingala). It turns out to be a lengthy analysis of the linguistic origins of the language, and no help to me at all.

Finding Delphin is a tremendous stroke of luck. I eventually give up on the Internet and telephone the Embassy of the Democratic Republic of Congo, in Washington, D.C., for advice. I explain my situation, and get no further than the man who answers the phone, because it turns out that he happens to have a nephew who has recently moved to Toronto. This receptionist puts me in touch with his nephew, Delphin, by e-mail. Delphin and I finally meet, one snowy day in March, in the subway station nearest my apartment. He looks like a young Samuel L. Jackson, huddled against the cold in a totally inadequate black leather jacket. We are both shy about discussing how he is to teach me and particularly the issue of payment. The situation has no precedent. But eventually we fall into a routine. Every Monday afternoon, Delphin comes to my apartment and teaches me for an hour and a half, 2 hours, or until I reach saturation point and make him stop—"Ekoki! Ekoki! Oyo ezali ya mingi!" (Enough! Enough! This is already a lot!).

Not only does Delphin know Lingala, but he is an experienced teacher in the opposite direction (teaching French to Lingala-speaking Pygmies), a journalist by profession, and generally good at languages. Aside from Lingala we speak only French, but presumably he could manage perfectly well in English since he is living in English-speaking Toronto and taking a course on computers. So gradually, over the winter and the spring, I learn Lingala. Of course I have nobody to practice it on except Delphin. My family and friends get annoyed when I speak to them in incomprehensible Lingala, so I get into the habit of speaking Lingala to my cat, Daisy. I develop one party trick which only Delphin can appreciate. You see, my cat speaks one word of Lingala. I scoop Daisy into my arms and demand in Lingala, "What kind of animal are you? Are you a fish? Are you a bird? Are you a turtle? . . ." Until eventually she mews in protest:

"Niaou!"

"That's right, you're a cat!" (It just happens that the Lingala word for a cat is *niaou*.) Delphin laughs obligingly every time.

Lingala is a strange language. It has very few words, so each word has several possible meanings depending on the grammar and context. *Lobi* can mean either yesterday or tomorrow. *Mbula* can mean either rain or year. Delphin begins each lesson practicing polite greetings at great speed: "Mbote, sango nini?" (Hello, what news?)

"Sango te. Ozali malamu?" (No news. Are you well?) Lingala lacks a word for yes, so you have to repeat back the question with the grammar adjusted for the first person singular: "Nazali malamu. Yo mpe?" (I am well. You also?)

As the weeks go by our lessons become more relaxed. Delphin delights in introducing me to some of the subtleties of African culture. He teaches me how to tell, when bargaining over a price, whether the salesman really means the price we have reached, or whether he is actually prepared to go lower. He explains the crucial words at the end of a Lingala sentence that make the difference between "Sure, I'll show up sometime tomorrow or maybe the next day if nothing else comes up" and "I'll be there at dawn tomorrow no matter what."

Organizing my old e-mails one day, I take another look at all those messages from people who were part of the long chain of contacts that eventually led me to Claude. I am excited to come across an old message from Dr. Jean-Philippe Chippaux. The name had meant nothing to me at the time, but now, more familiar with the reptiles of the Congo, I recognize him as the world's greatest authority on west African snakes. I feel I owe him a thank you and a follow-up report at the very least, so I contact him, and soon we are engaged in happy correspondence about snakes. Jean-Philippe, like Claude, works for the IRD, and he studies snakes as a hobby. He was posted for a long time in west Africa, which is how he came to study the snakes of that part of the world. But he has recently been moved to Bolivia. To my delight, he invites me to join him there for the month of May to undertake a project looking for a relationship between altitude and the incidence of snakebite.

Snakes turn out not to be abundant in the cold foothills of the Andes, and I end up spending a lot of time as a houseguest of Jean-Philippe and his wife in La Paz. Jean-Philippe is a physician by training, and an excellent scientist, with particular expertise in the treatment of snakebite. He does research, he tells me, instead of practicing medicine, because he prefers it to dealing with patients. After hearing about a few case histories involving snakes, I can understand his frustration.

Jean-Philippe gets up early and puts in a long day. Over dinner he and his wife and I discuss topics of general interest. But the best part of the day is after dinner, when I get Jean-Philippe to myself to talk about snakes. We sit together with a bottle of red wine between us and discuss and debate such topics as the definition of the loreal scale on the head of colubrid snakes, how to count dorsal scale rows most accurately—conversations only a handful of people in the world would understand or find interesting. As the level in the wine bottle drops, my French starts to deteriorate, and Jean-Philippe becomes increasingly eloquent, so I sit back and listen. I love these evenings, and learn an enormous amount listening to him.

A tremendous amount of misinformation and misunderstanding surrounds the treatment of snakebite. People believe in useless "traditional medicines," people believe all snakes to be venomous, people don't know the correct first aid for snakebite. Proper treatment, if the victim gets it, will vary depending on the species of snake, the severity of the bite, the amount of time that has passed since the bite, and how much the attending physician knows about treating snakebite. Snakebite is complicated to treat and to educate people about.

Misinformation and misunderstandings can lead to tragedy. Jean-Philippe tells me about a man who was brought into the hospital where he once worked to be treated for a snakebite. The man had been bitten on the hand, so his friends put a tight tourniquet on his upper arm, and took him on the 3-day journey to the hospital. By the time the man reached Jean-Philippe, it was clear that the bite had been from a nonvenomous snake. But the result of the tourniquet being in place for 3 days was that the arm had become gangrenous and had to be amputated—a case of an arm lost totally unnecessarily as a result of incompetent treatment in the field of a nonvenomous bite.

Efforts must be made to educate people about snakebite, but sometimes a little bit of knowledge can do more harm than good. The man who runs the antivenom institute in La Paz struggles constantly against the local "traditional medicine" used to treat snakebite. This is a potion, an infusion made from local plants and animals, which the victim drinks. It is probably harmful only in that it creates a false sense of security and may prevent the victim from seeking proper help. And in Bolivia, in contrast to the Congo, competent medical treatment is available. Anyway, the director of the Antivenom Institute made a great effort to get remote clinics to stock antivenom and to teach the clinicians how to administer it intravenously. Unfortunately, the result was that the next bite victim was still given the traditional potion—but administered intravenously!

About 600,000 people in Africa are bitten by venomous snakes every year: 20,000 of those die, and among the 580,000 lucky survivors are people who lost a hand, who suffered permanent nerve damage, and so on. I've never seen any statistics on the number of deaths per year that result from the incompetent treatment of harmless bites. It would be interesting to know.

I tell Jean-Philippe that I don't carry antivenom in the field because (1) there isn't one available for the venomous species encountered in the Congo and (2) it has to be refrigerated. Actually, he tells me, there is a new antivenom being developed at a lab in Mexico. It is a polyvalent antivenom, containing antibodies against the venoms of the 10 most dangerous species in Africa, and it comes freeze-dried in a powder, so that it doesn't have to be refrigerated. When you are ready to use it you simply dissolve it in saline solution to make liquid antivenom. The product is not approved for use yet, but if I mention Jean-Philippe's name the lab developing it might be willing to give me a free sample.

He also gives me some advice on how to administer antivenom under field conditions, should that ever be necessary. "An intramuscular injection is too slow," he tells me. "It needs to be intravenous." Then after a moment's thought he adds that if it wasn't possible to give an intravenous injection, an intraperitoneal injection ought to work as well. I don't think I'd have any difficulty getting a needle into the vein on a bite victim's arm to give an intravenous injection, but the idea of an intraperitoneal injection—driving a long hypodermic needle straight into someone's abdomen and as deep as it can go—makes me shudder even when Jean-Philippe assures me that there would be no danger of puncturing the intestines since they would just slide away from the tip of the needle. In any case, it's highly unlikely that I'll ever have to deal with a snakebite victim. Everyone thinks of my fieldwork as being dangerous because of the snakes, but I've said time and time again that more mundane dangers—malaria, murder, crashes of small planes—are much more likely. Finally, Jean-Philippe gives me a copy of his new book about the snakes of west Africa, which ends up being tremendously useful in my next expedition.

George at the Smithsonian sends me boxes of equipment once again. He also has some advice about the fixing of specimens. Instead of preserving large snakes whole, which produces specimens which weigh a lot and are likely to rot, he tells me to dissect out the body, leaving only the head attached to the skin, and roll the whole thing up in a strip of formalin-saturated cheesecloth. As for amphibians, since many of the features used to identify frogs are inside the mouth, fix them with a piece of a plastic drinking straw propping their mouth open, so that they will harden with the inside of the mouth visible. I ask George for injectable Nembutal for euthanizing reptiles instead of chloroform. Obtaining Nembutal and shipping it to Canada turns out to be such a daunting maze of red tape that he looks for alternatives and discovers procaine. Procaine is supposed to work the same way as Nembutal, just an overdose of an anesthetic, and to order it off the Internet all I am required to do is tick a box promising that I am over 18. Gradually equipment is bought and logistics start to fall into place.

Then there is the issue of students.

Shortly after returning from my expedition, I was invited to give a lecture about my adventures, much like the one I gave to the herpetologists at the Smithsonian, to a group of undergraduates in the natural history club at McGill University. I show them pictures of my camp of Pygmy payottes and one tarpaulin shelter that caused my Bantu guide

The flooded forest

My 2005 camp near Ganganya Brousse

Florence in the "kitchen"

Etienne with an improvised headlamp

The red snake

Me with
Grayia ornata

Fixing specimens in my "lab"

The two giant cobras

Ange cataloguing *Bufos*

The Impongui children

Romuald in a pirogue on the Likouala aux Herbes River

Lise with a
dead *Lamprophis*

Me with a giant millipede

The first brick pile

Me swimming in the flooded forest near our camp

Ange collecting frogs at night

Catching the rhinoceros viper *(Bitis nasicornis)*

Lise and I skinning a 2-meter-long forest cobra *(Naja melanoleuca)* captured in the flooded forest near our camp

Ange standing up in the pirogue

Anuarite
with machete

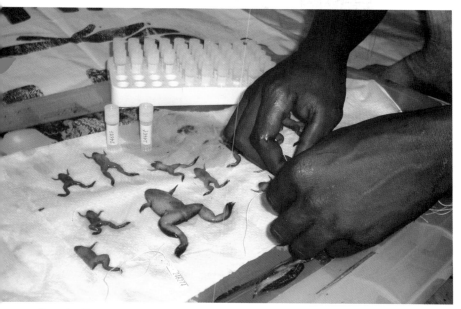

Preparing *Xenopus*

Leaving Impongui:
the man with his
arms upraised is
Uncle Marcel

Hemidactylus fasciatus

Hemidactylus pseudomuriceus

Trachylepis maculilabris

Trachylepis affinis

Lygosoma fernandi

Ptychadena perreti

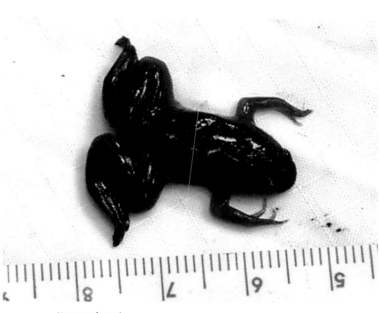

Xenopus fraseri

Silurana (= Xenopus) epitropicalis

Hymenochirus curtipes:
the strange little bumpy frog from
the day we took the nets down

Cryptothylax greshoffii

Hoplobatrachus occipitalis:
a large and common
African bullfrog

Bufo regularis: the commonest toad at both campsites

Bufo camerunensis: not *"Bufo jacksoni"* after all, but a
known species

Aubria masako

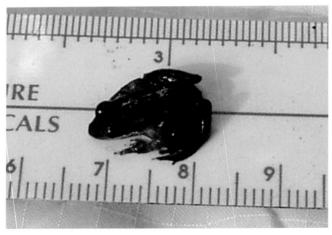

Phrynobatrachus hylaois: an LBF (little
brown frog)—I got help identifying this one

Lamprophis olivacea: my first specimen, collected in a Pygmy village in 1997

Grayia ornata

Grayia smithii

Boulengerina annulata: a water cobra 2 meters long

Mehelya poensis

Lamprophis fuliginosus

Psammophis phillipsii

Hapsidophrys smaragdina

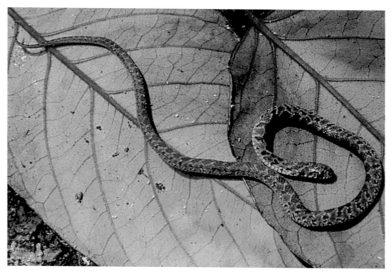

Dasypeltis scabra: the egg-eating snake

Python sebae: my badly behaved pet, Ariane

Typhlops lineolatus: the "5-minute snake"

Naja melanoleuca: collected by hand from the last brick pile

to quit on the grounds that the living conditions were too harsh. I show a photograph of the food prepared by my cook, which had resulted in my losing 10 pounds in the course of 5 weeks. And I show pictures of the animals I collected, some of which might turn out to be new species.

But far from being put off the prospect of fieldwork by my presentation, the students are so excited and enthusiastic they swarm me at the end of the talk for business cards with my e-mail and website addresses on them. One girl earnestly begs me to take her with me as my field assistant on my next expedition. I know just how she feels. I remember. And yet, I find myself telling her to do it on her own: "Leaf through the atlas until you find a place you're interested in and then just go there, and figure it out for yourself." "That's what I did," I tell her.

As I say the words, it dawns on me for the first time how much like my old professor I have become. I'll take risks myself in the field, but I don't want to have to worry about the safety of anyone else, and besides, if *I* had to teach myself, then that's what everyone should have to do. And somewhere, perhaps, there's another thought: What on earth do I have to teach anyone? I just do what I do. I don't know any methods or techniques—after all, I just figured it out for myself.

Reluctant as I am to have students tagging along with me, I have no choice. When he gave me my export permit last year, Dr. Tathy made it very clear that training Congolese students was a condition of my continuing to do fieldwork in the country. I do see the value of Congolese scientists learning to study the biodiversity of their own country, without being dependent on foreigners, but when it comes to my own expedition, I am not enthusiastic.

Resigning myself to it, I write the cost of two Congolese thesis students into my budget, and ask Dr. Pangou, at the Biodiversity Study Group at Brazzaville's Marien-Ngouabi University, to select the individuals. First and foremost, they must be excellent students, I begin my list of requirements, who are interested in learning about amphibians and reptiles. They must be in good physical shape, and most important they must be prepared to tolerate field conditions. They will work during the day as well as during the night, they will be dirty and wet, and the food will be awful. They will need to be cheerful and resilient.

If they can meet these requirements, they will have the opportunity to learn a great deal, to visit a habitat unlike any other in the world, and to have their names on the resulting publication in a scientific journal. At the end of this expedition they should be capable of carrying out their own herpetofaunal surveys independently. I will provide a stipend of 100,000cfa each for the 2-month period, as well as covering all travel expenses and providing modest food and accommodation. I will supply all specialized materials and equipment necessary.

I hesitate over the final paragraph of my e-mail to Dr. Pangou. I have very mixed feelings about affirmative action, but eventually I decide that in the case of field biology in the Congo it is justified. "Of course the candidates selected must be those best qualified. Nevertheless, I would be particularly pleased to train a young woman in herpetology if a well-qualified candidate should present herself." I hit "send" before I have time to change my mind.

I get no reply from Dr. Pangou, but soon I receive messages from the two students he has chosen, Lise Mavoungou and Ange Zassi-Boulou. Lise is 24 and doing an undergraduate honors thesis, while Ange, 31, is about to begin his doctoral work. I start corresponding with them 3 months in advance of the expedition, and try to start planning possible projects for each of them, assigning them homework that can be done by using Internet resources in preparation. When I push them to narrow down their interests, Ange decides that he would like to study amphibians, while Lise tells me that she is passionate about snakes.

I easily come up with a great project for Lise. I remember all the *Grayia* I got in my nets last year. There were enough of them that one could actually do an ecological study. Even if she just collected them in the nets, measured, marked, and released them every day, she would end up with the first data set on the natural history of African aquatic snakes. The skill Ange is going to need most is the ability to recognize the species he is likely to encounter in the field. Rather than overwhelm him with the hundreds of amphibians we may potentially encounter, I tell him to take the list of amphibians I collected in my report from last year, and use the various Internet amphibian databases to learn about just them.

Of course most of all I wonder what they are going to be like as people. Lise's curriculum vitae is full of typographical mistakes, and she sends friendly, casual e-mails. Ange writes with such formal and elaborate language that sometimes his French defeats me. I am surprised to find myself really looking forward to meeting them.

My first-aid kit is very well organized and includes the four ampoules of the new antivenom sent to me by the lab in Mexico. The lab people assure me that four ampoules is enough to treat a really serious bite. I store the ampoules in a small Ziploc bag along with needles and a 10-cc syringe, and bury the whole lot among the bandages, antibiotic ointment, and painkillers.

This year I have a better idea of what equipment I will need. Last year my 12-inch hemostat was my most useful snake-handling tool. Its only failing was that it was sometimes too short for me to get close enough to the snake safely. So I am delighted to find a 24-inch hemostat for sale on eBay. It turns out to be a disappointment, however, because the hinge is very near the pincers, so that opening them to any width requires using both hands to open the handles wide apart. A clumsy tool. Why can't somebody make a 24-inch hemostat with the hinge near the handles? My MP3 recorder for frog calls, sadly, is stolen from my lab, and I can't afford to replace it. I buy three Eternity flashlights—flashlights that don't need batteries but need to be shaken very frequently to keep them going. These seem like an excellent idea in case I run out of batteries for the normal flashlights, but in the event they turn out to be infuriating to use. I buy Lise and Ange each a backpack, a headlamp, and a notebook.

I soon discover that students can actually be useful. This year I want to make sure that I have the collecting permit I need arranged even before I arrive in the Congo. I also have a complicated problem with my travel arrangements. I am flying into Brazzaville on the evening of the sixteenth of October, but want to continue directly to Pointe Noire, where I plan to spend my first week. The airline that does the short Brazzaville to Pointe Noire flight is a little Congolese airline, and the only way to book a ticket on it is to go in person to its office at the Brazzaville airport and pay cash. There is no way to arrange it from Canada. Also I would like to drop off two large boxes of equipment in Brazzaville rather than take them with me to Pointe Noire and back. Ange eagerly takes on all this arranging of logistics. With Victor's help he gets to work on the permit. As for the travel plans, he buys the ticket with money I send him by Western Union, and promises that he and Lise will be at the airport to greet me and to take the boxes off my hands.

A couple of days before my departure, he writes to me, proudly reassuring me that everything is arranged: The permit will be ready tomorrow and he has booked my flight to Pointe Noire on the nineteenth. I would have found this reassuring had I not been told every day for 3 weeks last year that the permit would be ready "tomorrow," and had I been planning to arrive in Brazzaville on the nineteenth as opposed to the sixteenth. But it all gets sorted out in the end.

As my departure date approaches, Delphin has less and less Lingala left to teach me. We drift into long conversations in French. Delphin feels guilty about this because he worries that I am not getting value for money with my lessons. Clearly these lessons can't go on much longer. Delphin has taught me about as much as he can. I'll be sorry to lose him though, and I think he feels the same way. It would be nice if I could keep him as a friend, without the excuse of the lessons. I am surprised to realize just how much I am going to miss his companionship when I leave for the Congo. Aware that he hasn't lived in Toronto long, and doesn't know many people here, I start to engineer introductions to some of my French-speaking friends. I arrange for my sister to come over for a drink at the end of my Lingala lesson, and then invite Delphin to stay and have a beer with us.

My sister is blond, over 6 feet tall without heels, and a Crown prosecutor, who spends her days prosecuting murderers and gang rapists in the roughest part of Toronto. She speaks excellent French. Delphin is greatly impressed by her, and I find myself feeling a bit jealous as they converse—both of them correcting my French when I join in. My sister asks Delphin how he came to Canada and why. And Delphin tells his story—a story he has never told me.

Delphin was a journalist in the DRC, who ended up in the turbulent eastern part of the country, seeking out a newspaper that wouldn't censor his articles. The region was full of "rebel" soldiers from several factions, all unpaid and hungry. These armies survived by pillaging villages. The men fled their villages in fear of being killed, while the women stayed to protect their children and were raped by the soldiers. President Joseph Kabila sent in the Congolese army to protect the villagers, but these soldiers turned out to be just as bad as the rebels. It was the article revealing that the Congolese army soldiers were raping women and pillaging the very villages they were supposed to be protecting that got Delphin arrested and thrown in jail by Kabila's government.

Delphin still finds it hard to talk about the 4 months he spent in jail, so the details of conditions and treatment of the incarcerated in a prison in that part of the world are left to our imagination. It was when the village where the prison was was attacked that a sympathetic guard allowed Delphin to escape in the mayhem ("You have 30 seconds to get out of here—run."). And Delphin ran. He fled across the border into Rwanda, and from there, by a long and circuitous route, he made his way to Canada, where he applied for refugee status. When I first met him he had only been in Canada a month.

Suddenly my little adventures in the Congo seem terribly trivial. And how could I have spent so much time with this man every week for months without ever knowing about any of this?

The week before I leave for the Congo, Delphin comes over to my apartment one last time. Not for a lesson, not to meet one of my friends. Just to say goodbye. He promises me that he won't stay more than 10 minutes—"he knows I am busy," he says. We chat in Lingala. I give him a CD of Canadian music as a present. Soon we say our goodbyes. "Tikala malamu" (Stay well).

"Kende malamu" (Go well). And he is gone. But half an hour later the phone rings. Delphin has left the CD behind at my place. He comes back to pick it up. This time before he leaves, I stand on tiptoe to kiss him on both cheeks, as they do in the Congo.

"Where did you learn that?" he asks with a smile. And then he gives me a real kiss. A slow one, on the lips. "I love you," he says in English, and I hold him tight. He sits in the armchair and pulls me into his lap.

"Why didn't you tell me?" I ask as he strokes my hair. "You knew me for months, and never told me what you'd just been through until my sister asked you."

"I didn't want you to pity me."

That is the last I see of him before my departure.

chapter 12

back
to
the
likouala

"Docteur!"

"Ange!" He is short and stout with a friendly, easy-going face that is entirely out of keeping with the mayhem of the Brazzaville airport. I am enormously relieved to see him. After months of organizing by e-mail, my first meeting with my students is going to be a short one. I have only minutes to negotiate the chaos and get onto my connecting flight to Pointe Noire, and I am going to leave my big equipment boxes with them, as arranged.

A slight, slender figure darts out of the crowd toward me. Lise! I have a fleeting impression of hair in a mass of tiny braids pulled back into a ponytail, the ends dyed pink, wobbly high-heeled shoes, and an outfit with a lot of sequins on it. She kisses me on both cheeks, before being swallowed up into the crowd. Dr. Pangou is there as well, to help carry the boxes away in his car.

Claude greets me affectionately at Point Noire, but he looks exhausted. The French government is closing his center. He will retire and move to a village in France. Sylvie and their son have moved already, leaving Claude on his own to pack up the last few things—and to throw a really great party before he leaves. I have organized my trip so I can be there. He has found me a much cheaper hotel than last year, and drops me off there so I can have a quick shower before dinner.

I am hopelessly underdressed for the restaurant he takes me to, but when I make conversation with the waiter in Lingala, Claude is so impressed that my appearance is entirely forgiven. I tell him how I came to learn Lingala, and the great coincidence by which I found Delphin. ". . . And so he became my Lingala instructor," I explain, "and now, well, well, now he's maybe something more." Claude is absolutely delighted to hear this. Never before has he shown such enthusiastic approval for any aspect of my personal life. Within minutes of what seemed to me a very subtle and cautious hint of faint possibility, he is planning our wedding, and threatening to get in touch with Delphin himself, to give him some advice. "You will do no such thing!" I exclaim in alarm. "I'm not even going to tell you his last name."

But I don't stop thinking about Delphin. For a woman collecting snakes in the Likouala forest, a husband or boyfriend, even a fictitious one, saves an enormous amount of hassle. It prevents everything from unsolicited advice on how to arrange one's personal life to unwanted romantic advances. The Lingala word *mobali* does not distinguish between (1) a boy or man, (2) a friend who happens to be a man, (3) a boyfriend, (4) a fiancé, or (5) a husband. Since Delphin definitely counts as at least two of these, I don't feel entirely duplicitous in claiming him as my mobali whenever one is called for.

I put in several days in Pointe Noire, spending time with Claude, who is no longer kept busy running the center. The thing I have to do in Pointe Noire is retrieve all the specimens and equipment that got left behind last year. Following the instructions of George at the Smithsonian I have to skin all the large, heavy snakes I collected so that just the head and the skin, neatly rolled, will be shipped back to the States. Last year Claude had taken my 2.5-meter-long forest cobra out of the box with the others and moved it to a freezer on the grounds that it was smelly. "You didn't throw it out, did you?" I ask anxiously.

"No, we ate it in a pimento sauce to disguise the taste of rotting flesh," he teases, digging it out from the bottom of the freezer chest.

After my experience last year, I give in to Claude's advice and buy a cell phone. I hate these African cell phones. One morning the girl from the front desk of my hotel wakes me up with the frustrating news that the white man was here for me but has left, leaving me to try to make sense of the situation. "Claude? Claude? Claude!" I yell into the phone, getting a lot of hissing and crackling along with a faint and clearly uncomprehending voice in reply. "It's Kate. Kate. No, Kate! I am Kate! Claude? I am at the hotel. The hotel! Yes, I know you are not at the hotel; where are you? Where? I can't hear. Are you at the center? Are you at home? Me? No, I'm at the hotel. I can't hear what you're saying." I give up, "Okay, I'm going to the Center. Now. I. Am. Going. To. The. Center. Maybe I'll see you there."

Claude's going-away party is clearly going to be a major production, with all of the center's employees and their families invited. The preparations seem endless. We join the men setting up lights in the garden as they take a break for a bottle of Ngok. Claude gets me to try out my Lingala on them. "My cat speaks one word in Lingala," I say in Lingala, while we are all sitting on folding chairs in the shade. Everyone laughs—not at my joke, but just at the fact that I've said something in Lingala. It's funny the same way it would be funny if a dog suddenly started to speak. But I persist, and run through my whole routine, "What kind of animal are you? Are you a fish? Are you a turtle? . . ." The men can see where this is going, but laugh good-naturedly at the punch line anyway: "Niaou—that's right, you're a cat!" One of them translates the whole thing for Claude, who shakes his head. "We're going to miss Kate when she leaves," he says. "She's small, but she takes up a lot of space."

Claude has endless meetings with the woman he has hired to run the party, and he has the lights in the garden all taken down twice before he is satisfied with them. Finally it is the night of the party. The invitation is for 7:00 p.m., so I arrive fashionably late at 7:05 to find that I am the only guest. The guard at the gate approves of my Impfondo dress though. "Docteur!" he calls out in delight. Gradually, 80 people, employees of the center and their families, assemble at the trestle tables in Claude's garden. The first course of salad isn't served until after 9:00, and it is after midnight when a man stands up, clears his throat, and summons Claude to stand beside him while he gives a speech. He talks candidly of their initial resentment at Claude's intolerance of mistakes and his accusing everyone of laziness, their grudging respect as he worked beside them, doing even the hardest manual labor, and finally their pride in their work, which they know was good. As Claude stands listening to this, his lip starts to tremble slightly and he fusses with a cigarette and lighter. Another man gets up to speak about what Claude's leadership of the center has meant for him and his family. And then another man, and another. Claude is a diminutive figure beside these big men. "He's small," I think to myself, "but he takes up a lot of space."

I am only slightly hung over when Ange meets me at the airport on my return to Brazzaville, the morning after the party. It is a Sunday and Lise is at church. When we arrive at the Catholic Institute, I knock on the door of Père Joseph's office. He greets me politely, but clearly doesn't recognize me. Then suddenly a great smile spreads across his face as he places me. "It's the serpentologist!" Père Joseph can never remember my name, so he takes to calling me Serpentine for the duration of my stay.

Ange nervously accepts a *jus,* orange soda in this case, as we sit in the spacious foyer of the Catholic Institute, and soon Lise arrives from church and joins us. Finally we are actually meeting in person and the atmosphere is very tense. We are all desperately hoping we will like each other since we are committed to a lot of time together in very close quarters. "First of all," I tell Ange, "it's Katherine, not Docteur, okay?" He blushes and Lise giggles. It takes Ange days to adapt to this informality. They are not what I expected. I had expected Ange to be complicated and intense, and Lise to be friendly and easy-going. But Ange turns out to be cheerful and eager to please, and Lise reserved and hard to read. We're going to have some time to put in in Brazzaville before we leave for the field, but I assure them we'll find plenty of work to occupy us.

"We are completely at your disposal, Docteur," says Ange earnestly.

"Katherine!" I correct, smacking him on the shoulder. Lise laughs. But they both quickly get used to "Katherine," and even shorten it to the less formal "Kat."

I never did get a reply from WCS before my departure, saying I could work in the Lac Télé Reserve, and getting this permission is high on my long list of logistical things to worry about, so it is a huge relief to finally make contact with Hugo by e-mail. He warns me that the water is very high this year and that much of the reserve is flooded, but it doesn't sound as if he's actually saying we can't go there. He happens to be in Brazzaville, and agrees to meet with me the following day.

"I can't believe you didn't bring tents!" he begins, exasperated. "That was one of the problems last year—that you didn't have minimally acceptable living conditions for the guide!" He makes it clear that having tents will be a requirement if I want to work in the reserve. "The place you will be going is called Impongui. You don't have any choice. Everything else is under water. The Notable at Impongui," he continues (the Notable is the hereditary leader of a village), "he's about 90, but he's a good guy. Make sure you see him first. You'll have to pay for the boat to get there, of course. It'll probably take 4 and a half hours if you're lucky, and you'll have to pay 75,000cfa for the petrol." I start writing down "75,000cfa," "but of course that's just one way" he continues, "t's another 75,000 to come back." I cross out the first 75,000 and start changing it to 150,000, controlling a growing sense of financial panic. "And then of course the *pinancier* (boatman) has to be paid 15,000"—I lift my pencil again—"but depending on the current he might have to spend the night so you'd have to pay him for 2 days . . ." I give up trying to keep track of all these wretched cfa. "And there will be no, absolutely no, letting snakes bite you, like last year. Nothing like that. Is that clear? We don't want people thinking you're a witch like what happened before. We may want to send other researchers to Impongui in the future so you will not—not—do anything that could give people the remotest idea that you're weird." I nod solemnly. I can't get into the reserve without Hugo's support, after all. But have I ever been *anywhere,* anywhere in the world where people *didn't* think I was weird?

The unanticipated expenses are adding up. I hadn't expected the journey to the field site to be so expensive, and I dread to think what tents will cost. In the end it is my Congolese friends who come to my rescue.

"Buy them?" Victor exclaims when I ask him where tents are sold in Brazzaville, "but that's going to be really expensive! I have a tent; you're welcome to borrow that, and let me see who else might . . ." He ponders the problem and then remembers a graduate student who has one. The student is studying in Belgium at the moment, but surely he wouldn't mind if we used his tent. Victor also manages to come up with two mats for sleeping on: one inflatable, the other a sheet of rubber just thick enough to make a difference if the ground is slightly uneven. Dr.

Parra, of the Public Health Lab, shakes his head over the folly of camping for a month in the swamp forest in the rainy season, but offers to lend me a satellite phone. This is a very welcome offer. A satellite phone is so staggeringly expensive to buy and especially to use that I could never hope to own one. It certainly couldn't be used casually, but having one will mean that I won't be absolutely cut off from help in the event of an emergency.

I end up spending the whole first day running around on errands, trying to organize the logistics of the expedition. I had planned to spend the day with Lise and Ange, but though I feel bad about leaving them waiting around with nothing to do, I'm finding that I just don't have the time to provide constant supervision.

But I have underestimated them. When I finally arrive at the university that houses Dr. Pangou's Biodiversity Study Group's lab, sweaty and dusty in my African dress, I find that Ange and Lise have efficiently reorganized the equipment boxes. They have even saved the duct tape that held them shut, neatly spread out in long strips, sticky side up, along the lab bench so that it can be used again. They have unpacked the photocopied articles I brought, and are poring over them. North American students would have been quite reasonably indignant at having been kept waiting for 8 hours, but Lise and Ange accept it as completely normal that I have been delayed for a whole day by unexpected errands.

It is after 4:00 p.m. when I finally sit down between them with a pencil and notebook and start giving them a lesson on the interpretation of phylogenetic trees—diagrams showing the evolutionary relationships between animals. I want to teach them this since they can't read English. Most textbooks and scientific articles are written in English, but if they can understand these diagrams then they will be able to get something out of an article even if they can't understand the text. Other students passing through the lab join us, and soon I have moved to a dry-erase board and am explaining the basics of phylogenetic systematics with a fuzzy-tipped green marker with very little ink in it. I've taught before, but it's never been like this. Every scrap of an offhand comment is industriously written down by those students who have paper and a pencil. When I give them a problem to work on they go at it as though the fate of the world depended on their solution. More students squeeze into the room. It is the sort of reaction I would expect if I stood on a street corner and started handing out money. When I finally sit down, 3 hours have gone by, but exhilaration fills me with energy. The students swarm all around me, all asking questions at once, until I really am exhausted. I wash the green ink off my hands. The running water in the lab hasn't worked for years, so there's a bucket of water on the floor, with the bottom half of a mineral water bottle floating in it to use as a scoop. You rinse your hands by getting a friend to scoop water over them. The inability to get plumbing repaired combined with the ingenuity of the bucket and modified mineral water bottle solution is somehow totally Congolese. If the water stopped running in the zoology labs at the University of Toronto, all work would come to a stop. I go back to the Catholic Institute, where I fall fast asleep at 8:00 p.m.

The thrill of teaching such enthusiastic students soon degenerates into frustration as I discover how weak their background is. How can graduate students in biology not know the structure of DNA? How can they not know about surface to volume ratios? Why have they never dissected a frog? They really need an introductory course in biology, not to mention basic ecology, physiology, molecular biology. In fact, they also need to know the building-block subjects that come before: chemistry, physics, statistics.

I do my best to teach them a few of these things, but soon feel discouraged, and maybe they do too. Lise especially heaves great sighs of boredom and gazes into space instead of taking notes. I try to look on the bright side. At least with Lise you never have to worry that she's just pretending to be interested out of politeness. I am sure that Lise will perk up when I sit down with her and show her how to identify a snake, but when I suggest it she responds with one of her trademark sighs and asks if we can do it tomorrow instead. What they need is far beyond what I can provide, and I have to remind myself that I did not come to the Congo to teach elementary science at the Marien-Ngouabi University.

The only other guests at the Catholic Institute are a French group establishing a program to help child prostitutes in Brazzaville—girls as young as 12, turning tricks for 1,500cfa, just trying to earn enough to eat. The girls only see 300cfa of that money, the rest goes to the pimp. Sometimes families are even desperate enough to rent out their adolescent daughters in their own homes.

This makes for distressing conversation, and the French ask me about my work to change the subject. "Do you carry pierre noire with you?" asks one of the men. I feel tired already at the prospect of having to explain the failings of "traditional" snakebite cures once again. I tell him politely that I do not carry pierre noire because it is entirely ineffective in treating snakebite, expecting this to be the end of the matter. "Oh no, it's very effective," the man insists, "I've seen it work. I've seen snakebites cured by it."

"What do you mean you've 'seen it work'?" I ask, annoyed at having my expertise questioned. "If you mean you've seen it used on someone who was bitten by a snake and didn't die, then it was probably a nonvenomous bite in the first place."

"No, no, I've seen bites that were definitely venomous that were cured by applying pierre noire."

"Listen, not every venomous or semivenomous bite that produces any symptoms is necessarily fatal if it's left untreated. Lots of bites cause internal bleeding or muscle damage or whatever but aren't severe enough to kill the person. Look, if you've seen pierre noire, do you know the kind of suction it exerts? Have you touched it against your tongue?" He nods. "It barely sticks, right? Not a lot of suction. Think of it this way. A snake fang is like a hypodermic needle. Imagine sticking a

hypodermic needle into someone's flesh and injecting a bit of liquid"—
I explain that flesh is sort of like a chunk of steak, except alive, so fluids
are moving around in it—"then wait, say, half an hour—hell, wait 2
minutes—and *then* apply your piece of pierre noire. Do you think it's
going to suck the liquid back out? Do you? Think it through. It's just
common sense." I know I am being rude. I just get so irritated having
to explain this over and over again. I change the subject, trying to think
of something polite to say. "So what do you do for a living in Paris?"
I ask.

"I'm a surgeon." He shuts the door quite hard as he leaves the room.

As the day of our departure approaches I become increasingly worried
about what Lise and Ange are going to be like in the forest. Ange at
least has taken a field course before, and loved it. But this will be Lise's
first experience of fieldwork, and a month camped in the Likouala
swamp forest during the rainy season is going to be a hell of an intro-
duction. A visit to their rooms in the university dorms one day reas-
sures me a bit. Clearly they are used to a degree of squalor. Lise shares a
dorm room with two other girls in a crumbling building with unreliable plumbing and electricity. While we wait for Ange, she shyly shows
me a photograph propped up on her bedside table: Lise with short hair.
"It's cute," I tell her. "How long did it take you to grow it out?" She giggles.

"It's a wig."

Suddenly I start seeing what are clearly wigs on all the well-dressed
women in Brazzaville. Now that they've been drawn to my attention,
they are completely unmistakable. So this is how they manage to keep
their hair looking so neat while mine is always a sweaty tangle by the
end of the day. I look at Lise's tight braids with new eyes. Are *they* a wig?

I hold a formal meeting with Lise and Ange. The living conditions are likely to be very rough, I warn them. They are going to get wet and they are going to get muddy. Herpetology is not like ornithology. They may not get clean and dry again until we return to Brazzaville. The boat that drops us off is as expensive as our airfares. It will come back to pick us up in a month, so once we are there we are there for the duration. There will be no going back early. Is that clear? They both nod earnestly. Even so, I tell them to give it some serious thought. If they're going to change their minds the sooner they decide the better. I pause and wait before going on. They are quiet.

"Okay then. Consider yourselves warned." I smile and the tension in the room breaks. "When you pack, bring lots of clothes. Stuff takes forever to dry there and putting on wet clothes is miserable, not to mention sleeping in them. Bring a good strong pair of shoes or boots," I say, thinking of Lise, "because we're going to be working with venomous snakes. And expect them to get wet. As in walking-around-in-the-water-for-3-hours wet. Oh, and bring something to read." They look doubtful. "Not just your scientific books and papers, but something entertaining. This is not a field course. I will not be providing activities continuously. There may be a lot of waiting around, and I want you to be able to entertain yourselves, so bring mysteries or thrillers or whatever it is you read for fun. And finally, pack whatever little luxuries or treats will keep you happy—chocolate, photographs, whatever. I'd rather pay for excess baggage on the plane than spend a month in the forest with someone who's miserable."

To my surprise, this speech doesn't seem to discourage them. In fact I have the distinct impression that hearing about these realities has got them excited and eager for the adventure to begin. I think things are going to work out after all.

"Kat," Lise asks me the day before our flight to Impfondo, "what are we going to do for water when we're there?"

"To drink you mean? Boil it."

"Euwh" (look of distaste); "can't we bring bottled water instead?"

"For a month?!"

"Well, I have a very delicate stomach. I only drink bottled water even in Brazzaville."

I tell her to go to the pharmacy and see if she can buy water-decontamination tablets. They're a nuisance to use and they taste worse than boiled river water, but she doesn't know that, and to my relief this solution seems to satisfy her. She's going to be awfully thirsty if it doesn't.

The next morning at 8:20 I am pacing around the foyer of the Catholic Institute in a state of increasing fury. I clearly told Ange and Lise 8:00 at the latest: "8:00 and I don't mean 10 past, is that clear?" 8:25 rolls around. I find a scrap of paper and am writing a terse farewell note when they appear, with an explanation about having difficulty finding a taxi in the rain and then realizing that it would be unforgivably rude to leave without first paying a courtesy visit to Dr. Pangou. "I was about to write a note to you and leave for the airport on my own. No, I'm not joking. The pencil was touching the paper when you arrived. I have spent half an hour going out of my mind with worry because you didn't arrive at the time we agreed on. I don't care what the reason is. The point I'm trying to get across is as follows: I am going to the Likouala to study snakes. I am not leading a safari tour. I am not even teaching a field course. You are coming along as my assistants. If it goes well you might learn something along the way, but you are here to *assist*. To help! Not to be yet another thing for me to worry about! Okay?"

But soon all is forgiven and we are eating sandwiches in the grimy departure lounge at the Brazzaville airport. As I turn off my cell phone, which will be useless from here on, I remember that Dr. Parra never did get back to me about the satellite phone. Too late now. But at 10:00 as we set off across the tarmac to board our 9:00 flight, somebody is shouting for me. Running toward me, across the runway, from the terminal, is Dr. Parra. He is waving something above his head: a satellite phone.

We land in Impfondo 2 hours later, and soon the truck is arriving at the Epena end of the familiar asphalt road. "Bit different from the last time you were here, Kate?" asks Hugo as the truck turns off the road into the WCS compound. I stare in amazement. Hugo wasn't exaggerating when he said the water level was high this year. The whole place is knee to thigh deep in dirty water. And that's not counting all the ditches. In some places lines of bricks have been set out as stepping stones, and sticks have been driven in in places—markers of some kind, but I don't know the system. The people who work at WCS are used to picking their way around by the shallow places, but I fall into unmarked ditches three times in the first day. The same ditch three times in fact, as Hugo can't resist pointing out. But the oppressive sun of Epena has its uses and my clothes dry quickly on the line.

Hugo has assigned me and Lise and Ange to an outbuilding with three rooms so that we can be together. Lise remarks that the rooms put her in mind of the Marien-Ngouabi dorms, and I know things will be all right. To my relief, they both seem perfectly contented with the bathroom arrangements. The toilet is what is euphemistically called a traditional toilet—a hole in the ground that you crouch over—and has a door with a broken latch which swings wide open if you let go of it. More seriously, because of the flooding, the surface of the contents of the traditional toilet is almost level with the floor. A flimsy partition separates the toilet from the shower, so the stench is the same in both. I have gradually learned that in most of the Congo the word "shower" actually means a place with a drain where you can dump buckets of water over yourself. The word implies no expectation of water coming from above through a tap. Ange and Lise wade across the compound, through thigh-deep water, to fill buckets from the well, and then modestly retreat to the smelly shower to wash. I prefer to get up before dawn and have my bucket shower on the front steps, in the privacy of darkness.

Lise emerges from her room just as the sun is up and the first employees are arriving. She has dealt with her hairdo by encasing it in a tight string net. She is wearing backless, pink, sequined slippers, but doesn't seem to mind wading around in the muddy water in them. "Good morning, Kat." I don't often get Lise on her own. I think I make her nervous, and I wish I didn't. In an effort to make friendly conversation I ask her what she has brought as recreational reading. The only book she has with her turns out to be an abridged edition of the New Testament. Is that really all she's brought for entertainment, I ask anxiously? Oh no. She digs through her suitcase and produces a cassette player, beaming. "I brought this to listen to."

"What kind of music do you like?" I try to hide my alarm.

"Oh lots of things—I like Celine Dion. And Christian rock music. And I really like Celine Dion."

"I don't suppose you have earphones?" I ask without much hope. Of course not. I'm afraid it's going to be a very long month.

At the Impfondo market I start to gain a new respect for Lise and Ange. We have been sent to the market with Ruffain, who has a computer printout listing exactly what WCS calculates should be needed by an expedition of three researchers and two guides. I find the heat and chaos of the market almost unbearable and am ready to buy anything I am told to buy just to get the trip over with, but Ange and Lise are made of sterner stuff. When we need to buy cooking pots, Ange holds no fewer than 15 of them up to the light to check for tiny cracks or holes before finding two that meet with his approval. As we start buying the dishes, it turns out that both Lise and Ange have thought to bring their own cup, plate, bowl, spoon, and fork, so we don't need to buy as many as expected. From time to time, especially with the "kitchen things,"

Ange's confidence falters and he concedes that we need a "woman's opinion." This means Lise's. Quite reasonably, nobody has the slightest interest in my opinion. Lise examines many different kinds of plastic buckets with lids (all to me utterly indistinguishable) and discusses them earnestly with several different shopkeepers before approving two for me to buy. Lise confidently insists that we can't possibly need as many Maggi cubes or as much Nido as Ruffain's list suggests.

Only I know what kind of wire mesh is suitable for building drift fences, and I decide that we need 50 meters of it, but Ange takes the tape measure from the salesman and measures it himself all over again, arriving at an entirely different result, leading to a lengthy debate. Meanwhile, Ruffain is bargaining over the cost per meter. I am quite enjoying watching all this until we go to buy the foam mattress. The salesman demands a ridiculous 19,000cfa, and then won't back down in spite of our combined efforts. We end up paying the 19,000cfa, but at that point Ruffain banishes me to wait in the truck. At the sight of me the salesmen are asking mondele prices, and Ruffain is getting fed up bargaining with this handicap. So I am watching from the truck when Ange takes all 50 sardine tins out of their cardboard box in the grocer's to count them, and finds that there are only 48. There is a terrific row over the 2 missing tins of sardines. But by the end of it all 50 tins are in the box, and there seem to be no hard feelings. Ange has given his visiting card to the grocer, whose son-in-law is thinking of moving to Brazzaville.

Back at WCS we sit on the steps outside our rooms and discuss strategy for Impongui. Lise and Ange have both taken a course called Stage Village ("Village 101"), in which they learned all about the complicated political structure of a village, as well as what is considered polite, and how to show respect. It sounds like a very useful course. The Chief of the village, they explain, is appointed by the government and changes every year or so. The real power lies with the Notable, the hereditary leader of the village. Hugo had mentioned that the villagers are building a school in Impongui, and that it would be a good thing when we agree on a fee to pay to the village for letting us camp there, to put it in terms of so much cement or so many bricks for the school rather than cash, which might just get squandered by the Chief. I suggest that we offer them our two tarpaulins when we leave, to make a roof for the school. Negotiating is going to be difficult because of me. The villagers in the Lac Télé Reserve are used to well-funded, large-scale expeditions, and believe that all mondeles are infinitely rich. I'm already planning to let Ange do most of the talking, with his Lingala and his Stage Village, and now I also suggest that all money appears to come from him. We will plan ahead. If we expect to need 2,000cfa for a meeting I will give him the money ahead of time. Nobody will ever see me handle money.

We have a couple of days to put in at Epena. I use the time to teach Lise and Ange to navigate using the GPS. We wade around the WCS compound, eyes focused on the little arrow on the screen. Eventually they get the hang of it. Hugo has given me the useful tip that the Notable of Impongui would appreciate "traditional gifts": wine, soap, salt, cigarettes, matches. It sounds like an improbable assortment of things, but I take his word for it. Wanting to avoid the mbote gauntlet myself, I send Ange and Lise to the village shopkeepers' stalls on their own to buy the gifts and tell them to navigate to the shop and back using the GPS.

On my way from the well to our rooms I come across Emmanuel, the elderly guide who came into the forest with me last year, just for the first 2 days, to help get things set up. He is cutting lengths of bamboo into strips. He doesn't speak any French and last year I'd only been able to communicate with him through an interpreter. "Mbote," I greet him. No surprise there—everyone knows "mbote." He replies politely, "Mbote."

"Sango nini?" (What news?), I try, as I said at the beginning of every lesson with Delphin. He pauses, a strip of bamboo in his hand, and slowly smiles.

"Sango te" (No news).

"Ozali malamu?" (Are you well?) He doesn't seem surprised, as I had expected, just approving, as though I have finally come to my senses. I go on to ask him what he is building, and understand his reply when he tells me he's building a fence. He never does inquire how I have come to know a little Lingala. "Tikala malamu" (Stay well), I say as I pick up my bucket and continue on my way, feeling absolute joy. When I think about it, this has been my first real conversation in Lingala. Until now I've only spoken Lingala to people who speak perfect French but who let me practice on them for a laugh.

On Monday morning we are all awake before dawn. We've been told the pinancier might leave early, and we're hoping he will. Getting off to a late start will mean being out on the river in the midday sun. (This, admittedly, is only a problem for me. Somehow, despite the months of organizing, I forgot to pack both sunscreen and mosquito repellent.) We want to arrive at Impongui in time to go through all the formalities with the villagers and still have enough daylight left to pitch camp. But Ange and Lise and I are the only people in a hurry, so the hours go by and we wait. Lise sings Christian pop songs in Lingala. Ange compulsively reorganizes our boxes of equipment into jigsaw-puzzle arrangements ensuring that nobody but he will ever be able to find anything in them again. As for me I just work myself into a frenzy of worry as it gets later and later.

It is after noon by the time our big, motorized pirogue finally casts off from Epena. We are on the point of leaving when someone notices that the peanut butter has been forgotten. Ruffain fetches it, a plastic bucket a foot deep in crushed peanuts, covered with a plastic lid that once belonged to some other bucket of an entirely different shape. We are just about to cast off for the second time when somebody points out that we don't have life jackets. Lise and Ange immediately put their life jackets on, fasten all the straps, test the emergency whistle, and sit in the chairs set up in the pirogue. I, being from Ontario and used to canoes, throw my life jacket into the shallow puddle collected in the bottom of the pirogue, and kneel on it, keeping my center of gravity low so as not to tip.

The Likouala aux Herbes River is wide, and full of grasses, which the pirogue pushes aside as it cuts through the water. Although we are going downstream, the current is almost imperceptible. The trip is much faster than predicted because the water is so high that the pinancier can take short cuts through what looks from a distance like dry land. This means going straight, instead of having to follow all the twists and turns of the river. Even so, I get so sunburned in the first half hour that I will have bleeding scabs on my nose and ears for the first 3 weeks in our camp. Only 2 hours after leaving Epena, the pinancier points to a little opening between the trees along the bank. "This is Impongui," he says.

chapter 13

this
is
impongui

As the nose of our pirogue approaches the little landing spot I start to worry. Can you do this? Just show up unannounced at somebody's village with a whole lot of equipment and inform everybody that you are staying for a month? What if the people at Impongui turn us away? We have no backup plan. The first people we see are a group of children who come rushing down the steep bank to greet us. They immediately start unloading our pirogue, as though motorized pirogues full of strangers and their equipment arrive at Impongui every day. I struggle to keep my footing on the slippery riverbank, while trying not to drop my big expedition pack in the water. A little girl takes it from me and darts effortlessly up the muddy slope. Soon the children have been joined by some men and all our belongings are being neatly stored in what seems to be the largest house in the village, facing a large cleared area of packed dirt. This building is made of cement bricks, while most of the houses are built of sticks and mud. A few well-fed cattle wander around. As I walk across this open area, the people sitting outside their houses respond to my "mbote" with such enthusiasm that I add, "Sango nini?" (What news?) and get a cheerful "Sango te!" (No news!) in reply. The children are sent to bring chairs, and soon the three of us are sitting down with most of the men of the village. We have asked to see the Chief, but he is not here yet. Apparently one of the several cows that wander the village has died in the forest and the Chief is one of the men busy butchering the carcass. Eventually a man of about 20 arrives. He is wearing button-fly jeans with the top button undone and a sleeveless white undershirt. "You are the Chief?" Ange asks doubtfully. Behind us some other men are carrying dripping chunks of meat into the house. Ange starts off on a speech in Lingala, holding forth at great length about how much we are "touched in the heart" by the kindness with which we have been welcomed. Just when I am beginning to despair of his ever stopping, he moves on to explaining our project—what we want to study and why, and how we hope to go about doing it. The Chief and the other men listen to all this, and then retire to discuss it in private.

It is after 3:00 p.m. and the sky is overcast. Getting our camp set up in time to sleep in it tonight is looking less and less likely. The men return in half an hour or so, the oldest man extending his hand. "We haven't properly said 'mbote' yet." There is a round of mbotes. Then the rain starts. All the chairs are moved indoors into a big circle, where there is to be more talking. Ange and I will have to explain the project all over again, and figure out how it will all work with respect to the village. Ange tries without success to interest Lise in taking notes. We explain that we will be here for a month and would like to hire two guides to work in the forest and to prepare meals. Our offer of the tarpaulins for the school is received with approval, and Ange adds 5,000cfa up front for the Chief.

We have been asking all along to see the Notable, and finally we are led through the rain and darkness to a little shack of mud and sticks, the size of a small garage, with its roof caving in, and stakes driven into the ground along one side, apparently to prevent the wall from collapsing outward. Inside the air is thick with smoke from an open fire, and only Ange and Lise and I go in because the space is so small. Once again children are sent to fetch chairs, or rather small stools. The Notable receives us with grave formality. He looks just as ancient as Hugo had said he was. We shake hands and give him the bag of "traditional gifts," which he sets aside without opening, and 2,000cfa, which he puts away discreetly with a slight nod. He listens patiently to Ange's long explanation of our project. I am able to follow Ange's Lingala just well enough to correct him when he gets something wrong. Only when Ange has finished does the Notable speak. Since it is raining and already dark, he suggests that instead of trying to set up a camp, we sleep in someone's house tonight. We must come back to him tomorrow. In the meantime he will consult with his ancestors about how best to arrange things.

We eat peanut butter (really a hard paste of crushed peanuts rather than what I think of as peanut butter) for supper, straight out of the bucket, using sticks as spoons, since nothing is unpacked. We are told we can sleep on the floor of the house that we saw the meat being brought into. We get out the three mattresses and I assign them. I give the expensive, thick foam mattress to Lise, considering her the most likely to complain about being uncomfortable, the inflatable mat to Ange, as the next most comfortable one, and take the rubber mat for myself. People are still walking through the room carrying chunks of flesh as I drop off to sleep.

The next day it takes ages for the "village committee," headed by the

Chief, to get organized for us. Apparently there has to be another meeting, a more formal one. Will we never get our camp set up? I sit in the shade of the overhang outside the main house with nothing to do but watch the little dramas of village life. It may be a poor village, as Hugo said, but Impongui is well kept. The first thing people do in the morning is to vigorously sweep the area of packed dirt around their houses, even if there is not a leaf or a twig in sight. I am reminded of people in Toronto who fuss in just the same way to keep a tiny lawn perfectly watered and free of dandelions. The village children seem to work rather than play, and appear perfectly contented. Any adult who needs an errand run or a task done simply tells the nearest child to do it. It doesn't seem to matter much who the child belongs to. A baby has somehow been left on the ground not far from where I am sitting. It is screaming and crying. I feel as if I ought to do something about it but what do I know about babies? I am hoping that a mother will come for it soon, but it is a boy of about 10 who eventually carries the baby away on his hip. The Chief comes out of the main house with a wheelbarrow piled high with the raw meat from yesterday's cow, to be divided up among the villagers. Half a dozen delighted children scurry after him carrying all the glistening entrails in a metal basin. Lise and Ange join the group around the wheelbarrow. They each buy some meat and give it to one of the village women to smoke on the fire until our departure in a month's time. Meat is expensive in Brazzaville, they tell me. It gets later and later. Ange is getting even more impatient than I am. A man comes by to tell us that a meal is being prepared for us, which is very hospitable of him, but as Ange points out, "We came here to work, not to party."

Finally the meeting gets going. It is held in the large open area outside the house of the Notable. Or rather it is held on half of the large open area. The other half is the place where the Notable's ancestors are buried, and nobody walks there. A long semicircle of chairs has been set out, enough for us and all the villagers who make up the village committee. Across from the semicircle, the Notable sits in a chair on his own, holding the long spear that is his badge of office. There is another Notable with a spear as well. Impongui was formed by three villages coming together, each with its own hereditary leader, so there are three Notables. The third is sick and has been sent to Impfondo. But our Notable from last night is the one whose ancestors are buried in Impongui, and so it is he who has the last word. Sitting on the ground between the two Notables is a Sage, one of the old men of the village. He must act as interpreter between the Notables, because they are not allowed to speak directly to each other.

Everything from yesterday is gone through all over again. Ange gives another 2,000cfa to the Notable as a mark of respect. He does this by placing the note on the ground halfway between him and the Notable. Somebody from the village committee picks it up and carries it to the Notable. Overnight, the Chief has come up with an idea. Instead of hiring two guides for a month, could we instead hire three teams of two guides for 10 days each, so that six people from the village can benefit from the employment rather than just two? I tell him that that sounds fine in theory, but that we will have to spend our first few days training the guides to do our work. If we have three teams we'll have to start from scratch with each new pair, and lose a lot of time. The only way I could see it working would be if all six came for the first 3 days to learn together.

But what really takes time is the financial negotiating. We have offered the tarpaulins, and expect to end up adding a bit of money to that. I am only following a fraction of these Lingala negotiations, but I do catch the figure "200,000cfa" and panic. I can't possibly pay 200,000. After all it's taken to get from Toronto to here it will all be over if they insist on 200,000. Ange catches my eye and under his breath tells me not to worry, it will work out. He launches into a long and persuasive speech. The gist of his argument is that we are mere students, *bana na kelasi*—schoolchildren (Lingala uses the same word for doctoral students and postdoctoral fellows as for kindergarten children) with very little money. Even the mondele is not infinitely rich. It takes Ange a good hour and a half, but in the end the agreed sum is 2,000cfa. There seems to be no sense of in between. It is like Lingala: big or small, good or bad, near or far, a lot or a little, no words for intermediate states. Does it not occur to them to consider a middle ground such as 20,000cfa because there is no Lingala word for a state between a lot and a little, or conversely does the word not exist in Lingala because they lack the concept of it?

The last thing to settle is the issue of where the guides are to sleep. I want them to sleep in the village rather than squeeze five of us into the tents that we have. Ange assures the village committee that the guides will still have their meals with us. "We'd planned all along to share our meals—in fact all our dishes and cutlery are in fives."

It is well into the afternoon by the time the meeting is finished and we have had a meal of stew made from the cow butchered yesterday and fou-fou. It all tastes pretty good because we have not eaten anything except peanut butter since yesterday. The meal is in what I've been thinking of as the main house, but which turns out to be the house of Romuald, who is to be one of our guides. Romuald has two wives and seems to be the father of a large percentage of the village children. He was the Chief last year. Charles, the other guide, is also at the table. He is a Sage, like the man who acted as interpreter between the two Notables this morning, elderly and missing most of his teeth. We all soon get into the habit of addressing him as "Old Charles," which is what everyone else calls him. Employment is very scarce, and work as a guide highly sought after, so you end up hiring quite distinguished members of the community to do relatively menial jobs. I thank Romuald and the Chief for the meal, and Ange thoughtfully calls out to the wives who are hovering in the background, "And a big thank you to the hands that prepared it."

🐾

Finally we set off, but not before a final courtesy visit to the Notable. We find him outside his house with a group of other old men—the Sages. Each of them is holding a bar of soap and a box of matches. The Notable has shared his gifts. The site for our camp has been decided by the Notable, and the location is to be kept secret. I had made a big deal of the great danger of the chemicals among our equipment to curious children, but I think the Notable is more concerned about making sure there will be no problem of theft. It will certainly be nice to have some privacy in our camp. All our equipment, unloaded yesterday, has to be loaded back into a pirogue. Standing in the stern, Romuald paddles off with the teetering stack of boxes and bags. The rest of us follow Old Charles out of the village, and into the forest. There is no trail, but he cuts one as he goes, and he seems to know where he is going. We eventually end up in dense forest at the edge of water. Impongui is on one side of a peninsula extending out into the Likouala aux Herbes River, and we must now be on the back of the peninsula. The water beside us is technically the river, but it has overflowed into the forest along its banks, so that it looks very much like the flooded forest beside my camp last year, only with much deeper water. Romuald is out there somewhere with the pirogue. Old Charles asks me if this place is satisfactory, and when I tell him it looks fine to me, he shouts to Romuald until he finds us and lands the pirogue where we are waiting.

Romuald arrives smiling and holding a dead *Grayia*, found drowned in some fisherman's net. The chin is quite yellow, and I think it might be *Grayia smithii* rather than *Grayia ornata*, which was all I got at Ganganya. Interesting. I must process the specimen as soon as possible so it doesn't rot, so I hope the camp will be ready soon. Old Charles starts clearing the forest, pausing from time to time to check with me how large an area I want cleared. I'm trying to imagine where the tents and the "house" will go. "House" is perhaps a rather grand name for two tarpaulins hanging over some branches hammered into the ground, but since it's clearly not a tent, that's what we call it, just as the corner of it where we work on our specimens gets called the "lab." Romuald unloads everything from the pirogue. I give the tarpaulins to the guides and tell them to make a house with them: use one tarpaulin for the roof, the other for the floor and walls. They start hammering in posts and cutting wood for beams, and I leave them to it. Lise and Ange and I put up the tents. These are the high-tech modern tents borrowed from Victor. The first one is very simple to put together: aluminum rods with elastic inside them that fit into two sleeves, making two arches that give the tent shape so effectively that it can be picked up and moved without dismantling it. But the next tent is very confusing. There seem to be too many rods for the number of sleeves, and the sleeves and rods turn out to be several different lengths. We are taking them all out for the third time when I look up to check on the progress of the house. They have built the beginnings of a house about the size of the Notable's. It is an impressive structure, big enough to accommodate all five of us standing up, but they have used one tarpaulin for each side, so that there is nothing left to cover the floor. This is a problem because I am going to sleep on this floor. "Forest floor" sounds misleadingly sterile, conjuring up images of linoleum or concrete. In fact, the floor of the Likouala forest, recently cleared of vegetation, is a lively assemblage of living, breathing, and moving things, none of which I especially want as my bedfellows. Romuald has an old piece of tarpaulin at home that he will bring tomorrow. As for today, it's almost dark, so I will sleep with Lise tonight.

Just as we are starting to think about food, the rain begins. The guides already have a fire going, and we congregate inside the house. It reminds me a bit of the day I set up my camp at Ganganya last year. Old Charles cuts some wood and builds a bench against the far end of the inside of the house. We unpack the boxes of food, and, darting out into the rain to tend to the cooking, Lise makes a pot of rice, and I make a sauce out of corned beef and tomato paste. Ange digs candles into the dirt floor of the house, and we eat by their light. When the rain starts to let up the guides go back to the village for the night. "Tikala malamu!" (Stay well!)

"Kende malamu!" (Go well!)

The next day starts, like every subsequent day, with Romuald's coffee. Using only a campfire, rainwater, an aluminum pot, and coffee from the Impfondo market, he produces something not unlike Starbucks espresso. Romuald scoops the thick coffee out of the pot taking care not to stir up the dregs, fills all five cups, and then adds several heaping tablespoonfuls of sugar to each one. The sugar is kept in a bowl with a plate covering it as a lid, but tiny black ants get in even so, and as the days go by, there is less and less sugar and more and more ants. Ange's coffee is special. Not only does he have his own plastic mug, brought from Brazzaville, but he adds lime juice to his coffee, explaining that this is a habit he picked up from west African friends. Limes are easily found growing in the forest around the camp.

After all the days wasted waiting in Brazzaville and then at Epena, there is no time to be lost. As soon as the camp is functional the pitfall traps and fishnets must be set up at once. So far I have had a remarkable lack of success with pitfall traps. I have jealously read accounts of other herpetological collectors who report pitfall buckets almost brimming over with exotic species of leaf-litter frogs and lizards, every morning. But these accounts are light on details of the precise construction of the pitfall traps in question. Apparently making them is something that everyone is just supposed to know how to do. This year I am determined to get it right. I'm also planning to do it on a larger scale. The day we stocked up on supplies at the Impfondo market, I bought nine plastic buckets and 50 meters of wire mesh, of the sort used to make window screens to keep mosquitoes out. I have it all carefully calculated. The roll of wire mesh is about a meter wide—wide enough to cut into two long strips to make a drift fence 100 meters long. Nine buckets will allow a bucket every 10 meters, with 5 meters of fence extending beyond the buckets at the two ends. I have even brought a staple gun from Canada, thinking using it might be an easier way to attach the mesh to the sticks used as fence posts than laboriously tying everything with vines. While we were waiting in Epena, I got Ange to hammer 10 holes in the bottom of each bucket, so that water rising from underneath would not cause the bucket to float up out of the ground, though I couldn't help thinking how distressed villagers would be to see good buckets ruined in this way. Lise and I cut the wire mesh into two strips, all 50 meters of it, stabbing our fingers on the sharp cut ends of the wire, and persisting with the folding scissors bought in Toronto's Chinatown despite getting terrible blisters after cutting barely 3 meters.

I explain the design of the trapline to the guides, leaving it to them to choose a promising location in the forest. Old Charles leads the way, cutting a broad trail as he goes. Ange thinks Old Charles's trails are *too* broad. "What does he think? That we need boulevards?" I keep thinking he's started clearing the line for the traps, but apparently we have not yet arrived at the place he has in mind. He goes on and on through the forest. At last Old Charles announces that this is where the line is to start. He cuts a first picket for the fence, and at my instruction drives it into the earth about 5 meters from the edge of the water. Then he starts clearing a straight line inland. I tie the end of a ball of string to the picket and follow Old Charles's cleared line, unrolling it until I have measured 5 meters from the picket. Here I stop and tie a knot of orange flagging tape around the string to indicate the location of the first bucket. As Old Charles cuts the line through the forest, I crawl along in his wake measuring string and tying flagging tape, and Romuald follows me with the shovel, digging a hole astonishingly quickly at each flagging tape marker. Ange brings up the rear, sinking a bucket into each hole. It all goes very quickly. Crawling along with my measuring tape and string I suddenly realize that I am marking the place for the last bucket. Romuald has almost finished digging the hole for the second to last, and Old Charles is back at the beginning of the line, cutting sticks to use as pickets for the fence.

The staple gun is a great success. Old Charles is hammering in pickets, Romuald is unrolling mesh, and Ange is stapling it in place. Lise is drifting around looking bored, which is what she has been doing all morning, so, leaving the men to this three-person job, I take Lise back to the camp and set her to work boiling water, since I had noticed our supply of drinking water was running low. The people in Impongui collect rainwater for drinking rather than using the river water. Our system in the camp is that the guides bring a big plastic jug of rainwater each morning and we boil it for drinking and use it as is for cooking. "But what do they do for water in the dry season?" I ask. Apparently in the dry season they get their water from an underground spring which comes out near where they land the pirogues. In the rainy season the water level rises in the river, so that the spring is submerged. Hence the rainwater. Lise never did buy water-decontamination tablets, but she hasn't said a word about water quality since the day before our departure, and has been drinking the boiled water like everyone else, without complaint. Everyone is repelled by the disgusting idea of boiling the brown forest water to drink as I did last year.

On our way back along the trail to the camp, we pass a spot at the edge of the water which is so beautiful that I can't help but stop for a few moments, and point it out to Lise. I'm not sure why it seems so special. It is typical flooded forest habitat, which I love, but there's no shortage of views of flooded forest around here. Perhaps just because there is a gap here in the forest along the dry-land edge, emphasizing the enormous scale and depth of the water and trees. "This might be a good place for setting up nets to catch water snakes," I suggest. "I wonder if it's shallow enough that we could check the nets just by wading in?" But Lise tells me she's afraid of the water and that she can't swim. "I could teach you to swim," I offer. "Here?" she looks incredulously at the dark, swampy water, and shakes her head vigorously in disgust.

We return to the trapline to find that the staple gun has jammed, which has brought construction to a temporary halt. I walk back to the camp again for the dissecting instruments, and eventually Ange manages to fix the gun using one of the pairs of Chinatown scissors. Fence in place, the men are under the impression that the job is finished, but the really laborious work is just beginning. Around every bucket, the space between bucket and hole must be carefully filled with earth, so that the rim of the bucket is exactly level with the forest floor. The bottom edge of all 100 meters of fence has to be filled in with earth so that nothing can pass under it. All this digging around in earth dug up from the forest means a lot of encounters with turned-over nests of frantic biting ants, and I crawl the length of the trapline several times, filling in holes, shifting leftover earth into the surrounding forest, and camouflaging the trampled area along the fence with leaves and twigs. I am finally satisfied with the result, but there turns out to be 6 meters of wire mesh left. I measure the whole fence again: 100 meters exactly. I am baffled after Ange's careful measuring in the market, but I guess it doesn't really matter. It is 2:00 p.m. and now that the trapline is done we all notice for the first time how tired and dirty and hungry we are. Romuald asks me to give them a mark on the job. "A mark?" "Out of 20. Like in school." "25!" I am convinced that this will be my first pitfall trapline that finally works. I can hardly wait for the flood of specimens tomorrow morning.

Lise has prepared a big pot of spaghetti back at the camp, without being asked. We fall upon it ravenously. Then I let the guides leave, but taking with them the fishnets to string. They point out that it will be easier to string them in the village than here in the forest, where they will get tangled in leaves and twigs.

Nets were the most important part of my daily routine last year, but this year the water is too deep for wading and the nets have to be checked by pirogue. Romuald takes to doing this on his way to the camp in the morning, so I am deprived of that pleasure. He will come and fetch me, he assures me, if there is a live snake in the net. I choose the first site for the net, after Romuald and Old Charles have paddled me around showing me various options. I choose a place where the water is fairly thick with vegetation, trees, and hummocks of plants close enough together that I can imagine snakes swimming easily from one to the other and getting caught in my net in between. "Why is the net so short?" I ask, puzzled. Romuald has just tied the far end of it to a bush and it seems like less than the 250 meters I bought in Impongui. I don't get a straight answer until much later. The two guides had decided that my size #1.5 nets were not deep enough, so instead of setting out 250 meters of shallow net, they took it upon themselves to double it up and sew the two halves together, making a deep net only 125 meters long. "But snakes swim along the surface!" I exclaim in frustration. "I deliberately bought long, shallow nets." Ange says mildly that Romuald is known to be the best fisherman in the village, and clearly thinks I would do well to follow his advice. "I'm not doubting that he's an excellent fisherman, but fish are not what I'm trying to catch." I never manage to get enough control over the use of the nets. Romuald, meaning well, regularly moves the net to a place that looks more promising to him, not even mentioning to me that he has done this until days later. We get disappointingly few water snakes.

Old Charles has built us a lab desk to work at in the house out of branches lashed together with vines. It even has a bench to sit on and is big enough for two people with a bit of a squeeze. But the surface of the desk is made of branches lashed together, and the formalin jar is in constant danger of tipping over and small tags and dissecting instruments keep falling through onto the ground. Romuald has brought an old piece of tarpaulin for me to put on the ground to sleep on. The sheets we bought in Impfondo, one for each person, which seemed quite expensive at the time, turn out to be three packages each containing a flat sheet, a fitted sheet, and a pillow case, so we are able to use some of the sheets to cover the open end of the house, with the hope of reducing the number of flies, wasps, mosquitoes, and bats that make their way in. Last night was fine, and Lise's tent and big mattress are going to be very comfortable accommodation for one, but I am looking forward to having the house to myself. I could share a tent with Lise, but I think we would both go mad if I did. Sleeping in the house, I have no privacy to retreat to, but I like being in the center of things, keeping an eye on the provisions and the equipment. I stretch out on the piece of tarpaulin, pull the mosquito net around me, and fall fast asleep.

I am woken just at dawn by a strange rustling sound. I doze for a while, not giving it much thought until I feel something tickle the back of my neck. I brush at it, and my hand comes away covered with tiny white ants. Now I am awake, and the rustling noise turns out to be coming from my sleeping mat, which is a swarming mass of ants. I must have been lying in it for hours. My skin is covered with ants, my clothes full of them. I get up and run outside the house in absolute panic. No ants outside. I run to the water, wading in until I am out of my depth. I swim underwater and run my fingers through my hair for a long time before I am confident that I am free of them. That leaves my bed. I know it's ridiculous to have such a horror of ants, but I shudder at the idea of going back into the house, and at this point I am ashamed to admit that I am not above pleading for a manly rescue from them. The guides haven't arrived yet, so I wake Ange. "These aren't ants," he corrects me from inside the house. I am waiting tremulously outside until they have all been got rid of. "They're termites."

"I don't care what they are—I don't want to sleep with them!" He shakes the mat and tarpaulin free of termites and hangs them both over the roof of the house. Then he spreads shovelfuls of ashes from the fire all over the floor of the house to kill the ones that are left. This leaves the inside of the house in a cloud of ash. I spend the rest of the night sitting outside with the mosquitoes.

The camp takes shape over the next few days. I am especially pleased with my swimming spot. By some great stroke of luck, the big pirogue that Romuald used to convey all our belongings here has been left, one end pulled up on land, behind a screen of trees, right in front of the camp. The other end extends out into the water. Duck-diving to the bottom, feeling the pressure change in my ears, I estimate the water is a good 2 or 3 meters deep at the end of the pirogue. Definitely deep enough to dive in head first off the end. If you swim far enough, the dark, forested water gives way to the bright sunlight and grasses of the broad Likouala aux Herbes River, which it is continuous with. I swim off the end of the pirogue several times a day. Lise and Ange view this as complete folly. They prefer to fill a bucket with water and retreat with it into the privacy of the forest to wash.

The pitfall traps are a great disappointment the next morning when I get up early to check them myself before anyone else is awake. Nothing in them except five giant millipedes and two shrews. Nine buckets and not so much as a toad! The millipedes are easy enough to remove, but the first shrew bites my hand when I catch it to throw it back into the forest. I use my 12-inch hemostat to grab the second one. I cheer up a bit over coffee. The plan for the morning had been to investigate a marshy area that might have frogs, but Romuald tells me that he saw a snake yesterday, fleeing into a pile of bricks in the village. The bricks are for a church which is to be built some day. If we moved the bricks we might find the snake. This sounds to me like a splendid idea and I am happy to change our plans.

For our trip to the village, I dig a red and white beach volleyball, bought in Toronto on Canada Day, out of the equipment box, and inflate it to give to the children. As we walk along the trail I work out how to say in Lingala, "Don't hit it with feet. Hit it only with hands, because it is not strong." Impongui is so small that even after just a few days we are starting to get to know people, so greetings are more elaborate than a mere "mbote."

"Mbote, mama," I say to the oldest woman in the village, scrawny, and terribly hunched.

"Mbote, koko," she smiles at me. It is the first time I have heard someone use the word *koko*. It means both "grandchild" and "grandparent." A child sent by someone wordlessly hands me a plastic bag containing a dead *Calabaria reinhardtii*. Mottled with scales of rust and black and perfectly cylindrical, it is a harmless burrowing python with a blunt tail which looks so much like its head that it sometimes even tricks would-be predators into attacking the wrong end by waving its tail enticingly. It is one of the three animals that get called "double-têtes" (double heads) in this part of the world. I am disappointed to see that this specimen has had both head and tail chopped off and discarded. Double-têtes of all kinds are inexplicably thought to be deadly venomous. One of them, the tiny, blunt-ended *Typhlops* is universally feared. I have heard it referred to as the "5-minute snake," because, supposedly, if it bites you, you have 5 minutes to live. I just don't understand. The head is so small it is hard to see how it could open its mouth wide enough to bite, and in any case it has only a few tiny teeth—certainly no fangs! It occurs to me that a pretty good gauge of how much a species is feared is the condition of the specimens when they are presented to me. My one specimen of *Typhlops* had been chopped into five pieces by the time it got to me.

I am absorbed by the headless ground boa and hardly notice that a child has started screaming in the distance, until Romuald chuckles, "She's afraid of Katherine." I look up and see a girl of about 3, in a blue dress, outside a mud and stick house across the cleared area from where I am sitting. I smile, wave with both hands, as is local custom, and utter my most unthreatening "mbote," but this just causes her to howl even louder. I remember my father telling me about the time he took me to the Toronto Zoo when I was about the same age as this girl. I burst into tears at the sight of the orangutans. I suppose they looked to me almost like people but with something horribly wrong with them, and somehow at 3, that was terribly upsetting. I must look like that to Perséphone, this little girl, who has never seen a white person before—almost human but with something disturbingly not quite right about me. She is one of the children I soon get to know by name, because she reacts this way to the sight of me the whole time I spend near Impongui, in spite of all my efforts to ingratiate myself.

Romuald's idea of finding the snake by moving the bricks seems slightly less splendid when we arrive to find that the pile of bricks for the church is almost as big as a church. They are big cement bricks, each weighing 10 kilograms or so, and quickly counting from top to bottom and along the sides I estimate that there are at least 2,000 of them. They look as if they have been there for some time. Plants are starting to sprout from the top of the pile and some of the bricks are broken and crumbling. I must look as daunted as I feel, because Romuald, who is already starting a new pile for the bricks that have been moved, suggests that I go and sit in the shade and wait. They'll let me know if there's a snake, he assures me. The children will help him. The children have already started attacking the big pile. I'm certainly not going to lounge in the shade while these little kids do my work, though getting out of the mid-morning sun is certainly tempting. It's only going to get hotter in the next few hours. But when I see the woman who called me "koko" hefting a brick, slacking off is out of the question. Soon I am happily absorbed in the work. Everyone is pulling bricks out of the sides of the pile, so I climb to the top to pass bricks from the top layer down to the children below. The child working the hardest is a little girl who stands silently behind me, conveying every brick I remove to Romuald to be added to the new pile. She is too shy to answer me when I ask her her name, but Lise finds it out. She is Anuarite, 10 years old and one of Romuald's brood. I tear out tufts of vegetation to free the bricks. Each one I turn over is a surprise to look forward to, though admittedly the most frequent surprise is a nest of vicious, biting ants, though sometimes a giant centipede or an enormous, hairy spider, both of which are said to have a terrible bite. Ange makes a great fuss of crushing them with the useless 24-inch hemostat, which I have let him carry.

If we were millipede experts rather than herpetologists we would be in paradise. The giant millipedes of central Africa are glossy, gentle, slow-moving creatures, about the size and shape of a hot dog. I am rather fond of them, but I have never met a Congolese who looks on them with anything other than complete revulsion. The brick pile is full of them. Standing on top of the brick pile I wave a giant millipede above my head, shouting in Lingala at the children below, "Who wants it?" They look at me as if I've gone mad. I swing my arm so it looks as if I'm throwing it at them and they scatter with screams of horror and delight.

After a couple of hours of exhausting work the pile of bricks doesn't look much smaller than when we started. I'm greatly regretting not having brought drinking water with me from the camp. Anyone in the village would give me rainwater, but it wouldn't be boiled, which might or might not matter. I call to Lise, who is sitting in the shade again after being ordered to work at the brick pile three times so far, and try to send her back to the camp for water, but she says she doesn't know the way. Although I'm thirsty, I'm so absorbed in the work that I hardly notice my skin blistering in the sun. Fearing that the dead ground boa might rot more quickly in the heat, I pull the bag out of my waistband and hand it down to Anuarite to go and put in the shade beside my backpack. I am getting used to the habit of using children as convenient little servants.

A brick tips over and crushes one of my fingernails. Another falls on my foot. At least I have boots, unlike anyone else. An enormous cockroach comes out of the pile and runs up my trouser leg. For some reason I seem to be dirtier than anyone else. By 2:00 p.m. we have found no snakes, and spirits are flagging. We are at about the halfway point, with Romuald's new pile of bricks roughly the same size as the remains of the original pile. Perhaps the snakes go out during the day and then come back in at night, Romuald suggests. Maybe we should stop and come back tomorrow, early in the morning. "But they'd be just as likely to go back to the new pile as the old," I point out in exasperation, "and then we'd have to move all the bricks in both piles."

Well into the afternoon only three layers of bricks are left to move. We haven't found a single snake, and it's not looking promising. Ange suggests calling it quits. He's probably right that we're not going to get anything, but after all those bricks I can't bring myself to stop with only three layers left to go. I turn over a brick and find a toad, *Bufo regularis*, very common in the village, and easily obtained without moving enormous piles of bricks. Since arriving in Impongui, the Lingala Delphin taught me has been serving me well, but nobody seems to understand the word he gave me for toad: *ligorodo*. The local word must be something different. I turn to the little boy moving bricks beside me, and brandish the toad. "Kombo na yango ezali nini?" I ask him in my best Lingala (The name of this is what?). The boy gives me a pitying look and answers me in French.

"Crapaud" (toad).

We are moving the very last layer of bricks when the first snake streaks out from among them. It is a *Mehelya*, harmless and easily recognizable by its square snout and its body, which is covered with black scales stretched tight, so that white skin is visible between them. The area around the brick pile is completely open, with no cover, and I easily catch the snake, even grabbing it behind the head in one snatch. I get three more snakes among the last of the bricks, another *Mehelya* and two house snakes *(Lamprophis)*. Then as a bonus there are two large, banded geckos of a species I've never seen before. All three of these end up being the only specimens of their respective species that we get in all the rest of our stay. At the very end there is a common skink, *Trachylepis*. I catch all the lizards neatly, without breaking their tails.

Can this be only the beginning of our first week? What a difference from last year with that awful period at the start, of finding nothing. And largely thanks to Ange's skill at negotiating, the people in this tiny village (population 250) really seem to care about our project. Nobody in Impongui ever asks to be paid for contributing a specimen or helping out with work like moving bricks. In fact, the people of Impongui are so kind that they often send presents of pineapples or manioc to our camp, as well as specimens, care of the guides. Part of this enthusiastic participation is in a competitive spirit. I mention that I had carried out a study like this last year at Ganganya Brousse. Soon people are asking me excitedly how many specimens we have so far and how many we got at Ganganya, keeping note of the statistics. Definitely things are going better than last year. Moreover, having had the experience of identifying all the specimens I collected last year, I now recognize many of the animals we find, and even if I'm not certain of the species, I at least have a pretty good idea what genus they belong to.

Exhaustion suddenly catches up with me, and I retreat to the shade, full bags hanging satisfyingly from my belt. Lise has had the excellent idea of bringing a bag of candies, and gives one to each of the children. They accept these with shrieks of delight, and start a rowdy game with the beach volleyball. They have been lifting bricks all day like the rest of us. Where do they find the energy?

Back at the camp it is almost dark, and since I want to photograph the snakes and the geckos I decide to wait until tomorrow to fix them. Lise retreats to her tent.

Ange has his notebook out and is busy making an inventory of our food, counting tins of tomato paste and kilo bags of rice in preparation for organizing a menu for the rest of the month that will ensure that we don't run out of supplies. Already, in the first 4 days, Romuald has got through a kilo of sugar making the coffee. We are going to have to give up the luxury of having a second cup of coffee in the afternoon. Ange is especially indignant to find that we are missing a sack of smoked fish, which is on our supplies list but which must have got left at WCS. I do my best to appear disappointed. In the course of going through the supplies, Ange finds that the termites have started eating through the cardboard boxes. He rearranges the rubber equipment boxes so that all the scientific equipment somehow fits in one box, so as to use the other for all the food that had been in cardboard boxes. The damp cardboard that remains, he props up near the fire to dry out, since it might be useful for something. Sure enough, it turns out to be just the thing for covering the bumpy branches of our lab table, making a smooth and usable surface. "Ange?" I say, watching all this activity and remembering also his expert negotiating with the village committee, "I am the scientific director of this expedition," he looks up from his list, "and you are the administrative director." He grins and nods agreement.

"Exactly." It is a perfect division of labor that serves us well for the rest of the expedition.

"Goodnight," I call after him as he closes the sheet behind him.

After the termite incident there is no question of my sleeping on the ground any more. Old Charles builds me a bed out of branches lashed together with vines. Even with my rubber mat it is phenomenally uncomfortable. Generally I'm so exhausted that I manage to sleep on it even so. It's certainly better than sleeping in a swarm of termites. I often wake in the night because the sticks I am lying on dig painfully into my shoulder and hip, and I find I can guess what time it is to within an hour or two, in complete darkness, by the sounds of the forest. The background noise of the forest changes gradually throughout the night, from the frogs starting at dusk to the first birds at 3:00 a.m. Lise and Ange add background noise that I could do without.

Lise's tape deck is not something that I manage to tolerate for long. To be fair, she usually plays it at such low volume that it is only really audible if you are standing right beside her tent, but there is something about that music, just hovering at my threshold of hearing, that drives me crazier than it would blaring at top volume. I confront her over it one morning. Lise has brought her tape deck out of the tent and is playing it while we wait for the coffee to boil. Christian rock music in a mixture of French and Lingala floods the camp. I tell Lise that the first time I went into the field, I also brought recorded music, but when I got there I just couldn't bring myself to play it—it seemed like noise pollution in the midst of the natural sounds of the forest. This approach turns out to be way too subtle for Lise, so I try something more direct: "Look, you can listen to the tape deck whenever you want in Brazzaville, but here, just for a few weeks, you have the opportunity to listen to the sounds of the animals of the forest instead." I might as well not have spoken.

"This next one is my favorite song," says Lise enthusiastically as another one begins. Clearly I am not getting through to her, so in the end I just lay out the bottom line:

"I have come a long way to listen to the sounds of the forest, and I don't want to hear any more recorded music. Is that clear?"

I don't often hear the tape deck after that, but both Lise and Ange create a tremendous amount of noise even so, pushing me close to the brink of insanity. Lise shuts herself in her tent and sings Christian rock and Celine Dion, especially when I am trying to get to sleep. It's somehow even more annoying than the recorded version, but I don't feel I can forbid her to sing in the way that I have forbidden her to play her tape deck. Ange's repertoire consists largely of catchy election campaign songs from Kinshasa, where elections for the position of president of the Democratic Republic of Congo are going on right about now, while we are in the forest ("Votez, votez, votez, Ka-bi-la"). Ange too sometimes sings at night, but usually inflicts his repertoire on everyone during the day when he is in a particularly good mood.

Our camp on the bank of the Likouala aux Herbes River is like paradise—but a paradise to which insects have been added. At my camp last year I got to know ants, wasps, and flies. We have all of those here too, plus a few extras. I am kicking myself for buying tarpaulins that are royal blue—not that there was a lot of choice in the market in Brazzaville. I had forgotten that blue attracts tsetse flies, a lesson learned from a pair of blue cargo pants worn on my first trip to the Congo. Large and black, tsetse flies give a painful bite, and are also the vector that spreads sleeping sickness. The blue tarpaulins draw them into the house as though to a beacon. They buzz lazily around, slow enough to give the impression of being possible to successfully swat, but actually capable of a frustratingly quick getaway. They are worst on sunny afternoons. If I have any paperwork that has to be done in the house I retreat under the mosquito net, in spite of the heat. Sometimes they do no more than drive me to distraction by droning around and around the house, but if I ever have my skin accidentally in contact with the mosquito net, they will bite me through it. Often they get themselves trapped along the peak of the roof between the two overlapping tarpaulins, and buzz madly, sometimes for days, the sound amplified by the vibration against the walls of their tarpaulin prison.

The mosquitoes are such an obvious presence as to be scarcely worth mentioning. They appear in enormous numbers, every evening at 6:00 p.m., without fail, just as darkness falls. That is also a hot and sticky time of day and it's hard to choose which is worse: covering up with socks and long sleeves and going under a stifling mosquito net, or going for a cooling twilight swim, leaving skin exposed and then being kept awake night after night by the terrible itching, scratching until the skin is torn and open to infection. And more seriously, running the risk of malaria.

But the rulers of this camp are the termites. Termites look like tiny white ants and are always found in enormous numbers. The only good thing that can be said about them is that they don't bite—at least not human flesh. Termites eat things—anything. We suffer a termite incident at least once every day, requiring all belongings to be moved away from them so that hot ash can be scattered over the area they cover. We do our best to control them, but during our time camped near Impongui they eat holes in the sheets used for doors, the cardboard boxes our food is stored in, the cover of my field catalogue, most of a pocket handkerchief that lands on the ground for all of 15 minutes, much of a plastic raincoat that goes missing overnight, and enough of a leather belt to make it unwearable—and those are just a few examples that spring to mind.

At sunrise, I check the pitfall traps. Once again there is nothing in them but shrews and giant millipedes. I watch one small shrew escape through one of the holes at the bottom of the bucket. If a shrew can get through, then so can a lot of other animals. Perhaps that's the problem. The holes are too big. I get the guides to use the leftover wire mesh to cover the bottoms of the buckets, holding the circles of mesh in place with duct tape.

As the routines get established, the days become calmer, and I start to enjoy being camped in the Likouala forest again. I love the system of having a camp in an undisclosed location, and having the guides live in the village. I also love the selfless helpfulness of the people of Impongui, who collect any specimen they come across, and get them to us by dropping them off at Romuald's house. The guides come first thing in the morning, before breakfast, and often have the afternoon off and come again at dinner time, and they seldom come empty-handed. So these specimens alone keep us almost continually occupied.

It astonishes me to hear that Lise, who claimed to be "passionate" about snakes, has never touched a live one before. So the day after the brick pile, I take one of the house snakes *(Lamprophis)* out of its bag to give her some practice handling one. You could hardly find a less threatening species to begin with. But as soon as I open the bag, Lise rushes to the other end of the camp in a panic. It takes the better part of an hour to coax her over to where I am standing. "How are you going to be a herpetologist if you're afraid of snakes?" Ange berates her. "No, don't give it to me!" he says in alarm, and then, recovering himself, "I already know how to hold a snake." The furthest I get with Lise is to have her touch the tail gingerly with the tip of her finger while I hold the head firmly away from her. Maybe she'll do better with the next one. The procaine turns out to work very well, and I much prefer euthanizing snakes with a quick injection that just seems to put them to sleep, rather than messing around with chloroform as I did last year.

Not many things seem to interest Lise, but I noticed back in Brazza- ville that she quite often had Jean-Philippe Chippaux's new snake book open in front of her. Of all the literature I brought with me, that book is the most accessible, being not only in French but also written at a fairly general level, and Lise, though bright and capable of really doing well, I am convinced, if only she would make an effort, does like things that are easy. But at this point I'm at my wit's end to find any way of getting

Lise to learn about snakes. Most of the book is made up of identification keys for west African snakes, including some species that get into the Congo. An identification key, or "dichotomous key," is a series of questions. You start with the specimen you want to identify in your hand, and answer questions about it. Each question has two possible answers to choose between, and the answer you choose leads you to the next question, also with two choices. When it works properly, your answers to the series of questions should eventually lead you to the answer—tell you what species your specimen belongs to. Here's an example, translated from Chippaux's book *Les serpents d'Afrique occidentale et centrale* (p. 83):

> "1. 17 or more dorsal scale rows......................2
> (or) 15 dorsal scale rows................................3"

Let's suppose the dead snake in your hand has 15 dorsal scale rows. You would go to question 3 (p. 83):

> "3. Fewer than 180 ventrals; fewer than 45 subcaudals....4
> (or) More than 180 ventrals; fewer than 45 subcaudals....5"

And so on. Sometimes there are dozens of these questions before you get to a question for which the answer is not the number of the next question, but the name of a species. The principle is simple enough, but obviously you have to know what ventrals and subcaudals and dorsal scale rows are. And the names of all the other scales on a snake.

I finally persuade Lise to try using the key by promising that I will hold a formalin-fixed snake so that she doesn't have to touch it, as she works through the series of questions, learning the names of the scales as she goes. By the third step she seems interested, by the fifth she gets fed up with trying to count scales on a specimen while someone else is holding it and takes it from me, formalin and all, and by the seventh she is completely absorbed, even when the question requires something tedious like counting all the ventral scales (all the scales along the underside of a snake—generally more than 100), and when she gets to the end and I tell her that the snake is indeed *Dasypeltis,* and she has got the right answer, she is happy and excited for the first time since I've known her. Perhaps there is hope for Lise after all.

chapter 14

snake
medicine

Lise and Ange soon learn how to formalin-fix specimens, to take tissue samples, and to write catalogue entries. They seem to think that they've just about mastered herpetology. But I am supposed to be training scientists, not technicians. Of course they need to know these basic techniques, but last year Etienne, a villager with no education whatsoever, learned how to do most of this. I am expecting considerably more from graduate students in biology. They need to learn to recognize the species they are collecting, or at least to be able to tell the genus of the most common and most distinctive-looking species. I teach Ange, who is supposed to be specializing in amphibians, to recognize the big African bullfrog, *Hoplobatrachus,* by the ridge that runs across its head behind the eyes, and *Ptychadena,* which turns out to be the most common frog here, by its long back legs and capacity for enormous leaps. The toads, also very common, all belong to the genus *Bufo,* although we may be dealing with several species, and then of course there's *Xenopus,* the African clawed frog, slimy, largely aquatic, and, it seems to me, unmistakable because of its distinctive shape—big webbed feet, hefty hips and thighs, wide mouth, and spindly arms. But Ange, so capable and so dedicated, has great difficulty telling apart even the most obvious specimens, even when the animal is a species he has seen several times before. It is a great struggle for him to learn these, and even at the end of the month he can not reliably recognize a *Xenopus.*

Lise, on the other hand, intellectually lazy and afraid to touch a live animal of any kind, turns out to be quite good at recognizing snake species. Each time I collect a snake, we sit down together and work through the key, with me making sure that she arrives at the correct identification. She never needs to be told what a snake is more than once. Without fail, when we get the second specimen of a species she's seen once before, she confidently identifies it at a glance.

The camp is built, the pitfall traps and nets are in place, the people of Impongui are sending in specimens, and we're still feeling buoyed up by the success of the brick pile, but something important is still missing: night searching. We have all got into the habit of collapsing into an exhausted sleep at 6:00 p.m., when it gets dark and the mosquitoes appear. I announce over breakfast that the guides will have the afternoon off, but that after supper we will be going out in search of frogs, and anything else we are lucky enough to catch. The guides know the area, I don't, so I tell them to give some thought to good places for catching frogs at night.

Our first night outing is a farce. It takes a full hour after my planned departure time of 7:00 p.m. to get everyone into the pirogue. If rivers are the highways of Central Africa, pirogues, carved by hand from a single piece of wood, are the cars. The WCS pirogue is the only one I ever see that has an outboard motor. Having an outboard motor also means having a transom on the stern to attach it to. In a normal pirogue there is no difference between bow and stern, so you don't even need to turn around to change directions. A pirogue is propelled by a pinancier, standing up in the stern (well, posterior end), with a single long oar used as something between a paddle and a punt pole, depending on the depth of the water. Often there is a second pinancier in the front end. Having grown up in Ontario I am very used to canoes, which at a first glance seem quite similar to pirogues. I never do quite get used to the difference between the two. The main difference is weight. I amaze Romuald by telling him about my country, where lakes are so numerous and pirogues so light that you carry your pirogue on your head to get from lake to lake. Used to light canoes, I am always afraid that a landed pirogue has not been pulled up far enough to prevent it from floating away. I worry especially about the big pirogue that I swim from—that it may float away with me in it, stark naked, and without a paddle. But my greatest fear is of tipping over. The pinanciers paddle standing up, which you certainly couldn't do in a canoe. I suppose in the Likouala aux Herbes River it allows them to see where they're going over the grasses. They do it with such obvious competence that I don't worry too much, but Ange drives me mad insisting on standing up in the pirogue, with the center of his considerable mass to my mind too high for safety, and by sometimes also incompetently wielding an oar. I have clearly heard Old Charles tell him politely, "Tika" (Stop it), but Ange seems to have got the idea that in the Likouala there is something unmanly about sitting down in a pirogue. I am annoyed by the delayed departure on the evening of our first night search, even before we get into the pirogue. Ange insists on standing up the whole way apparently to assert his masculinity, and Lise, who can't swim, does the same, but in her case in order to avoid getting her tight gray pin-striped trousers wet in the little bit of water in the bottom of the pirogue. If we were to capsize, which would I save, I ponder—the digital camera or Lise? I sit in the bow as the pirogue cuts silently through the water and grasses, until Ange points out to me that the grasses are covered with ants, and so, by now, am I.

We land according to plan at the pirogue landing place, which has a promising long, shallow, grassy shoreline, only to discover that all the village children are there, playing some rowdy game. Romuald suggests that we go closer to the village and search for some other landing spots until this place has become more "calm." Then it turns out that the batteries are nearly dead in the flashlights of both guides. Lise and Ange are going to waste even more time going to see the Notable to thank him for some plantains he sent as a present. Knowing that the Notable can be almost as long-winded as Ange, I anticipate that this visit may take some time, so I have Lise give her headlamp to Romuald until she returns. We set off in the direction of the village. Lise and Ange soon rejoin us. The Notable had already gone to bed.

I catch a *Ptychadena* in the vegetation under a tree, and it is at that point that we discover that only I thought to bring plastic bags. While everyone else is figuring this out, the frog slips out of my hand and escapes. This is not serious. *Ptychadenas*, smooth, streamlined green frogs with long legs, will turn out to be even more common than the toads.

Romuald goes on ahead, leading the way in the bright beam of Lise's headlamp, which he is greatly taken with and has not given back. Lise is making do with the smallest of the Eternity flashlights, barely adequate for reading in bed. Romuald knows the area well, but I do not, and it all looks especially unfamiliar when all I can see is what the narrow beam of my headlamp catches, so I don't immediately realize that he is leading us right through the village. This is exactly what I wanted to avoid. We're unlikely to find anything in the midst of all this human activity, and we don't need the swarm of noisy children getting roused up and joining in. But I don't know where I am, and he is ahead almost out of earshot, and all I can do is follow and make the most of checking whatever bushes and grassy borders I pass. You never know what you might find.

Romuald seems to be taking the opportunity to make a social visit to each of his neighbors, so groups of people, sitting outside their houses enjoying a quiet evening, find themselves suddenly blinded by the unfamiliar headlamp beams. Only I have used a headlamp before and know that headlamp etiquette involves turning off the light or pointing it in a different direction when you look someone in the face. We continue to prowl around the village. I feel embarrassingly conspicuous. While trying not to lose sight of Romuald, I find an area that is grassy rather than packed dirt, and follow my beam into it. The grassy area is quite large, and I find a small brick structure of some kind that looks like a possible hiding place. I climb on top of it and start pulling at loose bricks. I happen to look up for a moment, and as my headlamp sweeps around the area, I suddenly realize that this is the village cemetery and I am standing on top of, and pulling bricks out of, somebody's tomb.

I hastily rejoin the rest of the group, and at last we are away from the village. Lise looks totally dejected, shaking the inadequate little Eternity flashlight every 15 seconds, and stifling a yawn as she pretends to scrutinize the ground. Romuald is far away from us. I give Lise my headlamp. I don't imagine for a moment that she'll actually catch anything, but she should at least have a chance. Old Charles trails along after us, as though he could see anything with his fading flashlight.

In the end Romuald and Ange, who have the headlamps (not counting my headlamp, which Lise has), catch a few of the common African bullfrogs. Romuald is very pleased with them because they are such big specimens. Since we have only one plastic bag, along with a lot of cloth snake bags, unsuitable for amphibians, we have to head back to camp. In the last 10 minutes I order Lise to go over to where Ange is standing so she can at least see the frogs. I want to force her to get her feet wet.

Ange has caught the most frogs and is noisily boasting. I make him give me his headlamp just to show him how impossible it is to find frogs with one of the Eternity flashlights. Against all my protestations, he stands up in the pirogue all the way back to the camp, singing and loudly bragging about having caught more frogs than anyone else. Poor Lise doesn't need this. She looks miserable enough as it is about the results of the outing. Back at the camp I get Ange on his own and tell him to stop it. He has spent a month on a field course, while this is Lise's first time ever in the field. Even so he can't contain himself. "I caught three things!" he crows.

"Yes, and we've all heard about it more than three times." And aside to Lise, I add, "And this from the only person who had a headlamp for the entire evening."

Before the next night outing I take Romuald aside. I explain to him that the night work has two objectives: obviously the first objective of obtaining specimens, but equally important training. Lise especially needs to learn how to catch frogs. I know that we would get far more specimens by giving a headlamp to him, but I want to give it to Lise. The most useful thing Romuald could do would be to help her to catch a frog herself, for example by pointing out to her a frog he sees rather than immediately catching it himself. It doesn't matter if some get away, I assure him.

Future night outings go a bit better. I veto the village as a place to search and insist that we stick to the field and to the marshy shoreline. The guides have new batteries in their flashlights and everyone brings plastic bags. We never catch anything very interesting, just the big bullfrogs, *Hoplobatrachus*, long-legged and agile *Ptychadenas*, and the occasional gecko. But Lise is making minimal effort and no progress whatsoever.

One night I notice one of the common toads at the edge of some crumbling foundations. Right out in the open; no way it could possibly get away. "Lise!" I call. She drifts over. "Here's a toad for you to catch," I tell her when she arrives. Lise squeals girlishly, glancing over her shoulder at Ange and the guides, the audience of men, with a helpless grin. "Lise, you are going to pick up this toad." Another squeal, and a check over her shoulder to see that the men are laughing. Doesn't she get it, I ask myself? Doesn't she see that they're laughing at her because she's making a fool of herself? "Pick it up." There is no joking in my tone. She bends awkwardly at the waist to reach the toad. "Crouch down!" I yank her down by the sleeve, exasperated. "Now pick it up." She extends thumb and forefinger, starts to close them around the toad, then lets go, snatching her hand back with a loud shriek, followed by a giggle over her shoulder at the men. I have had it. "Lise, you will pick up this toad if we have to stay here all night. I'm not kidding!" She picks up the toad again with thumb and forefinger and lifts it about 2 inches off the ground before dropping it with a scream. The men are laughing, and this makes me furious. The toad starts to hop away. I grab it and put it back in front of Lise. "Lise. You will pick up the goddam toad this minute or I'll fucking make you eat it! There will be no more—absolutely no more bullshit! Do it!" She makes a clumsy grab at the toad, then stands up, giggling at the men. To my consternation, the toad seems to have got away. Then I look up. Lise has the toad in her hand. "You did it!" I exclaim.

"Do you mind giving me a bag?" She thrusts the toad at me and stalks off after the others, looking furious.

I get held up putting the toad in the bag, and catch up with the rest of the team at the pirogue landing. The children who were there earlier have gone, and there are lots of frogs in the shallow water among the grasses. I arrive just in time to hear Romuald say to Lise, "Osimbi?" (Did you catch it?) in incredulous Lingala.

"Nasimbi" (I caught it), Lise replies nonchalantly, as though she caught frogs all the time. She demands imperiously that someone get her a bag.

The evening's work is over. Ange and I hang back as the rest pile into the pirogue. "Did she really catch that frog?" I ask him.

"Well . . ." he demurs, "it went up her trouser leg."

Our first weekend has already arrived. Ange plans to pay the guides every Saturday. I've counted out the money and given it to him to give to them, and I can tell he's looking forward to paying them, knowing how pleased they will be. They've worked hard for it this week. So we are surprised when Romuald declines, saying he'd rather be paid the full sum at the end of the project. Old Charles says the same. Ange finds out later that Romuald needs the money—a whole month's wages—to pay for a memorial for his mother, who died 2 months ago. Something I never understand here is the way that people who can't afford the cost of the medicine that might save a person's life feel the social obligation to spend an enormous sum on the funeral that follows. Romuald's entire extended family, from as far away as Impfondo, will all descend on Impongui for a 3-day party in his mother's memory. He will have to provide food and drink and shelter for all of them for the duration, and then of course there is the monument that must be built in the cemetery to pay for, and so on, and so the costs add up. Getting paid the full sum at the end will ensure that none of it gets spent, given, or taken away before the memorial is paid for.

Romuald has invited us to a lunch of *saka-saka* on Sunday. Saka-saka is a dish that is a lot of work to prepare since it involves slicing leaves into strips as thin as cut grass. Saka-saka can be made either with peanut butter or with smoked fish. The former is delicious, the latter revolting. You have to be very careful ordering it in a restaurant because the menu never specifies which way it has been prepared. The arrangement that Ange makes with Romuald is that we will contribute ingredients—peanut butter, onion, garlic, and rice—and Romuald's wives will prepare the meal. This is a nice idea, but we can't afford a whole day without work. The pitfall trapline has been a total failure so far, and I want to move it. The guides have suggested setting it up in a spot not far from the village, parallel to the water instead of perpendicular to it.

So we dig up the buckets and roll up the fence. Sunday morning finds us setting it all up in the new place, in the forest along the shore near the marshy area used for landing pirogues. I hope there won't be too much disturbance from human traffic nearby. Since we have built the trapline once, setting it up a second time goes surprisingly fast, with everyone knowing what to do. Old Charles clears a path, followed closely by me with the string and tape measure and flagging tape, followed by Romuald digging holes for the buckets and Ange unrolling the fence. We are almost finished when we are interrupted by a shout—there is a snake in the village! I take off at a run with Ange close behind and Lise following us as quickly as is possible, picking her way around the cow pats in backless sequined slippers. But the men waiting for us at the edge of the village don't seem to be in a hurry. Where is the snake? I want to know. Isn't it going to get away? Why not? Nobody seems capable of explaining. When we arrive in the center of the village it all becomes clear. A crowd has formed in a wide circle, at the center of which is a large rhinoceros viper pinned to the ground through its tail by a fishing harpoon. The wound from the puncture is bleeding onto the dusty ground and the snake is hissing and striking randomly. Its thick body is covered in a velvety skin with a diamond pattern in improbable red and lavender. Ange is carrying all the snake-catching equipment, which I had forgotten in my excitement, and I take the 24-inch hemostat from him. I easily get control of the viper's head, and then pull out the harpoon as gently as possible, and get the heavy snake into a bag.

I am delighted. In my new Lingala I tell the crowd that we are very happy to have this snake and that it is the first one of its kind that we have found. It is probably the first one reported from the Likouala region, and found in Impongui. But I am forgetting an important lesson learned last year: Avoid excessive displays of enthusiasm. Ange is with a couple of young men I don't recognize, standing a bit apart from the crowd. He interrupts me urgently and discreetly. The men who brought the snake are demanding a reward. It turns out that these men are from Djeke, another village, not Impongui. They had heard that there were people in Impongui who are buying snakes and they want a reward. My heart sinks. It has been going so well up till now, with people volunteering specimens and none of the annoyance of bargaining and having to pay for animals. If we pay these men, everyone else from here on in will expect to be paid for every specimen found. In fact everyone who has given us a specimen before now will want to be paid retroactively. We just can't let that get started. "I know," says Ange, racking his brains for a solution. "Katherine, how badly do you want this snake?"

"I have to have it."

"Okay." He goes back to the men. After a few minutes of conversation he comes back to me again. "They're saying that if they had known we wouldn't pay them for it, they would have eaten it."

"Well that's easy," I feel a glimmer of hope, "tell them that all I want is the head and the skin and the stomach contents. They can have the meat. I'll even fillet it for them."

"I don't think that will work—I think they're just making an excuse. They're asking for 6,000cfa. Let me see what I can do." Ange goes back to talk to the men. The crowd gradually disperses. Lise and I stand together out of earshot. The sun beats down. My arm is tired from holding the heavy snake bag safely away from my leg. Ange and the men are still talking. Occasionally Ange darts over to ask a question or to report progress. "Here's what I'm suggesting: Since they're not from Impongui, I'm putting it in terms of paying them for their journey to get here, making it clear that we're not paying them for the snake. They're still asking for 6,000 but I think I can get it down to 2,000." Another 45 minutes go by. Ange and the men are still talking. I am starting to worry that I may faint if I have to stand in the sun any longer. I can overhear enough to understand that Ange is having a hard time getting them over the assumption that all mondeles are fabulously wealthy. "It's true that technically she is white," he reasons with them, "but she's part of our study group at the Marien-Ngouabi University. Moreover," he plays his trump card, "her husband is Congolese, from the DRC." Moments later Ange is clapping one of the men on the shoulder with a jovial laugh and calling to me to take a group photo. The men are smiling and posing with Ange for the picture. Ange is giving a business card to each of them and making them promise to call him if they are ever in Brazzaville. "We've settled on 2,000 for their journey. Do you have any money on you?" I don't. None of us brought money with us to go out and build pitfall traps. In the end we have to borrow the 2,000cfa from the Chief. Ange waves cheerfully to the men until their pirogue is out of sight, and then heaves an exhausted sigh of relief. I have never known anyone capable of negotiating with such relentless stamina as Ange—he can wear anyone down with his dogged reasonableness, and though it may take hours, at the end of it he always ends up great friends with his opponent, the issue in dispute long forgotten.

It is a huge relief to sit down out of the sun at Romuald's table, the snake bag on the floor between my feet. There is water in a pot on the table, and one of Romuald's wives leans over kindly to whisper to me that it is boiled. Bowls of food that have been covered with overturned plates to keep them warm during the long negotiations are uncovered and passed around. I accept a lump of fou-fou. I still don't like manioc, but I'm getting to the point of not minding fou-fou. The fish skeleton soup I pass along without taking any. I help myself to some rice and a stew. I have my mouth full of it when somebody tells me it is stewed pangolin. A pangolin is an elongate mammal, covered with hard scales except for its soft underbelly. It rolls into a ball to protect itself. In the stew, its flesh is rubbery lumps. And of course there is the saka-saka.

Romuald's wives have prepared it with peanut butter and no fish at all, and it is delicious. I eat much more than my share of it while trying to appear not to.

Once my immediate hunger is satisfied I start to pay attention to the people around me: Lise, Ange, Old Charles, Romuald, and Romuald's Uncle Marcel. An odd social dynamic is at work. The men are engaged in a conversation about Brazzaville politics, and it is clear that Lise and I are not meant to be involved. Old Charles may be my employee, but in this context he is a man and I am a woman. Romuald's two wives are hovering in the shadows, but there is no expectation that Lise and I could strike up a conversation with them, since we are, in this context, their husband's colleagues first and women second. So Lise heaves a sigh of boredom and I half listen to the conversation of the men. Instead of the back and forth I am used to thinking of as conversation, they each take turns to talk for a very long time without interruption. When the meal is over we move to chairs in the shade outside, and the conversation continues. Uncle Marcel produces a box of wine for us to share. I am half listening to the men, just picking up a fragment here or there. "What kind of man, I ask you, what kind of man goes on twelve journeys in one year?" Uncle Marcel is not expecting anyone to interrupt him with an answer.

". . . So you see, the economy of the city—the strength of the city—depends on the village . . ." Ange is holding forth at great length on Congolese economics.

After a couple of hours we are all well fed and slightly drunk on Uncle Marcel's wine, but I insist that we go back and finish setting up the pitfall trapline. It is agreed that since the trapline is close to the village, Old Charles will check it every morning before coming to the camp. It makes sense, just as it seems efficient to have Romuald check the nets on his own. But later I regret not having insisted on supervising these tasks more closely. Once the trapline is set up in its new place, we return to the camp for an afternoon nap.

The cooking is a problem, and Ange and I are working at cross-purposes. Cooking for us was in the guides' job description, but the only thing Romuald seems to know how to cook is fou-fou and a soup of the small bony fishes that our nets seem to catch a lot of in the places he has chosen for them. Old Charles can't cook anything at all. Ange tries to encourage Lise to take over the cooking. After all, if I'm the scientific director and Ange is the administrative director, what is Lise's role? Lise seems to accept the cooking duties without complaint, even with Ange constantly criticizing and correcting. ("Next time you make spaghetti with sardines, don't waste our cooking oil on the spaghetti, use the oil from the sardine can. See? This is what's in a sardine can—few sardines, lots of oil.") I am not pleased with this arrangement. Lise was not brought here at enormous effort and expense to work as a cook. She is here to train as a scientist. I don't want her pushed into the role of cook just because she's a woman. I take her aside and tell her that her cooking is appreciated, but that I would like to see the energy she puts into cooking redirected into our scientific work. She is a scientist, I tell her, not a cook. But unless Lise cooks, we end up living on fou-fou and fish skeleton soup. And since I can't bring myself to eat the fish skeleton soup, I am living on nothing but fou-fou.

Although it is not actually raining the following day, the morning is too overcast for taking good photographs, which is a pity because the guides have arrived with some interesting specimens from the village. The villagers have been tremendously helpful catching any reptiles and amphibians they come across in the course of their day, and making sure the specimens reach us in our hidden camp by sending them to Romuald's house in the village, but it is terribly difficult to get collecting data to enter in the catalogue. People don't know that in addition to the specimen I need information: Where was it caught? How? At what time of day? In what kind of weather? Often it is hopeless. Romuald receives a dead snake in a bag from one of his wives, who was brought it while Romuald was out by a child sent by the sister of a woman whose husband came home with it after checking all the fishnets that he has set up in many different places . . .

So I am very pleased when Romuald brings me a small viper, dead, in a muddy plastic bag, to get the detailed answer that the village children saw it swimming in the water at the landing spot this morning, and killed it by bashing it on the head with a pirogue paddle. "The children?" I say, alarmed, "tell them to be careful—this is a venomous snake—very dangerous." I dread the possibility of a child getting bitten by a venomous snake because of me. I can't see the snake well through the muddy plastic, but it is clearly a viper, and it is small. A glance at its head scales rules out *Causus*, the night adder. I suppose it is probably *Atheris*, a genus of smallish arboreal vipers. Strange, though, that it was found in the water. I hand it over to Lise and Ange to identify using the key. That will be good practice. Lise has had much more practice keying out snakes than Ange, and I have set this up on purpose, so that for once Lise will feel a bit of confidence while working with the older and more experienced Ange. It takes them a very long time, and three times they call me over for help, and turn out to have completely misunderstood something fundamental and headed off in entirely the wrong direction. So I am not terribly surprised when they announce that they have finished, and identify the snake as *Cerastes*. "No, no," I head over to see where they've gone wrong this time, "*Cerastes* is a sand viper found in the Sahara Desert. Their range doesn't come anywhere close to the Congo." But before I can sit down with them and work back through the steps to figure out where they went off course, we are interrupted.

I don't immediately recognize the Chief, dressed for work in the forest, in tattered clothing and carrying a machete. Ange asks him politely how he found his way to our camp, but I know Ange well enough that I can tell he is angry at the intrusion. The Chief says vaguely that one of our guides (I know Old Charles is the culprit) has a distinctive machete cut when he clears a trail, and it is this that allowed the Chief to identify the trail leading to our camp. It is starting to rain, so we have no choice but to invite him into the house. His timing is inconvenient. Not only am I dying of curiosity over the viper, but we have several other specimens waiting to be processed, and I will need to make the most of what little light is left today to photograph some specimens that can't wait for tomorrow. Ange politely tells the Chief that we are very busy. It takes quite a lot of talking before the Chief gets to the point of his visit. Today is the day that the second team of guides should have started; that is what he has come to complain about. We had all forgotten about that suggestion at the first meeting of having three teams of guides instead of the same two throughout. I said at the time that the problem would be training each new pair from scratch. The only possible solution was to have all six guides work at once for the first 2 days. Only Romuald and Old Charles were ever assigned to us and we assumed the notion of six guides had been abandoned. But the Chief himself was supposed to have been in the second team, and now he is demanding again that we hire six guides in series instead of keeping the same two. Ange discusses the problem with him for a long time. Eventually Ange manages somehow to convince the Chief that they are both in agreement that we should stick with Romuald and Old Charles, and the problem lies with the village committee. They go over and over the same arguments as the rain beats down on the tarpaulin.

Suddenly I notice a small and slippery frog on the ground, disappearing under the bed. I dive after it and Ange tries to help by holding a lighted candle under the bed to help me see. Lise, reclining on my bed, is shouting at Ange that he's going to set the branches on fire, but then she sees the frog down the crack between the bed and the tarpaulin wall, and I catch it. Afraid it will slip free from my grasp, I drop it into a bag along with the handful of earth I grabbed with it. I'm eager to get a proper look at it, but the Chief is showing no intention of leaving anytime soon, and the rain is getting heavier. "Can I lend you a rain jacket, Chief?"—this seems to me like a pretty blatant hint. "I'm afraid the termites have eaten some holes in it but it should still help to keep you dry in this rain." Although he has a good laugh over its chewed-up appearance, he accepts it, but still stays for ages. The solution finally agreed on is that there will be a meeting tomorrow morning to discuss the situation.

"Is there really any reason why I need to be there?" I ask Ange when the Chief is gone. I resent the time wasted and in any case the whole thing will be in Lingala and I'll only understand half of what's going on. Ange is happy to handle it on his own. Lise and Romuald will go with him, but I will stay in the camp. We go back to work on the mystery viper. I work through the key myself, but I too end up with *Cerastes*. Impossible. A real mystery. I am absolutely baffled.

The next morning, Ange and Lise are sleeping in. At 7:45 I shout outside their tents to wake them, reminding them that they have a meeting with the Chief and the village committee at 9:00. The guides arrive with more of the nasty little fishes from the nets as well as a drowned *Grayia* which smells as if it has been dead for some time. I immediately seal it in a plastic bag in the hope of discouraging the swarm of flies it is attracting. Romuald makes the coffee, and then sets off for the meeting along with Lise and Ange. Old Charles is left at the camp with me.

Bracing myself for the stench and the flies, I carefully skin the *Grayia*. As soon as the body is removed and I have checked for stomach contents (none), I give it to Old Charles to get rid of somewhere far from the camp. Soon I have the skin saturated with formalin, rolled up and labeled in a plastic bag, but it takes a while for the flies to dissipate, and the rest of the day to get the smell off my hands. The rest of the work is more pleasant, though I am disappointed when I examine the frog I caught under the bed while the Chief was here and it turns out just to be a *Xenopus,* not another *Hymenochirus*—the rare small bumpy frog that I found a pair of last year. The meeting goes on long enough that I am able to get all the work of preparing and storing specimens out of the way, though I curse Ange's organizing every time I have to search for something in the crammed equipment box. As I work I drop dirty plastic bags, little scraps of muddy toilet paper from wiping the frogs clean, and leftover bits of plastic straws on the ground around the desk. I leave the dirty dissecting instruments on a tray. It is nice to have assistants who will pick up after me.

They are still not back from the meeting when I finish the work. Old Charles occupies himself blocking off the old trail leading to the first site of the pitfall traps, to avoid having accidental intruders finding the camp, washes the accumulated dishes, and cuts wood for the fire. "Cutting wood for the fire" here does not mean bringing back a whole lot of small logs, as I am used to expecting, but rather searching for some time and then cutting a single enormous chunk from a big tree, which will smolder for a week or more. Finally Old Charles lies down on the bench and looks on as I cook a pot of macaroni. Apparently he views this as women's work, though he does step in to rearrange the fire when a log gives way and the pot almost tips over. The result of my efforts is a solid lump of macaroni, which gets even less appetizing as it cools off while we are waiting for Ange, Lise, and Romuald to come back from the much-longer-than-expected meeting. Oh well, at least my efforts will ensure that nobody prepares fou-fou and fish skeleton soup for lunch, and I will get a filling meal. I give in and tidy up the debris around the workspace myself. There is a bit of sunlight filtering through the trees, so I hang out some washed but still damp underpants in the hope of getting them a little drier. Not having clothespins I hang them from the line looped through the leg. They look so exactly like a group of bats roosting that I laugh. I point it out to Old Charles since there is nobody else here to share the joke with. "Bats?" he doesn't get it, but it starts a train of thought. "We get bats here, you know.

They're edible." I find it hard to believe there's much meat on a bat, but Old Charles indicates his chest. I suppose it makes sense they'd have good-sized pectoral muscles, since, like birds, they have wings.

"They must be pretty hard to catch."

"No, no, not at all. They all roost together in a hollow tree. All you have to do is make a fire to smoke them out and put up a net, and the whole lot fly into it. You can get 100cfa each for them. Then they sell them in Brazzaville." I am distressed by the thought that anyone would kill off a whole population of bats—probably all the bats for miles around—for a lousy 100cfa (about 25¢) each. I'd pay a hundred times that to have them left alone. And this is in the middle of a wildlife reserve. I feel suddenly sad and discouraged about the future of the whole forest.

"How much do they get sold for in Brazzaville?" I ask. Old Charles is not sure but speculates that it might be as much as 500cfa per bat.

We get talking about the forest, mostly in French but with a bit of Lingala mixed in. Old Charles knows the forest around here very well. I ask him about Lac Télé. Lac Télé is the lake that gives the wildlife reserve its name, famous for being the home of Mokele-Mbembe, the Congolese equivalent of the Loch Ness monster. It has been the destination of many well-funded foreign expeditions hoping to find the monster, none so far successful. Old Charles has been a guide on several of these expeditions. I wonder if those foreigners knew that "Mokele-Mbembe" translates roughly from Lingala into "a story that isn't true" (or so Delphin had told me). The village of Boha, not at all far from Impongui, controls access to Lac Télé, and I suspect that those expeditions in search of the monster are a major contribution to the economy of Boha. Old Charles tells me that it is a 3-day hike from Boha to Lac Télé. The people of Boha had once proposed building a road, but this idea had been vetoed. Old Charles assures me he can take me to Lac Télé if I want to go. I'm tempted. It doesn't seem right to spend a month in the Lac Télé Reserve, especially so close to Lac Télé itself, and never go and see it. But I can imagine that the people of Boha, accustomed to foreign expeditions, would expect to be paid a lot more than two tarpaulins for access to the lake—certainly more than I can afford. Old Charles describes Lac Télé with awe. It is more than a kilometer across—so big that there are even waves. I think of my apartment in Toronto, overlooking Lake Ontario, and doubt that I would be much impressed with Lac Télé. It's just as well to convince myself that I don't want something that I can't have anyway.

Old Charles tells me about other strange places he's been to in the forest. Places with huge trees, much bigger than the ones here. He complains about an employer on one of the Lac Télé trips who made him work all day with only a 15-minute break and then gave him half a tin of sardines for dinner. I agree, with sympathy, that this is totally unreasonable. I find myself telling him about Delphin, how he was arrested by Kabila's corrupt regime, in the DRC, the other Congo, and how he escaped. Old Charles shakes his head in sympathetic indignation. "They're villains there in the DRC—a bunch of villains." He tells me more stories. Eventually he pauses as though something has suddenly occurred to him. "It's strange, isn't it?" he says, looking at me oddly, "I mean, that you can actually have a conversation—a normal conversation—with a white person." He ponders this. "Well," he eventually concedes, "I suppose, if you think about it, they are people, just like anyone else."

More than 3 hours go by before the others return from the meeting. Ange launches excitedly into an account so detailed that I fear it will take as long as the meeting itself, and I try to get him to summarize it. The Chief had started the meeting with the village committee an hour ahead of the appointed time and in somebody's house rather than in the presence of the Notable, getting people all stirred up and indignant long before 9:00, and automatically making an enemy of the Notable by this clumsy effort to hold a meeting behind his back. Ange recounts the entire dialogue as it took place—with the Chief and the committee on their own, with the Notable on his own—and relates the progress of the official meeting, when he eventually got everyone together in the presence of the Notable to argue about whether we could keep the same two guides for the whole month or whether we should be forced to accept a new pair every 10 days. It sounds as if it was all quite dramatic, and I shudder when I hear that Ange threatened that we would pack up and leave immediately if we didn't get our way. Anyway, thanks to the intervention of the Notable, and Ange's eloquence in turning the village committee against the Chief, everything turned out well in the end, and we can keep Romuald and Old Charles. But the thing that pleases me the most is that they caught a tree snake, our second *Psammophis,* on the way back along the trail. Apparently Lise was the one who spotted it, but it was Romuald of course who knocked it out of the tree with his machete, and Lise who immediately recognized it correctly as *Psammophis.*

One evening, the guides return from the village bringing the usual plastic bags of toads and skinks, but also the exciting news that a sitatunga, an endangered African mammal bearing some resemblance to a deer, had wandered into the village and had been killed. As the meat was being divided up, the Notable had said, "Don't forget our visitors," so a chunk the size of a football has been sent with Romuald, dripping blood from its manioc leaf wrapping. Ange puts it on the smoked-fish rack above the fire, which Romuald built, with a piece of cardboard over it. A week later it is a shriveled, blackened lump the size of a small fist, and Ange seems very satisfied with this result. Eventually he reconstitutes it by boiling it and makes a stew of it. It tastes okay, but I suspect that it's one of those things that only tastes okay because you're in the field and hungry.

After a lot of interruptions I finally turn my attention to the mystery viper, taking advantage of free time when Lise and Ange are both in their tents having afternoon naps, to work through the key on my own, quickly, and without explaining. Sure enough, the key leads to *Cerastes*. When I read the details of scale counts that define the *genus Cerastes*, the specimen still fits, but it doesn't agree with the description of any described *species* of *Cerastes*. It makes absolutely no sense. *Cerastes* are desert vipers that bury themselves in the sand, thousands of kilometers from here. This viper was found swimming in the flooded forest of northern Congo. I admit defeat. I can't wait to get back to e-mail in Brazzaville and be able to send a picture to Jean-Philippe.

One rare sunny morning enough light is filtering through the trees to allow good photographs to be taken. I am taking advantage of it to get some good pictures of two small egg-eating snakes, *Dasypeltis*, and now have them spread out on a tray for measuring when Ange calls out that we have a visitor. I hurry outside and am surprised to find the Notable, holding three enormous plantains as a present. We sit him down on the bench. He seems interested in seeing the camp for the first time and asks politely about our work. Wanting to show him how we are getting along, I bring out the plastic tray with the snakes spread out on it. I bend over to show it to him and realize a split second too late that any normal person, presented by his host with a cafeteria tray would be expecting—I don't know—canapés or something? Not snakes, anyway. The Notable recoils from them with a gasp. Ange gives me a reproachful look.

This time I don't manage to follow the Notable's Lingala at all. I will have to get Ange to explain it to me later. As for Lise, I can't figure out how much Lingala she knows. I've never heard her speak a word of it, but she appears to understand when people speak to her. Is she shy? Is she bluffing? At any rate she doesn't say a word during the Notable's visit. When he leaves, we thank him for the plantains and give him a tin of sardines as a present before Ange walks him back to the village.

Lise retires to her tent after they are gone, so I have to wait for

Ange's return for a translation. The Notable came to find us because something came to him in the night. It is something about our project, and something good that he wants to share with us. But he can only talk about it in the presence of his ancestors. We are therefore to come to his house tomorrow for a private meeting during which he will explain it all.

We leave early the next morning to meet with the Notable. He is sweeping leaves from the ground around his house when we arrive. Four small stools are already set up just outside the door of the hut, one for him facing three arranged in a semicircle for us. I take the middle stool in the semicircle with Ange on my left and Lise on my right. The Notable takes his place. Polite greetings are exchanged. Ange quietly places a 1,000cfa note on the ground in front of the Notable. He had asked me for this earlier, telling me that this token sum was an expected gesture of respect for an audience with the Notable. A slight breeze riffles the air, and Ange tactfully picks up the note again and stuffs it discreetly under the Notable's sandal to prevent it from blowing away.

The Notable begins, placing on the ground between us a clear plastic bottle that must once have contained some kind of cosmetic, half filled with a translucent, faintly yellowish liquid with a soapy look to it. I have no trouble with the Lingala this time. I pick up some key words in his first sentence: "Kisi . . . nyoka . . . makasi . . . mobimba" (medicine, snake, strong, healthy/whole/cured). I realize with dismay that this great insight the Notable wants to impart is some local potion for curing snakebite. The Notable talks for a long time. There is a man in the village of Boha who has developed a cure for snakebite. The man makes and sells his product, but won't divulge the recipe. But the Notable is the Notable of Boha as well, and because of his position of authority has access to the recipe. He has used the recipe to make a big batch of the stuff—enough for the whole village of Impongui. This is not magic, he emphasizes, this is traditional medicine. He points out that our work puts us in particular danger from snakes. He understands that we have our own medicine for snakebite, but if it were to run out, or if we ever needed it in the future it might be useful for us to have. I keep expecting him to hand over the bottle, but he never does. If he were to give it to us now it would drive the snakes away, which of course is the last thing we want to do during our study (this detail I have to get Ange to explain to me later). The Notable doesn't want just to give us a bottle of the concoction, he wants to teach us how to make it using the secret recipe. He explains how it should be administered. A snakebite victim should drink some of it, and some should be poured on the bite wound. If the person is really close to death drops of it can be poured into his eyes.

Then he launches into a long series of case histories—a man from Boha was bitten last year and looked as if he was going to die for sure, but when he took this medicine it saved him; once a man from far away, almost dead from a snakebite was brought to Boha for the treatment and was completely cured within a day . . . These accounts go on and on. To my left, Ange is listening intently, bowing his head every couple of minutes to say, "Merci mingi, Notable." To my right, Lise heaves a great sigh of boredom, staring into space and swinging her baseball cap between her knees. Every time I think he's finished, and say a respectful, "Merci mingi," the Notable goes on to yet another testimonial. When he finally finishes we thank him effusively, and Ange has the sense to say that he needs time to discuss the matter with his colleagues.

That evening, dinner over and the guides gone home for the night, we sit outside bundled against the mosquitoes in hot clothes. By the light of a candle melted onto a tree stump, Ange explains some more details of the meeting with the Notable that I had missed. The whole enterprise is starting to sound a lot more complicated than it had originally. Apparently the active ingredient in the concoction is the leaf of a plant which grows only in Epena. Somebody would have to be sent to

Epena to collect some, a long and tiring trip in an ordinary paddled pirogue, not like the motorized one from WCS that brought us here. Then the ingredient that serves as a "base" for the mixture is something Ange refers to as "parfum." "Parfum?" (perfume?) I ask doubtfully.

"Yes, I think it's some kind of eau de toilette for putting on babies." The parfum will have to be bought somewhere. I give Lise and Ange an hour to take a nap, telling them that we will then have a meeting to decide on a plan of action.

I speak first when we reconvene. "It seems to me there are several issues here. I'm afraid that all my reservations may end up being a moot point. The bottom line is that the Notable has been tremendously good to us ever since our arrival. He's been supportive of our work, he gave us a secret location for our camp, and he stood up for us against the Chief and the village committee when there was that problem with the business of the six guides. His offer to teach us how to make this snakebite cure is one of genuine thoughtfulness and generosity. We really can't afford to offend him in any way because the success of our survey depends very much on his continued goodwill."

That said, I have some concerns. This trip to Epena to collect plants, this parfum, the time spent learning how to make it—how much is it all going to end up costing in terms of time and money? We must find that out right away.

But the thing that bothers me the most is that I am a herpetologist, a specialist in venomous snakes. I don't simply believe that these "traditional cures" for snakebite are ineffective; I consider them actively misleading and thus potentially harmful. I don't want to be seen to show any support whatsoever for this "medicine." I don't want the Notable to be able tell the next person he tries to convince of the efficacy of the stuff that a mondele snake expert came from Canada to learn how to make it.

Ange speaks next. He entirely agrees that we can't afford to alienate the Notable. He will speak with the Notable again to find out how much money the ingredients are going to cost. As for my final concern, Ange suggests that from here on I have nothing to do with this venture. Only he and Lise will go and learn how to make it. I will stay out of it. It is Lise's turn to speak next, but she has nothing to add.

So Ange starts looking into the logistics. The trip to Epena is easily taken care of. We will send Old Charles, who is already being paid by us anyway. Conveniently, since he is a Sage, he knows what the plant looks like. The "parfum" will cost 2,000cfa, and the Notable will send someone to buy it, wherever one buys eau de toilette in the Likouala flooded forest.

The WCS pirogue that brought us from Epena had an outboard motor, but for Old Charles, paddling his pirogue, it will be a round trip of at least 2 days. Ange gives him his rations of tins of sardines and a bit of money to buy manioc, and we send him on his way. "Bring back five of the plants," Ange tells him, "roots and everything."

chapter 15

making
herpetologists

Time is going by, and I have to come up with thesis projects for Lise and for Ange. It is quite a challenge to come up with a project which will be an original contribution to science, and which they can carry out without access to a museum collection, or even a library, while at the same time making the most of the resource they do have: access at their doorstep to field sites never before studied by herpetologists. The project I had planned for Lise, catching, measuring, and releasing *Grayia* from the nets, is clearly not going to work out. She's afraid of the water and she's afraid of live snakes. But she does seem to quite like identifying dead snakes using the key. In fact it's the only thing she has shown any interest in at all. One afternoon Lise is sitting beside me at the desk counting scales on some formalin-fixed *Grayia*. We have found one specimen that the key tells us is *Grayia ornata,* but which doesn't have the usual coloring on the underside of the tail. I tell Lise about the strange reddish *Grayia ornata* I caught last year. We get into a long discussion about the variation in number of supralabial scales in the different species. There are four recognized species in the genus and all four of them can be found in the Congo. I tell her that it is a genus in need of revision—needs to be properly studied by someone. Lise looks up from the specimen in front of her and grins at me. "I guess I'm going to have to learn to swim."

At that moment we are interrupted by an angry shout from Ange. Apparently Lise had put some manioc roots in a pot of water on the fire before starting in on the *Grayia*. She was so completely absorbed counting the scales of the dead snakes that the manioc roots have boiled dry and burned into the bottom of the pot. Ange is furious. I am delighted. Perhaps I'll make a herpetologist of her yet. "Can we start the swimming lessons on Monday?" she asks.

"No," I say firmly, "we can start them this afternoon."

An hour later I shout at Lise's tent that I am going in the water and she can join me when she likes. Will she actually go through with it? I usually swim naked, but I've noticed that Lise is more modest than I am and uncomfortable being seen undressed even by another woman, so for the occasion of her swimming lesson I have sacrificed a bra and underpants from my dirty laundry to getting wet, as a gesture toward decency. I dive in off the far end of the pirogue as usual, and in due course Lise appears. She is wearing a white plastic shower cap patterned with little green flowers, a camisole, and a pair of knee-length support briefs that my grandmother would have dismissed as dowdy. But all this is concealed by a modest and voluminous cotton wrap, which she removes just as she steps into the shallow water.

The position of the pirogue is very convenient for a swimming lesson. The bow is pulled up on shore, and the stern is in water more than

2 meters deep, so there is a gradual slope, the water getting gradually deeper, as you walk the length of the pirogue, and walking the length of the pirogue is exactly what I intend Lise to do. Standing knee-deep near the shore she exclaims with surprise at how cold the water is. I wade out to her, reach out and take her by the hand. The right hand. Her left hand rests along the gunwale of the pirogue as I gradually lead her into deeper water. I am walking backward and she can see how deep the water ahead of her is by looking at me. The only inconvenience of walking the length of the pirogue is that the shallow water is the dishwashing spot, with a slick of grease, and a lot of prickly bushes against the side of the pirogue have to be walked through. This is why I just dive off the far end. At her second step—to above the knee depth—Lise gives a great shriek of combined delight and terror. She continues to shriek every step of the way, but absolutely refuses every time I suggest ending the lesson for the day. Holding her hand, I lead her to the deep end. At the point where it gets too deep to stand I tell her that it is too deep to stand, but she steps forward anyway, into the void, and sinks like a stone; it takes all my strength to drag her out and push her back into shallower water. She surfaces with a delighted shriek. Back in chest-deep water I get her to put her face in the water. "Take a big breath, then put your face under water and blow it out through your nose. Keep your mouth closed." After some difficulty coordinating the deep breath with the submerging she gets it right.

"Did I do it right that time?"

"Absolutely. Okay, you've done it once. Now you're going to do it five times."

(Shriek!) But she does it five times. Next I make her do the same thing with her whole head under water. She doesn't seem to mind submerging her hairdo, which will get soaked in spite of the hairnet. I make use of the edge of the pirogue to teach her a flutter kick. She has great difficulty staying horizontal rather than sinking into a vertical position, and she's clinging to the gunwale of the pirogue in a very awkward way that quickly tires out her arms. I work on getting her to relax her arms, and I gently support her outstretched body from underneath to try to keep her horizontal. I feel sure she must have had enough of this by now, but she insists on continuing. A few steps away from the pirogue I show her what to do with her arms—a sort of head-above-water breast stroke. The final step is flutter kick and breast stroke together. I support her gently from underneath as she thrashes about, but whenever I take my hands away she sinks. I am the one who finally calls a stop to the lesson. We are both shivering and covered in goose bumps.

"Do you think I'll really learn to swim?"

"You bet. We've still got 2 weeks. You'll be swimming like a *Grayia* in no time."

Ange seems slightly sullen when we reemerge from the swimming lesson wrapped in towels, spirits buoyed up by the experience. I realize that he must be feeling left out. From all that screaming and laughing it must have been clear that we were having a lot of fun, but a gentlemanly fear of seeing us undressed has prevented him from joining in. I think I know just how he feels. I've spent much of my professional life being the only woman in otherwise all-male groups. But it's been a bad day for him in other ways as well. He is still fuming over the ruined pot, which is going to impart a flavor of burned manioc to everything cooked in it from here on. Also his watch, which is clearly labeled "water-resistant," has stopped working after getting wet as he tried to scrub the pot clean.

Perhaps I could have chosen a better moment to explain the project I have in mind for him, but I am so delighted with the idea I have come up with that I don't think of delaying. When I call to him from the bench, he has taken the back off his watch and is trying to repair it with the end of a burning stick. He obediently puts it down and comes over to join me, but his reaction is not the wild delight I had hoped for when I announce that I want him to specialize in toads (genus *Bufo*). *Bufo* is the genus to which most of the amphibians we think of as "toads" belong. Large, warty, and, well let's say, not conventionally beautiful, they are found all over the world, and are often very common. I think studying the *Bufo* of the Congo could be a great project. There are only about half a dozen species to learn to tell apart, and usually, wherever you do herpetological collecting, *Bufo*s are something you are sure of finding. Common though they may be, they are not much studied, and I think finding out more about them could have implications for conservation. I tell him about the *Bufo regularis*, a savannah species, that I found mixed in with forest *Bufo camerunensis* in the forest of northwest Congo in 1997. Are these toads invading along logging roads? Are they a sign of environmental degradation? Ange clearly knows absolutely nothing about *Bufo*s. I tell him about *Bufo marinus*, the cane toad, introduced into Australia from Central America, which has become an environmental disaster, destroying native species. I tell him about their poisonous skin secretions, which kill many animals that try to eat them by causing their heart rate to drop, and I tell him that people in some places will even lick the skin of *Bufo*s in the hope of having a psychedelic experience. I tell Ange that if he could gather data on what species of *Bufo* are found in different regions of the Congo, he would be the first to do it, and the results might show some interesting and revealing patterns. And the project is feasible. There are already data from my own work near Pointe-Noire and in the northwest. There will be our results from the Likouala, this project and my work last year as a starting point. He can survey the area around Brazzaville and take advantage of the field station operated by the biodiversity study group in the Mayombe forest of the south.

But Ange looks disappointed, and his tone is whiny. "You have to understand," he begins, "that in this country we have no money for research. How would I find the funds to do fieldwork in the Cuvette region? And how am I supposed to work when I don't have my own laptop computer?"

"It seems to me that you've got an awful lot of work ahead of you before you get around to worrying about the Cuvette region. I know the Congo is an incredibly frustrating place to be a scientist, but you can either sit around and never do anything because the conditions aren't ideal, or you can get to work and do the most that you possibly can, even if it takes a lot of energy and determination. It's up to you which approach you choose. Now what about that forest around your dormitory at the university to start with? Has anyone ever studied the toads there?"

The forest around the Marien-Ngouabi University is a sort of herpetologist's adventure playground. There was once an antivenom institute on the grounds, with an extensive collection of live snakes. During the civil war of 1997 the building was destroyed and the snakes escaped. Many were killed and eaten by people driven to desperate measures by hunger, but many more survived, so that a lot of interesting species of venomous snakes still live and breed in that small forest.

I am disappointed in Ange. I had expected a more enthusiastic response. I don't sleep much that night, and every time I step outside the house I see a light on in Ange's tent. Taking on this project, I realize, will be a major life decision for him. He is awake the whole night thinking it over.

I am equally disappointed in Lise's reaction when I explain to her over breakfast the project I have planned for her. Lise has become very good at identifying snakes using the identification key in the book, but we have already come across occasional places where the key doesn't work. I would like to see Lise take the next step beyond using a key. I would like her to learn to question rather than passively accept the validity of published keys. I would like her to invent a key of her own. Lise and I had examined a snake which I recognized as *Psammophis phillipsii*. But when Lise followed the key in the book it led her to the wrong answer. We quickly figured out that the problem was that the key requires that *P. phillipsii* has an undivided anal plate, whereas the anal plate of our specimen was divided. Clearly this is simply a matter of individual variation. We have discovered that *P. phillipsii* may have an anal plate that is either divided or undivided. Lise's project will be to devise a new key to the genus *Psammophis* that doesn't use the condition of the anal plate as a character. All the information about the condition of other scales for all species of *Psammophis* is right there in the book that she is so attached to. It would simply be a logical puzzle, and with only eight species in the genus, it would be a very feasible project for a first attempt to create an original key. This is surely just the sort of work that Lise will enjoy and do well.

But as I finish my explanation Lise is staring straight ahead and looking absolutely furious. What I had not counted on is that Lise, though bright, is lazy—that she needs to be pushed to try anything new, and that she doesn't like things that are difficult. Ange tries to intervene. "You have to understand, Katherine," he begins, "that Lise is only doing an undergraduate honors project. We had thought she could just present the results of our work here as her project." Now I am getting angry. He is not doing Lise any favors by letting her slack off, receiving a degree that is meaningless because she has been allowed to get credit for a thesis just by tagging along on an expedition. An honors thesis should be an independent and original piece of work. Lise is perfectly capable of carrying out this project. What she needs is to be pushed to make an effort—to do the best she is capable of. And she's going to get a serious shove in that direction from me.

In the end they both rise to the challenge. Lise spends several hours in her tent. I assume she is sulking, but when she emerges, she calls me politely to the work table and shows me a carefully prepared table of species and scale characters. It's wrong in all sorts of ways, but when I explain these, she doesn't give up on the spot, but goes back to make another attempt.

As for Ange, he takes on the unglamorous *Bufo*s with energy, enthusiasm, and even affection. I try to assign to him any work that comes up involving toads. *Bufo regularis* is very common in the village and we end up with a lot of them. He is kept very busy formalin-fixing new speci-mens and frequently unwrapping ones collected earlier, to organize them and to ensure that the specimens are in good condition. He gets used to injecting their sizable abdomens full of formalin to prevent them from rotting inside, and to the habit *Bufo* have of copiously emp-tying their bladders, either when captured or sometimes while being fixed. I occasionally overhear him talking to the toads as he processes them. "I'm tucking you in now," he says wrapping a formalin-injected toad in cheesecloth, "so no going pee-pee in the bed, okay?" When we start to run out of cheesecloth, he sacrifices two of his own pairs of un-derpants for cutting up to wrap specimens—one pair purple polyester and not very good for absorbing the formalin, the other pair red cotton knit printed all over with "I love you." Ange grins, thinking of the laugh the staff at the Smithsonian are going to have when they unpack them. "Lots of clothes," he assures the toads. "Don't worry, little ones."

Old Charles returns in the evening 2 days after his departure for Epena. "So how did the trip go?" I ask him.

"Oh, fine, it went well."

"So you got the plants okay?"

"Well, not exactly . . ." Apparently the flood water in Epena is even higher than it was when we left, and it was impossible to find the plants. He has returned with no plants at all.

After the guides have gone home, Ange and I spend the evening fixing toads. Ange is sullen as he works, which is so out of character that it surprises me. We are going through toads collected last week, some of which are a bit revolting, it's true. Some that were wrapped in toilet paper instead of cheesecloth have mildew on them and need to be scrubbed clean and rewrapped. Others, fixed with their mouths propped open with straws, have large worms which seem to have died as the toads were fixed, and been fixed themselves while crawling out of the mouths of the dead toads. But that is not the problem. Eventually I realize that Ange must be worried about the failure of the expedition to get the plants. I know how Ange admires the Notable, and how he would hate to feel he was letting him down.

"Look," I point out, "the thing about the plants from Epena? It may actually be the best possible solution to our problem. We did everything we possibly could to do what the Notable suggested, and the reason we didn't get the plants was clearly beyond our control. And now we're off the hook and we have one less thing to worry about." And indeed, no more is said about learning to make snake medicine, but just before we leave, the Notable gives us a big supply in a 1.5-liter mineral-water bottle.

It is Sunday again, and saka-saka lunch has become a weekly treat. We sit in chairs in the shade outside Romuald's house while his wives put the final touches on the meal. Romuald hands us two dead snakes in a bag that someone has dropped off. "*Dasypeltis* and *Hapsidophrys*," Lise declares confidently, snatching the bag from me.

"Not bad," I say, with a smile, after examining the contents of the bag myself. Across the clearing from us, Perséphone notices me and bursts into tears, running back inside her house howling. Soon we are seated again around Romuald's table. I am happily tucking into a bowl of saka-saka and a lump of fou-fou, when three older children come mischievously into the house, one of them carrying a trusting Perséphone on her hip. The cruel older siblings have a great laugh at poor Perséphone's terrified screams at finding herself suddenly only a few feet away from me. Sitting outside again after the meal, I am bored by the men's conversation. Only Romuald, sensibly using the time to tie fishhooks at regular intervals along a long string, is not participating. Lise is bored too and demanding a swimming lesson. It is a beautiful day and perfect weather for it, so I use this as an excuse to have Old Charles take the two of us back to the camp, leaving the men to take their time.

We have almost reached the trail when a woman sitting on the ground weaving a basket says in response to our greeting that a snake has been seen in a house nearby. "When was it seen?"

"Not long ago." It doesn't sound promising. I am drowsy from the meal, the sun is hot, and I am looking forward to a refreshing swim, but I have to follow this up. Old Charles knows the house she means and leads us to it. I hope the house will be a small one. I also hope that it will be one of the few brick houses rather than the sticks and mud kind, which would be hopelessly full of escape holes. When we arrive it looks as if I may be in luck. The "house" is actually a small brick outbuilding, not much bigger than a spacious wardrobe. On the downside, the village children have caught up with us on the way over, and I am not having much success trying to impose even minimum control over the swarm. There is no furniture in the building, but the whole floor is knee-deep in prickly dried palm fronds of the kind used for thatched roofs. The only thing to do is going to be to take out all of them. I have my snake hook with me to use instead of reaching into the thatch with my hand, but I am regretting wearing sandals instead of boots. It is a one-person job. The only entrance to the building is also the only source of light, and as I systematically turn over and drag out each frond, I am constantly having to shoo away the curious crowd blocking the doorway and plunging me into darkness. After 45 minutes I am soaked with sweat and thickly coated with dust. My hands and feet are scratched and bleeding, and I have moved all the thatch outside, revealing no snake but a floor pitted with many deep escape holes leading who knows where. I admit defeat, and the crowd disperses disappointed.

When we finally arrive back at the camp, I am longing to get into the water. The only problem is that we are almost out of rainwater, and

Romuald, who forgot to bring a supply this morning, is expected to arrive by pirogue at any moment with a full jug. Heaven forbid that he should arrive while Lise and I are having our swimming lesson, and see us undressed. But I am hot and dirty, the hours of sunlight will not last much longer, and I say to hell with it, and even Lise agrees.

Lise shrieks just as much during the second lesson as the first. This time we start by reviewing the things we did last time—arms, legs, head under water, but then Lise tells me that what she really wants to learn is to jump in. Okay. I have her stand in the pirogue at a place where the water is about 3 feet deep. I stand in the water myself to show her the depth, and tell her to jump off the pirogue as she would if there were no water there, and the ground was at a 3-foot drop. I tell her to hold her nose as she jumps and not to panic if her head goes under water. The water is shallow enough that all she has to do is stand up. But she raises her arms above her head, hands together and extended. "What are you doing?" I ask in alarm.

"I want to jump in the way you do."

"What, dive in head first? You can't do that in shallow water like this—you'll break your neck."

"Then I'll do it off the end into the deep water," she sounds quite determined.

"Into the deep water? But what will you do when you land? You'll sink! You've got to learn how to swim before you can go jumping into deep water!" Where has all this reckless courage come from? She eventually resigns herself to jumping into water she can stand up in, and then we do some more work on moving arms and legs together in coordination while I support her to prevent her from sinking.

"I think I just need to practice," she says when we finally call it quits for the day.

"I think so too. One more lesson and I think you'll get it."

It is a good thing that we didn't wait for Romuald. He has still not arrived and minutes after we get out of the water torrential rain begins.

Ange is back from the village now. He and Lise retreat to their tents and I to the house. It will be dark soon. We need that water, and Romuald is unlikely to go out in this rain. It takes me a good 15 minutes to realize the absurdity of the situation—waiting for a delivery of rainwater that is delayed by a rainstorm. I dart outside and set out all the pots and bowls with their lids off. The rain doesn't last much longer. We end up with enough rain collected to boil for drinking, but have to use river water to cook the macaroni. Lise doesn't complain. "You watch though," she comments, "he'll probably arrive with the water the moment we start cooking it." And she turns out to be absolutely right.

chapter 16

the
home
stretch

Life in the camp gets harder as the end of the project approaches. Ange does yet another inventory of the food and concludes that we are going to have to ration it carefully if it is going to see us through. We've got into the extravagant habit of preparing two meals a day. From now on there will be no more breakfast unless there happen to be leftovers from the previous night's dinner. "Well, what shall we have for dinner?" Ange asks cheerfully that evening.

"Of all the choices we have? How about escargots, followed by filet mignon, and finishing with crème brulée?"

"I don't know how to prepare any of those things," he says anxiously, not sure that I am joking. We end up having boiled manioc root, a present sent by Uncle Marcel's wife. Everyone watches me take a dubious bite out of my piece. "It's like a cross between a chunk of wood and an overcooked potato," I tell them when they ask.

I suppose I could try to get the guides to figure out some way of making my bed less painful to sleep on, but whenever I consider it, it doesn't seem worth it at this stage. After all, I tell myself, there are only 20 (. . . or 10 . . . or 5) nights left so why bother? Very occasionally though, and probably just from exhaustion, I get a bit of really deep sleep, waking completely disoriented. One night I suppose I must be awake, because I can hear a continuous pulsing shushing sound. The darkness around me is so complete that it makes no difference if my eyes are open or closed. I wonder if a toilet is overflowing somewhere nearby, and start to try to remember where I am. The shushing is overlaid with occasional squeaks and clicks. All I know is that I am very comfortable and barely awake. My mind scrolls through the possibilities: The bed in my Toronto apartment with the left side against the wall? The futon on the floor of the squalid place I shared with two guys in grad school? Am I in a hotel somewhere? It takes what seems like a long time to arrive at the unlikely realization that I am lying on a pile of branches under a tarpaulin in the forest of northern Congo. By some miracle of geometry I have found a comfortable position. I am lying on my side in such a way as to avoid all the lumps left where an accessory branch has been roughly chopped off, as well as the bumps created by the different thicknesses of the branches. I am cushioned by a bunched-up pair of damp cargo pants stuffed under my hip, and my head is resting on my backpack in a way that somehow avoids the corner of the French-English dictionary. I don't dare break the spell by moving, even to check the time by the light on my watch. But something has woken me up. I give the matter some thought and find that I am thirsty. As soon as I realize I'm thirsty I can't think of anything else, and I am going to have to move to grope around under the bed for my water bottle. I resign myself to shifting position, and might as well check my watch after all. But as I turn I am stopped dead by a terrible smell, which I trace to my unwashed armpit. In spite of all that swimming I'm never really clean. Crawling around after the water bottle wakes me up completely. The water has tasted even worse since the day that Lise let the manioc roots burn dry in the pot. Now I need to blow my nose. I grope around unsuccessfully for my handkerchief and almost give in and turn on a flashlight. But does it really matter under these circumstances if I blow my nose on my shirt? Now a cut on my ankle rubbing against a stack of notebooks near the end of the bed is causing a stabbing pain that can't be ignored. And how have I not noticed until now that there is a swarm of mosquitoes around my head? How did they get in? I give up and feel around for my flashlight. I discover that I must have fallen asleep without letting the mosquito net down.

Lise approaches me quietly one morning to ask if I have anything for worms. She has had *Ascaris* intestinal worms before and knows that that is what she has. You feel nauseous at first, she tells me, and then your abdomen becomes distended. I have nothing for worms. How stupid of me, when stocking the first-aid kit, to have made all that effort to bring something like antivenom, which we are so unlikely to need, and neglect treatments for obvious and common things like *Ascaris* worms. I selfishly hope I won't catch them. Ange and Lise have also both come down with a strange skin condition. They have a rash, mainly on their feet and ankles, which is terribly itchy, combined with larger lumps, which are painful. At first they blame the river water which they have been washing with, but I point out that I swim in the river several times a day, and I don't have a rash. Their next guess is that they picked it up from the flood water in Epena. This seems more likely, though it doesn't explain why it has taken so long for symptoms to appear, or how I have escaped it. But whatever the cause, the antibiotic ointment meant for disinfecting cuts and scrapes, smeared all over the itchy area, seems to help. As for the larger bumps, they are a mystery. They seem to be something separate from the rash, since they don't clear up with the antibiotic ointment. I try lancing one on Ange's back with a sterile needle, but no pus comes out. "As soon as we get back to Brazzaville, I'm going straight to my dermatologist," says Lise. We are also running out of Band-Aids. I always go through an enormous number of Band-Aids when I'm in the field, and I packed an enormous number of them in the first-aid kit. But we are three people, not one. I hope there will be enough to see us through.

Perhaps the timing is just coincidental, but it seems that Old Charles started slacking off immediately after the big meeting at which Ange fought so hard to keep the same two guides. It was at about the same time that Romuald got into the habit of bringing Darcel, his 11-year-old son, to work with him, and with Darcel doing little jobs like washing dishes without being asked, Old Charles does even less.

We are down to our last D batteries for the guides' flashlights, and less seriously, out of sugar. Romuald thinks it might be possible to buy these things in Djeke, a larger village than Impongui, half an hour away by pirogue, across the river. So one overcast morning, Ange, Romuald, and Darcel go off on a shopping trip to Djeke, leaving me with Lise and Old Charles. I have some lab work to finish up that I have to do alone, so I tell them to go onto the trail to the camp and crawl around seeing what they can turn up in the leaf litter. When I finish my work an hour later, neither of them has moved. Lise is in her tent, singing, and Old Charles is sitting on the bench gazing into space.

I round them up and set off on the trail. After 15 minutes I tie a piece of flagging tape to a tree and tell Lise that she is to search around the trail from this point back to the camp. I get down on all fours to demonstrate, turning over moss and rotting logs and sifting through dead leaves. I leave her to it and continue another 15 minutes, at which point I mark a starting point for myself. Then Old Charles and I go on for a further 15 minutes, and I tell him to start here and gradually work his way back to my marker. I go back to my marker and start crawling

around. It is raining slightly and I am not finding any reptiles or amphibians, but I am very happily absorbed in the task, encountering
such wonders as a giant millipede wrapped around a clutch of eggs.
Only half an hour goes by before Old Charles arrives, empty-handed,
complaining that it is raining too hard and that we should stop for now.
Now that he mentions it, I notice that it is indeed raining quite heavily,
and I reluctantly head back to the camp with him. Lise is already back at
the camp, drifting listlessly around and poking vaguely at the undergrowth with a long stick. Old Charles goes home for the afternoon, and
when the Djeke group returns bearing sugar and batteries we notice
that when Old Charles left at 11:30 he hadn't even washed the dishes.
Romuald and Darcel end up doing them, and Old Charles only returns
at 5:00 p.m. to be served dinner.

Lise is absolutely livid when she finds out that Old Charles has been
delegating one of his jobs, filling the heavy, plastic jug with our daily
supply of rainwater, to little Anuarite, and telling her that Lise has
asked her to do it.

What really gets me angry is finding out that Old Charles has not
been checking the pitfall traps, but simply reporting that there was
nothing in them. Romuald figures this out by setting up a bent grass or
something that shows if anyone has gone in to the trapline or not. Old
Charles arrives later and later every morning. Ange keeps saying he's
going to have it out with him but he never does. Why does Romuald tolerate it? It is Ange who finds out the answer to that question. Old
Charles is the uncle of one of Romuald's wives, so Romuald can't afford
to risk making an enemy of Old Charles.

With only a few days left, I decide to move the pitfall traps one last
time. This time I want the trapline set up in the forest near the camp,
parallel to the shoreline. Romuald and Darcel arrive at 8:30 a.m. by
pirogue, with all the buckets and the mesh fence. Old Charles doesn't
show up until 10:00, and when he does, the two guides finally have a
screaming row. I can't follow it except that Romuald is complaining that

Old Charles isn't doing his share of the work, and something is being said about Darcel. Poor Darcel looks frightened. Ange intervenes, trying to restore peace. The explanation I eventually get is that the guides had agreed to meet at 7:00 a.m. to take down the pitfall traps, and then proceed to the camp. But Old Charles never showed up, and Romuald had to do it himself. It's a two-person job and he wouldn't have been able to do it without the help of Darcel. Darcel shouldn't be doing the work of the second guide, which is what Old Charles is being paid to do. Old Charles's excuse is that he is in terrible pain—all up the back of his leg and his lower back. "Terrible, terrible pain," he insists. He hardly slept last night. Ange steps in. I am so glad that disciplining the guides is not one of my responsibilities. It is completely unacceptable that Darcel should be doing Old Charles's work. If Old Charles was too sick to do the pitfall traps it was his responsibility to let Romuald know, or to send somebody in his place. We only have a short time left. Romuald has been doing most of the cooking because Old Charles doesn't know how, but at the very least Old Charles will never again leave the camp without first washing the dishes. Then Ange passes Old Charles over to me to give him something for the agonizing pain.

"Do you want something very strong, or very, very strong?" I ask him, taking out the Tylenol and Extra-Strength Tylenol.

"Very, very, *very* strong! I'm in terrible, *terrible* pain!"

The project is almost over, and it is probably not worth making an issue of it at this stage, but it infuriates me when Old Charles shows up at dinnertime, after an afternoon off, and expects to be served dinner. Dinner is to be spaghetti and Ange suggests that Lise prepare it. Lise is feeling so miserable from her assorted ailments that she doesn't want to eat and has retreated to her tent. I absolutely refuse to have Lise cook for a guide whose job it is to do such work. Old Charles is going to do it, I announce. Ange and Old Charles simultaneously protest that Old Charles doesn't know how to cook. "That's okay," I tell him, "I'll tell you what to do." I set him to work step by laborious step. It is agonizing to watch him fill the pot with water, spilling precious rainwater on the ground and letting ash get into the boiling water as he struggles with the piece of cardboard we use as a potholder. When he starts trying to get the plastic packages of spaghetti open, pulling at them in such a way that they look likely to tear open suddenly and send dry spaghetti flying, Ange can't stand it any more, but I give him a look that firmly forbids him to intervene. I do make the concession of stepping in after the pasta has been boiling for 10 minutes to taste a strand to see if it is done. I tell Old Charles to take the pot off the fire and drain the water out of it. He drags the pot over to the place where we dump empty sardine tins and torn specimen bags, a place thickly covered with swarming ants, and tilts the pot, using the lid to keep the spaghetti in.

"Stop!" shouts Ange, "you're about to . . ." but it is too late. A potful of spaghetti lands among the ants and garbage. More than three quarters of our carefully rationed spaghetti has been dumped. There is not enough left for dinner, never mind anything left over for tomorrow morning. There is only one thing for it. At this point Ange takes over, picking the spilt spaghetti off the ground and collecting it in the other pot, then laboriously washing it, handful after handful, with rainwater. It takes returning to the comforts of Brazzaville, and being well fed, before we are able to laugh about it—"Spaghetti à la dirt"—Old Charles's specialty.

Lise helps Ange prepare smoked fish for breakfast. It is a meal that doesn't count in our rations since it doesn't involve any canned food or dried rice or pasta. The resulting dish actually doesn't look too bad aside from the smoked fish. It is in a thick sauce of peanut paste and cut-grass-like *legumes*. They each serve themselves a bowlful. I hesitate. I think I will try it. This, I tell them, is a historic moment for me. I swore 9 years ago that I would never eat smoked fish again, and although I have tried, I just can't bring myself to eat it. But the way they have prepared it, it looks so good that I think I can muster up the courage to taste it. Ange goes to get me a bowl, but I stop him. I'll just have a taste of Lise's. I cast about for a spoon, but Lise hands me hers, with almost a smile. I put half a spoonful in my mouth and chew. It is pretty disgusting. The fish, which supposedly can be eaten bones and all, clearly have bones, and these get stuck between my teeth. The smoked fish imparts a fishy taste to the rest of the sauce, which would otherwise be not much different from saka-saka. But it is not absolutely inedible, and I am hungry. I fill half a bowl for myself and eat it.

The group is uncharacteristically impatient and unenthusiastic as I point out the place I have chosen as the last site for the pitfall traps. This upsets me until I remember the quarrel between the guides just over an hour ago, and the stress that Ange must be feeling over that incident. In fact the only person who seems to be working happily is Lise. She and I take on the job together of unrolling and measuring the fence, while the men cut a trail and bury the buckets. By the time the trapline is finished, the work has cheered everyone up a bit. Romuald asks me again to give them a mark out of 20 on the job they've done: "25!" I reply cheerfully, and then qualify that, saying that we'll have to wait and see what it catches us.

That night, though exhausted, I am just too hungry to sleep. In the dark I shake the Eternity flashlight and climb out from under the mosquito net in search of something to eat. After all, our supplies are all piled up just across from my bed. But all I find is stuff like rice and macaroni that needs to be cooked, or tins of sardines and corned beef, which are rationed and have been carefully counted. I come across the plastic bag Ange has been storing the smoked fish in. I've seen him eat the small blackened fishes as though they were potato chips, biting chunks off the crisp fish, bones and all. Am I as hungry as that? I reach gingerly into the bag and pull out a small, shriveled fish. I sniff it. All it smells of is smoke, but I just can't do it. I go back to bed hungry. The next day Ange takes all the smoked fish out of the bag to inspect them and finds that many of the larger ones are full of maggots. He carefully picks the maggoty parts out, shakes the loose maggots out of the bag, and puts the fish back in.

Romuald reports one afternoon that a man "kuna" (over that way) has caught a big snake on a hook. Last year I was always frustrated by the answer to my question, "Where?" because all I got was a vague "la bas" (over that way) and a wave of the hand. I thought at the time this was a translation problem, but now I know that "kuna" is as precise as Lingala can get. The man would have brought the snake, Romuald explains, but he thought he had to bring it in alive and decided doing that was beyond him. "Take me there," I tell Romuald, "I'll get it off the hook." But Romuald puts it off, is unclear about the actual distance involved, and promises to bring it the following day. I should have been more insistent, because when he arrives the following morning, in a swarm of flies, the 2-meter-long forest cobra he's holding is giving off a terrible stench. I have to wait and get a cup of coffee inside me before I can face the task of skinning it, but Lise doesn't seem put off in the least. By now we've skinned a lot of big snakes together and the routine is familiar. I start at the head, she starts at the tail, and we work our way toward each other, carefully separating skin from flesh without tearing it. The big #8 hook is far down in the throat, and gets removed with the body. The smell and the flies are so bad I am not sure I can stand to finish it. I am already feeling nauseous. But Lise seems to enjoy dead snakes in all forms and not only cheerfully does the dissection, but stays behind scrubbing the instruments long after I have left to try to scour the smell off my hands.

Ange is never separated from his notebook, which has come to serve many purposes beyond its originally intended use of recording all my pearls of herpetological wisdom. I can't guess how many pages have been devoted to inventory after inventory of our supplies. The eventual distribution of the equipment we will be leaving behind is a subject to which Ange has been devoting a great deal of mental energy since shortly after our arrival. As the weeks go by he is continually modifying the list and changing his mind. I have decided that it is not worth taking back our household equipment and any leftover supplies. This leaves buckets, dishes, the foam mattress, the cooking pots, probably some canned food, at least, to give away. Socially sensitive and ingeniously tactful, Ange agonizes over the list, trying to make sure that everyone will be pleased and nobody will feel offended. It would never have occurred to me that leaving behind a few buckets and pots and pans in a village could be so fraught with complications.

One particularly delicate problem is what to give the guides at the end. Romuald has done far more work than Old Charles, but their wages were settled at the beginning and so we have to pay them each the same. Presents left behind at the end are another matter. But Ange doesn't want any hard feelings. If Old Charles feels resentful, Romuald will ultimately suffer. Ange hits on a plan. The guides will get no presents at the end aside from each being allowed to keep his machete and his flashlight. The trick is this: give everything to the women. Old Charles is single while Romuald has two wives. Moreover, his two wives have prepared many meals for us. Giving a whole lot of pots and plates and dishes to Romuald's wives will be an indirect way of rewarding Romuald, and the fact that Old Charles has no wives to give things to will be a convincing excuse. But Ange continues to agonize over every plastic coffee cup, every fork . . . He worries particularly over the buckets. We have two ordinary buckets for carrying water, but we also have two plastic buckets with lids for storage of food. The buckets with lids are the preferred present, and he would like to give one to each wife, but he hesitates because one is bigger than the other. He wants to give the same thing to the two wives, and this, he worries, may be awkward. "Sounds perfectly straightforward to me," I tease him when he puts the problem to me. "Romuald has one wife who's big and fat and another who's small and skinny. You have a big bucket and a small bucket. The solution is obvious."

"That's exactly the kind of thing I'm worried about," he explains, despairingly.

One afternoon (yet another afternoon when I was supposed to decide where to move the nets) Romuald doesn't show up. Though it's unlike Romuald to be unreliable, Ange is becoming indignant by the time he finally appears, some time after dark. He had gone to Djeke to buy sugar, which we have run out of once again, the story comes out, and while he was there someone stole his pirogue. There is no way of locking up beached pirogues. This sort of theft would never have happened in Impongui, which is so small that individual pirogues would be recognized, but in the big bad metropolis of Djeke, apparently it occasionally happens. The following day Romuald cuts down a tree in the forest not far from the camp, and sets to work making a new pirogue, working on it whenever we give him a free moment. He tells me it takes a month to make a pirogue if you work at it full time, but that if you really go all out it's said to be possible to do it in only 2 weeks.

Life is not all bad. The first morning with the pitfall traps in the new location, I return to the camp from checking them, shouting excitedly for Lise and Ange, who are still in their tents. In one bag I have a frog, which Ange (with some prompting) recognizes as *Xenopus,* our second specimen of the slippery wet frog I caught under my bed that rainy day that the Chief visited us. But more interesting to Ange are the two toads in the other bag. They are *Bufo,* but definitely not the *Bufo regularis* that we have been getting in such large numbers from the village. These are small toads with rusty-colored sides and a pretty black and white pattern on their backs. Ange has the key to the *Bufo*s of Cameroon out at once and is puzzling over these new specimens. "If it's a new species I'll name it *Bufo jacksoni,*" he tells me, excited.

"Not because you think I look like a *Bufo,* I hope."

"No, no. You told me that you always name a new species after your mentor. You're my mentor." I am touched. It had never occurred to me that anyone would ever consider me a mentor. It feels like an honor and also a great responsibility.

"Well, let the pitfall traps be a lesson to you," I tell Lise and Ange, feeling suddenly that I ought to have something wise to impart. "The pitfall traps were a lot of work, and didn't get us many specimens. We could have got plenty of specimens more efficiently just by picking up things that are easy to catch in the village. *But,* if you go through the catalogue you will see that among those few specimens the pitfall traps caught are five species that we found nowhere else. Always remember that."

It is on our last Sunday morning that the mystery of Lise's hairdo is finally revealed. Sitting on the bench, she spends a good 2 hours unraveling all the tiny braids, which to my surprise come off, leaving her with a short scruffy frizz of hair which she says she will wash in Brazzaville. Hair extensions, she explains, throwing them on the fire. Since it is our last Sunday, this will be our last saka-saka lunch at Romuald's house. It takes some time to get going because it has recently occurred to Ange that the camp left unattended might be found by burglars. He fusses around piling the formalin jar and other unattractive items on top of the equipment box, and carefully selects the real valuables to be lugged along with us in our backpacks. "Mind you bring all the *Bufo*s with you," I tease him, stuffing the satellite phone into my pack.

"That would be a *really* unhappy burglar," he agrees, "to steal a box and find it full of pickled *Bufo*s."

We greet everyone we pass on our way through the village. It's not like the mbote gauntlet at Epena—we actually know who they are. I step around half a dozen children sitting on the path, each tending a tiny campfire—a perfect miniature of the one in our camp—and each with a sardine tin full of water coming to a boil on it. Nice to see our discarded cans being put to use. Romuald approaches me quietly while we are seated in the shade outside his house, waiting for lunch to be ready. "Have you seen the newborn?" he asks me. I have not. He leads me inside one of the mud and stick houses, where a young woman, looking very tired, is holding a new baby, its face crinkled and reddish. "She's beautiful," I say politely in Lingala.

"Her name is Kat-Lise," Romuald tells me. I assume he's joking, but recover myself quickly when I realize he is completely serious. "Because she was born while you were here," he explains.

"Lise and I will be her two godmothers," is the only thing I can think to say. This is even more of an honor than *Bufo jacksoni*.

We all fall ravenously upon the lunch, and this time there are no leftovers to take home for the evening. Sitting outside in the shade after the meal, Romuald serves palm wine. Viscous and sickly sweet, it is a magnet for flies, and the clump of leaves acting as a stopper for the bottle doesn't do much to discourage them. Luckily I know the Lingala for "only a little" and "that's enough." Lise and I are left out as usual while the men take turns holding forth. Lise sighs and leans back in her chair, but I decide to try breaking a social boundary and joining in—it's the last time after all. "My cat speaks one word of Lingala," I say in Lingala, taking advantage of a pause in the conversation. I tell my one Lingala joke and it is an enormous success.

I discover the following morning that the termites have started chewing a hole in one of the tarpaulins—the tarpaulins that we have promised to the village committee. I panic. What will we tell them if the tarpaulins have been ruined by termites? "Well, we'll just tell them that it was *their* termites that did it," says Ange indignantly.

As time runs out, I start to despair over my failure to teach Lise to handle live animals. I have saved a *Lygosoma* from the pitfall traps. It is a fairly large lizard, bigger than a human fist, and not as quick to escape or drop its tail as other skinks. Its hard scales are beautifully patterned in red and black. In fact it is really cute. I can't think of a less threatening reptile for Lise to practice on. But it is a nice specimen, and I don't want to lose it through Lise's clumsiness. I hit on a solution. We will practice handling the *Lygosoma* inside Lise's tent. The tent is small and completely sealed by zippers, and even if she drops it, it won't get away. But when I propose this sensible plan, Lise utters a scream of absolute horror. In fact she is so shaken by the idea of a live lizard being brought inside her tent that I have to put off the whole exercise until the following day, when she has had time to recover herself. As a compromise, I have her sit beside me on the bed, in the house, with me holding an open snake bag under the lizard in case it should get dropped. After more than an hour of squealing and dropping I am getting fed up, and I imagine the *Lygosoma* is too. "Okay, you are going to reach into that bag, grasp the lizard gently but firmly just behind the front legs, and lift it out. *And*, if it bites you, you will *not* let go. Is that clear? Its teeth are so small they won't even break the skin. Come on, enough mucking about. Just do it." After several hours of effort we move outside. With me carefully keeping an eye on the skink, and with a lot of prodding, she can pick it up off the ground and put it back. It doesn't seem like much progress.

Things are running out, things are breaking down. We are having trouble with the formalin. There is only about 200 milliliters of diluted 10 percent formalin in the jar. Some dust has got into it, and often clogs the needle when we are in the middle of injecting a specimen. I am ready to discard the dusty dregs of the formalin and mix a new batch, but Ange and Lise won't hear of such waste. They decant the dirty formalin into a bowl, rinse out the jar, and then pour it back into the jar, filtering it through a piece of Ange's "I love you" underwear.

Around 6:00 p.m. is the worst time of day, the time of trade-off between heat and mosquitoes, but we have a lot of specimens still to prepare and they can't wait for tomorrow morning. My long-sleeved jacket is stifling and does nothing to protect me from the swarm of mosquitoes whining around my head. Squinting through the first of the muddy plastic bags by the light of my headlamp and a candle melted to the corner of the table, I see what appear to be three dead *Trachylepis* lizards and a squashed *Ptychadena*. But when I open the bag two lizards leap out. The first, a *Trachylepis*, lands on the ground and is gone in an instant. The other, a gecko, lands on the sheet covering the open end of the house and with a quick grab I have it again. I check the bag again to make sure that the rest of the contents is really dead. Left hand occupied by the gecko, I manipulate the syringe of procaine one-handed, with the result that I stab myself with the needle. Blood drips all over the place, making everything slippery. The gecko bites me. A mosquito is stinging my neck, but I don't have a free hand to swat it. Then a moth flies into the candle flame and snuffs it out. It is hard not to cut corners when specimen preparation is so uncomfortable, but I know that if I do, I will always regret not having taken proper tissue samples and measurements, not having made detailed notes in the catalogue.

That job finished, we are all settling down for the evening. I am arranging the mosquito net around me and Ange is starting his nightly rearrangement of the house, while Lise leafs through the photos in Jean-Philippe's snake book. Two candles driven into the floor give the house a warm glow. As I reach under the bed for my water bottle, my arm brushes lightly against one of my boots. Suddenly I feel a terrible itching and in the dim light from the candle see that my hand is alive with a moving swarm which is making rapid progress up my arm. "Eeeeeee!!" I scream incoherently.

"What is it?" Ange turns in alarm.

"Ants!" I try frantically to brush them off with the other hand.

"Termites," Lise corrects me, holding the candle over my boots, which are crawling with them. She starts swatting at them with the sole of a sequined slipper. Ange grabs the boots between thumb and forefinger and rushes outside with them.

"It's because they're wet—the moisture attracts them," he explains. I gingerly turn over the corner of my sleeping mat and find that the whole bedframe is covered with them. Everything on the bed is rushed outside and shaken. Ange runs back and forth scattering ashes scooped from the fire in a bowl. There is quite a deep hole in the middle of the fire because we've needed so much ash for the termites. "Oh why, oh why can't you leave us alone?" Ange pleads. "Only a couple of days more and then you can have the place all to yourselves."

chapter 17

a
stressful
day

I wake up early on the morning of our third-to-last day. The air is still
cool at dawn when I strip off my clothes and dive off the end of the
pirogue. Mist is rising off the surface of the cold water around my
head, and the place looks somehow prehistoric, the first sunlight of the
day barely reaching the black surface of the water. I think I would be
only mildly surprised to encounter Mokele-Mbembe. The cool water
feels wonderful now that I am in it. Only two more mornings like this
left, I remind myself, then back to the greatly inferior world of indoor
plumbing.

My day starts to deteriorate when I climb back up into the pirogue
and find that it is full of seed pods which must have fallen off the

grasses as the pirogue cut through them on the Likouala aux Herbes River yesterday. Each pod has a point at each end, one for snagging onto clothing and the other for scratching nearby skin. While I've been swimming, my towel and underwear have been lying in a pile of them. I get dressed and set off to check the pitfall traps. Which is preferable— to be wet or to be itchy, I ponder? I'm disappointed to find nothing more than half a dozen giant millipedes, which I flick over my shoulder back into the forest, and two shrews, which I chase around in circles at the bottom of the bucket with my hemostat until I give up in frustration and remove them by hand, getting bitten in the process.

When I return to the camp, Romuald has arrived, accompanied by Darcel. He has already chopped wood, got the fire going again, and almost finished making the coffee by the time Old Charles shows up. Old Charles makes himself comfortable on the bench and waits for his coffee to be served. How can Romuald stand him? Lise gazes sleepily into the fire, and Ange, even more cheerful than usual today is loudly singing ("Votez, votez, votez, Ka-bi-la"). Romuald takes the lid off the sugar bowl and shows astonishment at finding inside it a lot of ants and very little sugar. Everyone stares into the sugar bowl. How can this be a surprise? Romuald puts sugar in the coffee every morning—yesterday, the day before yesterday, the day before that—how can he possibly be surprised that the sugar bowl he almost emptied yesterday is still almost empty today? For the syrupy kind of coffee that Romuald makes there's really only enough sugar for one mug. "Give it to Katherine," decides Ange magnanimously.

"No, no," I say hastily, eyeing the swarming mass of ants, "I'd rather just have my coffee plain."

"*Without sugar?*" everyone asks in incredulous unison.

"Yes, without sugar. After all, the coffee is the important part, not the sugar."

"I'll just give you a little bit," Romuald compromises, carefully flicking ants out of a teaspoon of sugar for my mug with a sharpened twig. Lise accepts her mug next, and the daily ritual continues as Ange squeezes a lime into his special mug. Romuald pours an inch of coffee into the second-to-last mug, and adds two overflowing spoonfuls of swarming ants. He stirs it vigorously and hands it to Old Charles. He pours coffee into the last mug, does his best to skim the ants off the surface and passes it to Darcel. Old Charles hastily tries to hand his mug of ants to Darcel and take Darcel's instead, but Romuald is too quick for him. For himself, Romuald dumps the dregs of the coffee from the pot into the sugar bowl and drinks out of that.

I told everyone yesterday that our plan for this morning was to take apart that brick pile in a shady part of the village—the one with ferns growing all over it. Ange has just been getting louder and louder all morning. He's moved on from Kinshasa election campaign songs to the other piece in his repertoire, an excerpt from a popular sitcom produced in the Ivory Coast. He repeats the dialogue over and over again, funny voices and everything. He's probably trying to distract everyone from the murderous tension between the two guides. It's not even 8:30 a.m. and I already have a stress headache. I retreat into the house, leaving them all to get themselves ready to set off for the brick pile.

But when I come out again 15 minutes later, nobody is showing any sign of getting ready to leave. In fact Romuald appears to be cooking something. "But the whole idea was to get there early so that we're not lifting bricks in the very hottest part of the day," I protest, exasperated. But they *are* getting ready, Ange assures me. They're just pausing to have a meal first. The meal is fish skeleton soup with big lumps of fou-fou, food that is fair game because it doesn't involve any of our rationed supplies. Though ravenously hungry, I just nibble the edge of a fou-fou lump dipped in the broth from the oily soup, as the sun gets hotter.

I decide that we will get to the village by pirogue, hoping that getting everyone on board and casting off will waste less time than taking the trail through the forest, which would allow people to turn back to do or fetch something while the rest of the party waits. Ange is still carrying on his singing and comedy routine. I already feel like throwing him overboard, and that is before he decides to stand up in the middle of the pirogue wielding a paddle for the whole journey. Luckily the only damage he does is to whack me on the back of the head with it, and we arrive at the landing without capsizing.

The village children descend on us in an excited mob before we are even out of the pirogue. As we make our way across the village to the brick pile, surrounded by them, I wonder if they are louder than usual today or if it just seems that way. The brick pile is a smallish one. The top layer is at about eye level to me, but it spreads out into a crumbling mound with a diameter of about 4 meters. It is shaded from the sun, and the bricks are almost concealed by the lush greenery sprouting from the mud between them. As I tear away handfuls of ferns and wrestle the first brick out of its place, I find that the pile is as much solid mud as brick, and probably one gigantic ant nest as well. I try to get the job off to an organized start by walking around the pile, assessing possible routes of escape. All the ground surrounding the brick pile must be cleared if we are to have a hope of catching anything that comes out of it. But while I am deciding on a strategy and whom to assign to what key locations, the children have started attacking the pile in a wild and disorganized way, and the members of my team are following their lead. Romuald is busy gathering up the bricks that have been moved and making a neat stack of them nearby. Ange seems to believe that his Ivory Coast sitcom is what the children are laughing at, and is spurred on to an even showier performance, not paying attention to the spaces he is moving bricks from. If there's anything under those bricks he's going to miss it. About a third of the children are tearing away at the bricks and flinging them aside, while the rest chase each other round and round the pile, screaming. Lise is playing with the children, and Old Charles is standing under a tree, hoping that in the chaos nobody will notice that he isn't doing any work. In fact aside from me, the only person taking the moving of the brick pile seriously is little Anuarite, a grave and silent presence at my elbow, carrying away each brick I hand her, and adding all her little strength to mine, prizing free the bricks most firmly wedged in the mud.

Everyone else seems to be having a wonderful time, but I am cross and irritable. Nothing has gone my way this morning. Nobody is doing what I want any of them to do. Nobody listens to me when I tell them to be quiet. This promising brick pile is going to be wasted because anything in it that we might have caught will easily escape in the confusion. Suddenly there is a tremendous scream from the other side of the pile. "What is it?" I demand, but the only reply is more screaming. Everyone rushes to where the screaming is coming from, leaving everywhere else unobserved. "Everything is going to escape," I shout, but nobody hears me over the racket. And then after all that screaming it turns out just to be a *Ptychadena*. But the first person to grab at it misses, and the frog leaps away from the pile, pursued by all the children and, ridiculously, by Lise and Ange and the guides, leaving only me at the brick pile. There turn out to be a lot of *Ptychadena*s among the bricks, but the fifteenth is received with just as much screaming and excitement as the first. After an hour the children have learned the scientific name and are referring to them as *"Ptychadena*s*"* instead of "frogs."

After 2 and a half hours of this I no longer care if we find any snakes at the bottom of the pile. I just want it over with so at least I can go back to the camp and be free of the screaming children. I start turning the bricks perfunctorily like everyone else, letting my mind drift away from the whole scene. I hardly react to the next round of screaming, but I do glance up from the hole I'm clearing and see that the excitement this time is not a *Ptychadena* but a snake. I glimpse a grayish body streaking away from the brick pile. In an instant I have recognized it as a house snake, and in another instant I am holding it in my hand. The gray body is glossy and iridescent. The eye has the characteristic vertical pupil. But I think it might actually be a different species of *Lamprophis* from the house snakes we got in the first brick pile. I am happy. Why was I finding the children's cheerful laughter annoying a moment ago? Ange already has a snake bag ready—he must have been paying attention after all.

The job is pretty much finished. Only a couple of layers of bricks are left, and I've got a snake, so this enterprise wasn't the total failure I had expected after all. I notice for the first time that my hands are scratched and scraped and muddy, fingernails torn. I start to look forward to a refreshing swim back at the camp. But then there is another cry. Everyone is shouting incoherently as ever, but in the middle of the crowd Ange is tugging at the cumbersome 24inch hemostat, trying to wrestle it free from his belt loop. Everyone gets out of my way and I catch sight of what caused the screaming: a coil of snake, no head or tail visible, just about to disappear into a crack. What I see is a mid-body coil of a black snake with large scales, skin stretched tight so that there is a bit of white skin showing between the scales. *Mehelya*. I recognize it as the same as the ones I caught in the first brick pile and grab hold of the disappearing coil. If I do anything else it will get away.

At this moment a lot of thinking gets compressed into a very short time. I pull the snake free of the bricks, expecting to see the square-snouted head characteristic of *Mehelya*. But the head isn't square it's rounded and foreshortened, and there isn't a clearly defined neck between head and body. The first thing that I really recognize as wrong is the bronze color of the sides of the head. The front third of the underbelly has broad yellow bands. Everything suddenly falls into place and I recognize the snake in my hand as a forest cobra.

Just letting go is an option not even to be considered among all these children. In the same instant that I shift my grip to get control of the head, the snake turns to strike. I see the mouth open. I see the sharp tip of the left fang prick my right thumb. And then I have a firm hold at the back of the head. The neck is spread into a hood against my grip. Viscous yellow venom is dribbling down my forearm and onto the cloth bag that Ange has given me. It has all happened so quickly that what everyone has seen is simply me grabbing at something between the bricks and then putting a snake into a bag. It's exciting enough to warrant lots of screaming, but no more exciting than any of the other things they've all watched me catch over the past month. "It's a forest cobra," I tell Ange.

"Oh. Did it bite you?"

"I'm actually not quite sure," I manage a convincing calm smile. "We're going back to the camp now."

"But there are still a few bricks left . . ."

"I said 'I'm not sure.' We're finished here. Absolutely no fuss, okay? Probably nothing to worry about. But we're going back immediately."

Ange manages to get everyone moving and we set off across the village to where we left the pirogue, followed by all the children. I'm glad I decided to take the pirogue and not the trail. At least in the pirogue, our entourage can't follow us. The pirogue seems to be much farther away than I remember. We walk and walk. It occurs to me that I ought to be keeping track of timing for my notes. My watch now says 10:30. So let's say I grabbed the cobra at 10:20. The walk gives me time to think. Time to make some decisions about what I'm going to do. But the trouble is that I don't know if the fang went in deep enough to inject venom or not, and deciding what should be done depends entirely on the answer to that question. Is there a puncture mark on my thumb from the fang? Impossible to tell among all the cuts and scrapes on my hands from moving the bricks, not to mention that I'm covered in mud and won't be able to see anything at all until I can rinse my hand. Very much in my thoughts is Joe Slowinski, a herpetologist killed a few years earlier by a misidentified juvenile krait, a snake so small that he couldn't tell if the fang had punctured the skin. We walk and walk. What would be the first symptoms of envenomation? I'm suddenly becoming aware of how little I really know about the medical side of venomous snakes. Am I imagining it, or is my right hand starting to feel numb and tingly? Would that be the first sign? To test it I make myself imagine that it was the left hand that was bitten, to see if I can convince myself that my left hand feels numb and tingly. I find that I can. My hands must just be numb from lifting all those bricks.

After what seems like an eternity but by my watch is only 10 minutes, we have reached the pirogue. "*Monsieur* Charles, could you hurry it up a bit?" Ange efficiently hustles everyone on board. As we cross the water Ange is not singing or reciting sitcom scripts. He is not even standing up. Romuald and Old Charles are paddling in the bow and the stern. Lise and I are sitting together in the middle. I certainly don't want the guides to suspect anything, but I take the opportunity to let her know what's going on. ". . . So you see it might have bitten me, but I just don't know for sure."

"Oh," she asks with mild interest, "are you going to inject yourself?"

"Yes, I think I will, just to be on the safe side. If I wait until I have symptoms it might be too late."

As soon as we land I tell Ange to send Romuald to Djeke by himself to buy sugar, and apart from that to give the guides the rest of the day off. "Oh, but can't I go to Djeke?" Ange has been looking forward to the trip.

"No. I'm going to need you here."

I can't keep count of the number of times I have worked through in my mind what I would do in the case of a snakebite emergency in a place where there was no possibility of proper medical help. I've imagined my way through every detail. Would I apply a pressure bandage, at the cost of precious minutes, if I had the antivenom right there ready to administer? Could I get an IV needle into the vein on someone's arm? What would I do if there was no way of knowing what kind of snake was responsible for the bite? Risk harming someone by giving antivenom to a person who had been bitten by a nonvenomous snake? And so on. The one part of the scenario that I have never considered is the possibility that the victim could be me.

So what do I do? A memory comes back to me from the Toronto airport the day of my departure for the Congo. My mother was there with me to help get all my boxes of equipment checked in. Before leaving me at the airport, she held me close. "Take care of yourself as though you were taking care of someone else," she told me.

I have antivenom thanks to Jean-Philippe Chippaux, and I have a satellite phone thanks to Dr. Parra. I consider the satellite phone. If I haven't been bitten then there's no point in causing a great fuss. But if I have been bitten I could call and ask for a rescue attempt. It would take some time for anyone to get here and then several days to backtrack my steps from Impongui to Epena to Impfondo to Brazzaville, and even in Brazzaville, as Jean's study showed, there are no facilities to treat a snakebite. I expect I would be dead long before I got treatment. I suppose I could use the satellite phone to call my medivac insurance and speak to a doctor. But what physician is going to know anything more than I do about snakebites and this new antivenom? The only one I can think of is Jean-Philippe, in Bolivia—the other side of the planet—and I don't have a number for him. How I desperately wish he was here to know what to do and to take charge.

It has never occurred to me to teach Ange and Lise how to treat a snakebite. Should I now teach them CPR in case I am in a condition to need it a few hours from now? No. I shudder at the thought. Anyway, the best they could hope to achieve would be to extend my life by a few hours, and with no rescue imminent what's the point of that?

I call Lise from the house, and rummage through the first-aid kit until I find my precious four vials of freeze-dried polyvalent antivenom. Each 10-cc glass ampoule contains the powdered antivenom which has to be reconstituted with physiological saline solution, which is injected through the lid of the ampoule with a hypodermic needle. The instructions with the antivenom expect you to be administering it in a hospital with bags of sterile saline solution. Saline solution has several ingredients, but the only ones I have available to me are boiled rainwater and salt. I send Lise to get a coffee mug full of water, a spoon, and the salt. "And quickly!" I tell her to mix a bit of salt into the water.

"How much?"

"Taste it. Keep adding salt until it tastes as salty as blood."

By now the guides are gone and Ange joins us. "It's probably nothing to worry about," I tell them again, "but I'm going to take two ampoules just to be on the safe side."

"Intramuscular is too slow," Jean-Philippe had told me, "it needs to be administered intravenously."

I draw Lise's makeshift saline solution into a 10-cc syringe and inject it into the first ampoule. I shake it until the powder dissolves. I draw the reconstituted antivenom back out into the syringe. I change the needle on the syringe for a smaller one, and look at my watch. Incredibly, only 50 minutes have gone by since the moment I grabbed that disappearing coil. I'm anxious that my right hand might start to be affected by the venom and I might not have the fine-motor coordination to handle the syringe. I'm working against the clock.

My snakebite kit is so well prepared that I even have a strip of rubber to tie around my upper arm to make it easier to find the vein. I get Lise to tie it and then squeeze my fist until the vein swells up. I slide the needle into the vein easily enough, but immediately find that I can't hold it still and in place long enough to inject such a large quantity of liquid slowly enough. An intravenous injection like this should really be administered in a hospital through a drip. This is not going to work. I must not panic.

My last resort is Jean-Philippe's other option, which I had immediately rejected with horror, when he mentioned it 6 months ago in La Paz. Intraperitoneal injection. "Ange," I ask without much hope, "if I gave you a syringe with a really long needle on it, do you think there's any way you'd be able to inject it straight through the wall of my abdomen? Right here," I indicate a spot on my waistline, between front and side. With only three layers of muscle to go through, it's the thinnest part of the abdominal wall.

"Sure, no problem."

"You're certain? You have to plunge the needle in as deep as it will go, with absolutely no hesitation."

Though reluctant to use up more time, I decide that cleaning the injection site with an alcohol swab is probably something I should do. And I end up being glad I did, since no fewer than five swabs end up grimy from all the brick dust. I change the needle on the syringe for a long one and hand it to Ange. I lie on my back, not sure whether it would be helpful to him for me to flex my abdominal muscles or to relax them. I feel the prick of the needle against the skin. "All the way in! All the way in! Don't stop part way like that!"

"But it is all the way." I lift my head up just enough to see that the needle is indeed plunged in to the hilt. Looking at it makes me feel slightly faint.

"Go ahead and inject it then." I gasp as he rams the plunger down as fast as it will go. When I said fast and without hesitation I meant putting the needle in, not injecting the antivenom. It feels icy cold inside and several internal organs feel as if they are being pushed away from their usual places. "Good job. Let's do another one." I'm watching the clock and I'm trying my very hardest not to become frantic. I hand him a second vial of antivenom, but he is still doing something with the first. "Ange, quickly! Inject this second ampoule!"

"No, wait, there's still a little bit left at the bottom of this one." He is chasing half a cc around the bottom of the vial with the needle rather than let it go to waste.

"To hell with the little bit at the bottom. Do the full one."

"There, I've got it." I clean and mark an injection spot on my left side this time. After it's done I just don't feel I can stand to have another injection like that. Not right now at least.

"Okay, here's the plan:" I address them both. "I am going to take the cobra out of its bag to photograph it, then euthanize it. I'll euthanize the other snake at the same time. Then Ange will inject me with a second vial of antivenom. I don't know how I'll be feeling. Do you think you can process the specimens without me? Sex, body length, tail length, and tissue samples for the snakes; just formalin-fix the frogs. Collection data same for all of them when you enter them in the catalogue." Knowing that these may be the last live snakes we get, I try to get Lise to handle the harmless house snake, but she adamantly refuses, and considering what she's seen me go through today as a result of snake handling, I don't feel inclined to push her very hard. Once the photographing and euthanizing are done, they tell me to rest and not to worry. Leave it to them.

As Ange plunges the next vial of antivenom into me, it dawns on me that for him this must feel no different from injecting formalin into one of his dead *Bufos*. No wonder he does it so unconcernedly.

Lise sits at the desk fixing the *Ptychadenas*, while I lie on my bed, waiting for the first symptoms from the cobra venom. I send Lise to fetch Jean-Philippe's snake book, *Les serpents d'Afrique occidentale et centrale*. I know roughly what cobra venom does, but I've never paid much attention to the clinical details. Now suddenly the few lines of information in the forest cobra entry that describe the effects of the bite seem desperately important:

"The venom is a neurotoxin with a length of 71–74 amino acids. Envenomation causes paralysis of the respiratory muscles leading to death by asphyxia" (p. 226).

Fuck the number of amino acids! I throw the book on the ground. I am not going to cry. I get out my notebook and try to record the timeline: time when the accident occurred, time the antivenom was administered, and so on, but my right hand has suddenly gone all weak and I can hardly hold a pen. Is this the effect of the venom or only fear? Lise works away on the specimens. She tells me that the cobra is a male and 99 centimeters long. What I notice about it is how much white there is scattered on its black scales. I've never seen that much white on a forest cobra. It was those white flecks that I mistook for white skin visible between black scales, and therefore thought the snake was *Mehelya*. It wasn't an entirely unreasonable mistake. It really wasn't, I assure myself. Could have happened to anyone.

Suddenly there is a shout from outside, and Ange comes running into the house with his shirt off, brandishing a leaf in front of him. "Look at this! Just look! It's a *maggot!*" Sure enough, perched on the edge of the leaf is a soft, white body, the size of a grain of rice. As Lise and I watch in mixed disgust and fascination it lifts up its front half and waves it from side to side. Where did it come from? Apparently Ange had been picking at his bumps, and when he squeezed one, out came this maggot. It turns out that *all* the bumps have maggots in them. Panic! My little problem is entirely forgotten. Lise and Ange rush outside where there is a bit more light and start frantically tearing open and squeezing the bumps to get the maggots out. I get up and join them outside. Squeezing is terribly painful. Lise is in tears as I squeeze a whole group of bumps just below her right breast. "Oh! *Ow!* It hurts so much! No, don't stop!"

Lise finds some on me as well. They show up better on my pale skin. She and Ange are flicking the maggots they remove into the fire in spite of my protests. I have a tissue vial filled with ethanol to preserve them in. When I beg Lise to at least let me keep mine, she is willing to humor me ("Wait, this one's a bit squashed—I'll find you a better one.")

But after half an hour of this I am suddenly hit by stomach cramps so bad that I can't stand up straight. In fact I can't crouch down either, or lie on my back, or curl up into a ball. I try without success to find a position on my bed of branches that isn't agonizing. "I have the worst stomach cramps of my life," I tell Lise and Ange. This impresses them considerably more than "I might have been bitten by a cobra but it's probably nothing to worry about."

"If you need us—if you need anything at all—you just give us a shout," they say when the specimens have all been fixed and they are going back to their tents. It is night now. I am completely consumed by the pain. I've stopped watching for symptoms of envenomation because I just don't care anymore. Ten hours after the accident I don't detect any neurological symptoms, and I think I should have felt them by now. The fang must not have gone deep enough to inject any venom after all. The opening of the channel in the hollow fang that the venom flows through is not quite at the very tip of the fang. If it was, the fang would not come to a sharp point. The venom exits the channel into the bite wound a fraction of a millimeter above the pointed tip—like the beveled tip of a hypodermic needle. That fraction of a millimeter must be what made the difference for me. I am desperate for something to do about the pain. I have Tylenol with codeine in my first-aid kit, but probably I should stop administering medicines to myself. I have done enough damage already playing doctor. But in the end I give in and take the pills anyway.

I think grim thoughts as I lie there in too much pain to sleep. By now I've pretty much stopped worrying that I'm going to die from a cobra bite, but that worry has only been replaced by another fear. Am I going to die of peritonitis? How could I have been so stupid as to use saline solution made in such an unhygienic way and then inject it right into my abdominal cavity? I see myself becoming another statistic on the long list of people who die every year from the incompetent treatment of nonvenomous snakebites, bites that would have had no effect whatsoever if they had just been left alone. Misidentifying a snake and having a very lucky escape only to kill myself by using a dangerous method to treat a bite that isn't even venomous. What more shameful way is there for a herpetologist to die?

If I'm dead in the morning it will be from the cobra. If I have a fever it probably means I have peritonitis. Eventually I do manage to sleep somehow. And I do wake up in the morning. I don't have a fever, and the stomach cramps are not quite as bad as they were. I get up and venture outside. Lise and Ange come rushing out of their tents when they hear me moving around. "Are you okay? Are you sure? We were so *worried*—you can't imagine!"

chapter 18

kende
malamu

The sun has already risen the morning I get up stiffly from the bed of branches and realize that I will never sleep on them again. Today is the day we take down the camp, and tomorrow is the day the boat is supposed to come to take us back to Epena.

Yesterday, feeling completely recovered from the cobra incident, I figured out the trick to removing the maggots. I finally remembered learning about something like them in an entomology course I took as an undergraduate. The flies lay eggs in damp clothing hung out to dry. If you don't iron it, or at least let the sun really dry it out, the eggs hatch and the tiny maggots burrow into any skin in contact with the clothes. Once they've burrowed in they start to grow. To grow and to wriggle around from time to time. Every time the maggot moves, it feels as if a large ant is biting you, but when you turn to swat it there is nothing there, except a lump getting gradually larger and larger. Ange had one that was especially painful. He wouldn't disclose its precise location except to say that it was difficult to get at, and that he wouldn't even consider anything so immodest as letting me or Lise squeeze it out for him. Anyway, after days of suffering, tearing great wounds open to infection in each other as we tried to extract the maggots, I remembered learning that these maggots breathe through a pore in your skin while growing in the flesh underneath. If you put a dab of Vaseline over the pore they suffocate and die, which makes them much easier to remove. "Do we have any Vaseline?" Ange asked.

"No." I admitted. Ange retreated miserably to his tent with the tweezers and the little mirror from the first-aid kit.

But I gave the problem some thought. What do we have that could block a pore? Maybe the medical adhesive tape, the strong white tape used for attaching gauze bandages? I don't think it is breathable. So last night we all put a piece of adhesive tape over each lump before going to sleep. The first thing I do on standing up in the morning is peel the strip of tape off the biggest lump, inconveniently located on my lower back. Tape removed, I squeeze the lump hard. A fat white maggot, slightly larger than a grain of rice, bursts out into my hand accompanied by a lot of pus. I repeat the procedure with one on my shoulder and another in my armpit. I keep meaning to save one, to leave it alone and let it develop into a fly. I long to have one with wings for my collection, but it's really hard not to pick at them.

Romuald arrives early, accompanied by Darcel and this time by Anuarite as well. Anuarite has been dying to see our camp all month and we had promised her she could come on the last day. But this means I'm never going to have another of those predawn swims in the misty flooded forest. The first job of the day is taking down the nets, and I insist on going along with Romuald to do this. He's using a borrowed pirogue which is so unstable that we almost capsize every time I have to turn around. How could I possibly have disentangled a live *Boulengerina* from a net under these conditions? We've been lucky, I suppose, that all the snakes caught in our nets this year have been drowned. Never a single live one. Yesterday I sent Lise with Romuald with the responsibility of choosing a site for the nets, and she seems to have chosen well since we get another *Grayia ornata*. I almost tip us over disentangling it from the net. The misty and silent part of the morning hasn't completely ended yet, and we are startled by a sound of breaking branches on the shore nearby. "A chimpanzee!" Romuald exclaims, and once he points it out to me I see it too—just a glimpse of a dark body disappearing into the trees.

After we pile the nets in the middle of the pirogue, we set off back to the camp. We go on in silence for a few minutes until Romuald can suddenly restrain himself no longer. "So who won?" he bursts out, "Ganganya or Impongui?" Apparently it is competitive spirit which has motivated the inhabitants of Impongui to be so helpful.

As soon as we land back at the camp, I call for Lise to show her the *Grayia,* but she is in the middle of brushing her teeth. "A *Grayia!*" she shouts, spraying toothpaste foam and adding confidently, *"Grayia ornata."*

"The supralabials are a bit unusual on this specimen . . ."

"Let me see!" The temptation is too strong. She hastily spits the toothpaste aside and abandons her toothbrush, to come and snatch the carcass from me, and take it to the lab to count scales. I leave her to it and get on with transferring the specimens on the hardening tray to plastic bags for storage. I am not pleased with what I am finding. A small frog which I can't identify and which we certainly don't have another specimen of, the sort of specimen that could well turn out to be a new species, has been overlooked and formalin-fixed without a photo or tissue sample, and stored among a large series of *Ptychadenas*. The *Ptychadenas*, moreover, have been carelessly fixed in a variety of awkward and grotesque positions rather than properly laid out to harden, webbings neatly displayed, as they should have been. These are the specimens that Lise fixed on her own the night of the cobra incident. It's not really worth complaining about it now, when there will be no more specimens, but I do anyway. This is unacceptable, and I say so.

Yesterday Lise turned down my offer of a final swimming lesson. I was sure that one more lesson was all it would take for her to swim, and I told her so, but she was firm. On our last evening both Lise and Ange begged off a final outing in search of frogs because they were feeling so wretched from their various ailments. If we'd been planning to stay here another week I don't think they would have made it. It frustrates me that Lise never did learn to swim or get over her fear of touching a live animal, and that apart from a few frogs Ange caught, neither of them ever caught anything by hand, something so basic to herpetology. Neither of them ever handled a live snake . . . I wish I could have done more for them . . . I wish . . .

But today is one of those rare sunny days, and a party atmosphere pervades the camp in spite of my bad mood. Lise is not as contrite as I think she should be about the *Ptychadenas*, and, joking around together while skinning the *Grayia,* she and Ange have carelessly broken the tail off the specimen. Old Charles, who drifted into the camp 2 hours later than Romuald, is sitting on the bench gazing contentedly into space. "What, *now?*" he asks incredulously when I tell him to go and get Romuald, who is in the forest with Darcel working on his new pirogue, and to take down the pitfall trapline.

"Yes, now!" Does he not realize that we have to disassemble the whole camp today? While the guides get themselves organized, I set off into the forest to take some last photos of the pitfall traps. I glance over my shoulder and find that Anuarite is following me, silent as a little ghost. When I speak to her she is too shy to answer. When I was working on the frogs earlier, in the house, she stood in the entrance watching me work, but turned away whenever I looked up in her direction.

I am feeling an acute lack of privacy. There are too many people in the camp, and unlike Lise and Ange, I don't have my own tent to retreat to. Darcel is fishing with a rod and hook off the end of the pirogue, preventing me from having a last swim. Anuarite is slicing bundles of leaves into thin strips to make the vegetable used for saka-saka. It doesn't look as if anyone is planning on leaving soon. Lise turns on her tape deck and floods the forest with Christian rock music. That is the limit. I order Darcel out of the pirogue so that I can have my swim. I just have to be alone, even if it's only for a few minutes. In spite of the intrusion of noise from the camp, I strip off my clothes and dive into the cool water. But even here there is no escape. I am just a few strokes away from the pirogue when I hear a splash behind me. Anuarite has left her dress beside my pile of clothes and followed me into the water. She still looks a bit afraid of me as we both stand naked and wet, back in the pirogue. I hand her my towel. She accepts it and dries herself, never taking her eyes off me.

Ange is organizing supplies, setting aside the two boxes of wine for the celebratory dinner we are to have tonight at Romuald's house. Old Charles offers to contribute a chicken to the evening's festivities. He asks for permission to make a quick trip back to the village to arrange it, and disappears for such a long time that it is Romuald and the children who disassemble the house, while Ange and Lise and I puzzle over the folding up of the tents. We will wash them properly with soap when we get back to Epena. The garbage hole is filled in. I want the fire to be extinguished, but everyone else rejects this suggestion as unnecessary. Ange has been planning all along how we will leave camp— leave it so that the forest will soon swallow it up again. He had planned to take down the frame of the house, but when the tarpaulins are off we find new leaves and twigs already sprouting from the branches that made up the frame, so we leave them standing. Ange has saved the tops of three of the pineapples people from the village sent us as presents, and he plants one in the spot where his tent was, one for the site of

Lise's tent, and one inside the frame of the house, commemorating the place where I slept. He is sure that they will grow into trees.

When Old Charles finally returns, everything is already packed and ready to be loaded into the pirogue and taken by Romuald to the village. It is time to say goodbye to our old home and head to the village ourselves, following Old Charles along the trail. We still have a final meeting with the village committee to get through.

Arriving in the village, we are surprised to hear the unfamiliar sound of an outboard motor. The pirogue from WCS, which we were expecting tomorrow, has already arrived. A man from WCS climbs ashore and soon explains. Apparently there is a desperate shortage of gasoline in Epena. Even in Impfondo there is none available. WCS managed to borrow some from the Catholic nuns and has saved just enough for the trip to Impongui to bring us back. The man from WCS is using the trip as an opportunity to videotape an interview with the Notable for a film about forest conservation. We will all go back to Epena tomorrow as planned.

The meeting with the village committee turns out to be a great anticlimax since nobody from the committee shows up. The Chief, we are told, has gone fishing. There is indignant grumbling among those present about the irresponsibleness of the young. Children are sent to find chairs so that those of us in attendance can sit in a semicircle across from the Notable and the second Notable, who are sitting up straight in their chairs, each holding a ceremonial spear, just as at our meeting the first day.

Ange begins. He has clearly been planning a long speech for some time. We are students ourselves he says, and want to reach out to our younger brothers and sisters, is the gist of his 20-minute address. He presents not only the two tarpaulins for the school that we had promised, but also a roll of string and our shovel to help with construction. We also express our gratitude with a donation to the school of 10,000cfa, entrusted to the Notable, and two gallons of palm wine to be shared by everyone in the village. All these things are placed, one by one, in a pile on the ground between us and the Notable. When Ange finally winds down, it is my turn to give a preliminary report of the scientific findings of the expedition. "Um . . . naloba Lingala kaka moke" (I only speak very little Lingala), I begin.

"Say it in French!" says everyone in exasperated unison. So, with Ange translating, I explain the difference between a species and a specimen, read off numbers of each collected, compare those numbers to the results from Ganganya last year, and finish with a final pitch about the importance of knowing more about snakes and frogs to the people who share the forest with them. I promise that a full report with pictures will eventually be sent to Impongui, but warn that it may take a long time. And that is the last formality of the day. The Notable tells us to come and see him before our departure tomorrow morning.

All our boxes and bags have been moved from the pirogue up the slippery slope from the port and piled in Romuald's house. Ange gets to do what he's been looking forward to for so long—paying the guides, and then calling the friends we have made in Impongui, one at a time, to Romuald's living room, to distribute as gifts the things we will be leaving behind. As soon as word is out that the guides have been paid, the whole village descends on Old Charles, who apparently owes a lot of people money. We have a final dinner in Romuald's house, washed down with my two boxes of wine. There is no sign of the chicken promised by Old Charles, something everyone notices but nobody comments on except Romuald, who merely mutters under his breath.

Old Charles is already drunk, and in an act of inebriated generosity has sent somebody to Djeke to buy drinks. Someone hands me a bottle of Coke. I can't get the top off it without an opener, and I am envious of Ange, beside me, who has somehow managed to get a beer instead. My bottle is passed around and the cap struggled with until it reaches the old woman who called me "koko," who opens it with her teeth. By dusk we have moved on to palm wine. Two tall drums have been set up, and two of the bigger children are banging out an elaborate syncopated rhythm on them, while the rest dance around them to the beat in a slow circle. One child much too small to reach the top of the drum is tapping a tattoo on its side with a stick. Night falls and the mosquitoes come out, but the party continues. Our two gallons of palm wine are long gone and someone has brought more. The Notable announces that he is going to bed, and walks along the circle of chairs solemnly shaking everyone's hand before leaving us.

I lean back in my chair and listen in increasing irritation to Ange, who has cornered the man from WCS, and is subjecting him to an embellished account of his negotiating prowess in dealing with the men who wanted money for the rhinoceros viper and with the village committee over the six-guides issue. These seem to have been the two highlights of the expedition for him. "So I decided to take the girl with me," he gets going on his account of the day of the 3-hour meeting, "and I said to Katherine, I told her, 'Katherine, I'm taking the girl with me to the meeting. You stay here in the camp,' I said to her, 'because if you don't get those snakes prepared they're going to rot.'" The man from WCS is alternately looking at his watch and rolling his eyes skyward, but this doesn't discourage Ange in the slightest.

"Ange!" I whack his shoulder affectionately. "Your account of the meeting is taking even longer than the meeting itself. Stop for a moment and take a breath and let someone else get a word in edgewise." The children have abandoned the drums and are now assembled in an excited crowd around Lise, who is teaching them to play cards.

Everything winds down just after midnight, which is very late by Impongui standards. Lise and Ange and I spread out our respective mats and mattresses on Romuald's bumpy floor. Even with the swarm of mosquitoes around my head it is much more comfortable than my bed in the forest, but I lie awake all night even so. Not that the night is long. In a couple of days I will be back in Brazzaville, and in a few days more in Toronto. It is almost Christmas. I'm longing for the opportunity to figure out what that mystery viper really is. And then there's Delphin. I've thought about him a lot over the past weeks, but maybe that's just because I've been speaking Lingala. What will it be like to see him again? Have I got too used to producing him whenever anyone inquires about my "mobali"? Did what happened between us that last night before I left mean anything at all? I suppose I'll find out soon enough.

Ange wakes up around 4:00 a.m. and starts shining a flashlight around. "Mice!" he starts busily moving things around. "Someone left food on the table. That's what's attracting them. They've been running over me all night!"

We are all up by 5:00. Romuald makes coffee for us all, even for Old Charles, perhaps out of habit. Hoping desperately that my last camera battery will hold out, I take pictures as promised of Uncle Marcel with his wife, and of course of Kat-Lise at her mother's breast. Many people bring us parting gifts of pineapples and immense bunches of bananas. Uncle Marcel lines me and Ange and Lise up in front of him and, starting with Ange, makes a little speech of surprising insight about the best qualities of each of our personalities, and extends his good wishes and hopes for each person's future. At the end of each speech he presents a gift. He speaks to Ange in Lingala and then presents him with a small wooden dagger with a coppery blade. Ange sweeps his hands in a slow, wide arc starting above his head, bringing his hands together in front of him, palms up, to receive the gift. I get a speech in French and a curious object, also carved of wood, sort of like a doll-house-sized one-legged stool. Lise's present is a spoon. Uncle Marcel carved all three objects himself out of wood, and probably some time ago, since they are blackened with dirt. "You can get them cleaned in Brazzaville," he assures us, "they'll come out really nice." I wouldn't clean that good Impongui dirt off mine for all the world, and I tell him so.

The Notable is our last appointment. We squeeze into his hut and stand in front of him. Like Uncle Marcel he speaks formally, addressing just me, in Lingala, but briefly and simply enough that I understand. He is glad that we came; he believes that work like ours has great value; and he gives us his blessing for a safe journey. He holds something out to me, and I sweep my hands in a respectful arc, as I saw Ange do with Uncle Marcel, before bringing my hands together in front of me to receive the gift. The Notable and I keep eye contact for a moment after he finishes speaking, and I say, "Merci mingi, Notable," closing my hands around something heavy and cold. "Kendu malamu" (Go well), he finishes.

"Otikala malamu" (Stay well), we all reply, backing out of the little shack respectfully. I contain my curiosity and only look at the object I am holding when we are out of sight of the hut. It is a blackened piece of iron, shaped roughly like a flat isosceles triangle. The base of the triangle is curved like an ax head, but blunt, and the top comes to a narrow point which is curved over into a small hook. I can't imagine what it's for.

Later, Delphin tells me that it is a standardized weight of iron, once used as a trade item. The shape allowed it to be easily beaten into an ax, a pointed blade, or anything else. In the DRC at least, Delphin's Congo, the Belgians once traded these with the Congolese for African artifacts and anything else they wanted. Delphin calculates that it must have been made before 1960, when the Congo declared independence, but no earlier than 1920, since before that King Leopold simply took what he wanted from the Congo without paying anything for it. The Notable must have lived through that era and held on to this piece of iron all those years. I spend a lot of time wondering why the Notable chose this object as a parting gift for a Canadian woman much too young and ignorant to have any understanding of its history or significance.

But the morning of our departure from Impongui, I just stuff it in the pocket of my backpack, as we finally head to the motorized WCS pirogue. Some people (including Ange) become tearful as we shake hand after hand and accept even more pineapples and bananas while simultaneously negotiating the steep and slippery slope down to the water. Perséphone, the little girl in the blue dress, takes one final look at me and starts to howl. Someone thrusts a final gift into Ange's hands, a freshly caught fish, very wet and loosely wrapped in a manioc leaf.

Before the camera battery finally dies, I snap a last photo of the crowd at the landing as the pirogue pulls away. And then Impongui is out of sight. Lise sits in the bottom of the pirogue like me instead of in one of the chairs. There is a huge maggot lump on her chin, giving her face an odd lopsided look. Her short hair is pulled back into a scruffy tangle at the back of her head, with no hair net to hide it. I can still see the rash on her feet in spite of the tattered remains of her pink slippers. And it occurs to me that we never did do anything about her intestinal worms. But for once she's smiling. Maybe she's just glad to be going home.

As the pirogue glides through the grasses of the Likouala aux Herbes River, Ange rummages in his backpack and finds a plastic bag to hold the dripping fish. "A herpetologist always has a little bag handy," he reflects, rinsing fish slime off his hands over the side, "because you never know what you might find."

epilogue

It is another Thursday morning in October. Two alarm clocks only barely succeed in waking me up in time to get to my first class of the day. How did I manage to wake up with no alarm clock at all, 15 minutes before dawn every morning at our camp near Impongui? I am lying on one side of a recently purchased queen-size bed. The other side is occupied by piles of papers and textbooks that I must have fallen asleep studying. On the pillow beside me, Daisy yawns, stretches, and utters her one word of Lingala. I get up and feed her.

A lot has happened since I left the Congo less than a year ago. The biggest change has been starting a new job as an assistant professor of biology at Whitman College, in Walla Walla, Washington. Toronto is most of a continent away, and Brazzaville is on the other side of the planet. Since the semester began I've been almost completely occupied just keeping up with the workload of my first year of teaching. Almost. The position came with generous research funds, though little time to spend them. When I go back to the Congo in the summer, I will not have to worry about the cost of tents, buckets, and sardines. I might even splash out and buy another dress, though I don't think I can use grant money for that.

It takes me less than 10 minutes, on my bike, to get to the science building. Pinned proudly to the wall outside my new office is an article which appeared yesterday in the online journal *Herpetological Conservation and Biology:* "Amphibians and Reptiles of the Lac Télé Community Reserve, Likouala Region, Republic of Congo (Brazzaville)" by Kate Jackson, Ange-Ghislain Zassi-Boulou, Lise-Bethy Mavoungou, and Serge Pangou. Eleven closely packed pages of charts, tables, and photographs, including, at the end, a photograph of each author.

"This is a scanning electron micrograph of the venom-conducting fang of a cobra," I tell my 10 o'clock comparative anatomy class. "The shape is highly derived, as you can see, but basically it's like any other snake tooth in terms of developmental origin. Okay, so tell me," I address a young man who looks as though he's about to yawn, "what germ layers it forms from."

"An epithelial-mesenchymal interaction between the epidermis, which makes the enamel part, and neural crest cells in the dermis, which form the dentine part inside." He must have been paying attention after all.

"Take a good look at the structure again. The fang is tubular — there's a hollow canal running through the shaft. Venom enters through this lumen at the base and exits, into a bite wound, through the orifice near the distal end." The students seem to be following. "Now the key word there is *near.*" I pause for emphasis. "The venom canal opens a bit before the tip of the fang, not at the very tip. Can you think of any reason why?" They can't. "Imagine if it were right at the tip. The tip wouldn't be sharp, see? Think of the tip of a hypodermic needle." They look doubtful.

"I never look at the needle," offers another student, looking slightly pale. I sigh.

In the library I run into a new assistant professor of Asian art. "Has the paperwork for your husband been sorted out yet?" she asks me, kindly.

"No, I'm afraid we're still just waiting." I don't bother to explain that Delphin and I are not actually married. We had planned to move here together at the beginning of July, and together unpack and start to build a life in Walla Walla, but 3 months later, he is still in Toronto, waiting for the travel documents he needs to enter the United States.

I check today's haul of e-mail. There is one from a forester in Pointe Noire who has taken to e-mailing me photographs of every snake squashed on the road or killed by a villager near his field site, for me to identify. The photographs are always of the most apalling quality. "If the size of the file is only 12 KB," I wrote back last time, exasperated, "the image I receive will be smaller than a postage stamp and out of focus. I can't perform miracles." But this one is in perfect focus. Just a severed head and neck, with a ballpoint pen lying beside it for scale. It only takes me a glance at the yellow bands on the black front of the neck. *Naja melanoleuca* is a species I will never again misidentify as long as I live.

The message I save for last is the first response to the pdf of the *Herpetological Conservation and Biology* article. I e-mailed it yesterday, as soon as it was published, to all my contacts in the Congo, as well as to Claude and to Jean-Philippe. Dr. Parra is the first to respond.

"Chère Kate: Congratulations on the publication of this article, which honors my country, the Congo, and which beautifully solidifies our collaboration. Thank you for citing us in the Acknowledgments section. We look forward to your return, and you will always be warmly received, here in the Congo—your country also."

acknowledgments

Financial and logistical support for the expeditions described in this book were provided by the Institut de Recherche pour le Développement, the Division of Amphibians and Reptiles, Smithsonian Institution, the Royal Geographical Society, the Wildlife Conservation Society, the Laboratoire National de Santé Publique, Brazzaville, the Silanes Laboratory, Mexico (manufacturers of antivenom), and the Group d'Etude et de Recherche en Diversité Biologique. I am especially grateful to the following individuals representing those orgaqnizations: Jean-Philippe Chippaux, Claude Laveissière, Victor Mamonekene, Henri-Joseph Parra, and Hugo Rainey. I thank the following herpetologists for help obaining hard-to-find literature and for expert assistance in the identification of some specimens which baffled me: Aaron Bauer, Manfred Beier, Adam Leache, Anne-Marie Ohler, Andreas Schmitz, and Richard Tinsley. David Blackburn deserves a particular word of thanks for examining, and succeeding in identifying, most of the difficult "LBFs" I collected. For assistance in the field, I thank Etienne Bokobela, Charles Dikassana, Romuald Essihé, and Florence Gonda. Collection permits were granted by the government of the Congo (DGRST and MEFE). I wish to express my great gratitude to the Notable of Impongui for the wisdom and efficiency with which he facilitated my work, and to all the people of Impongui.

For leading me to think of writing a book in the first place, my parents are largely to blame. My journal-keeping habit dates back to my infancy when they forced me to draw a picture and dictate an entry every day when I was too young to write.

As for making a herpetologist of me, nobody really knows how that came about except that the obsession predated kindergarten. Over the 30 years that followed I have learned my trade from herpetologists too numerous to list. Among my herpetological mentors, however, two deserve particular mention here, being themselves both eminent herpetologists and accomplished writers: Harry Greene, who unfailingly encouraged my efforts at popular writing, and Richard Wassersug, who nagged me until I published them. Hilary Davidson, a real writer, and Adam Summers, a scientific one, led me through the baffling world of book publishing, and finally to Ann Downer-Hazell, the editor of any herpetologist's dreams ("Snakes? Congo? Send the whole shebang"), the rest of the capable staff of Harvard University Press, and Nancy "the critter book editor" Clemente. Tuhin Giri, the world's most multitalented behavioral ecologist, drew the maps (though he says he'll be happy if he never draws another tree in his life). The photographs in which I appear were taken by a variety of people who kindly snapped away, when I thrust a camera into their hands and gave them a 5-minute crash course in photography.

Finally thanks to all the people, friends and family mostly, who read my book in bits and pieces and early versions and found kind and helpful things to say. I hope you enjoyed this book as much as they politely claimed to.

Index

Legless lizard. See *Feylinia*

Leptopelis rufus, 132

Lingala, 31, 51, 82–83, 86, 107, 114, 152, 193, 225, 226, 251, 256, 285; expressions, 5, 46, 52, 55, 116–117, 122, 179, 180–181, 190, 192, 206–207, 210, 214, 217, 224, 227, 238, 242, 253, 257, 312, 313; learning, 116–117, 178–181, 188

Lingala vocabulary: bana na kelasi, 214; kati, 117; kende malamu, 190, 217, 313; kisi, 257; koba, 116; koko, 224; kombo na yango ezali nini, 227; kuna, 281; ligorodo, 227; lobi, 180; makasi, 257; mbote, 46, 52, 55, 180, 206, 210, 224; mbula, 180; mobali, 192, 312; mobimba, 257; Mokele-Mbembe, 253; nasimbi, 242; nazali malamu, 180; ndako, 116; niaou, 180; ndoki, 5; nyoka, 117, 257; osimbi, 242; otikala malamu, 313; ozali malamu, 180, 206; sango nini, 180, 206, 210; sango te, 180, 206, 210; tika, 238; tikala malamu, 207, 217; yoka, 117

Likouala, 16–17, 24, 216, 233

Likouala aux Herbes River, 208, 215, 223, 231, 238, 290. *See also color insert*

Little brown frog. *See* LBF

Lizard, 101–102, 228. See also *Adolfus jacksoni; Chamaeleo jacksoni; Feylinia; Hemidactylus; Lygosoma; Trachylepis*

Lygosoma, 285–286. *See also color insert (Lygosoma fernandi)*

Mabuya. See *Trachylepis*

Mamba. See *Dendroaspis jamesoni*

Mehelya, 227–228, 294, 301. *See also color insert (Mehelya poensis)*

Millipedes, 223, 226, 232, 277, 290. *See also color insert*

Mokele-Mbembe, 253, 289

Money, 23–24, 28, 30, 33, 38

Mosquitoes, 79, 231–232, 286

Museum collections, 7–8, 68–69, 104; purpose of, 9–10, 11, 21, 102, 103, 128, 173–174, 175–176

Naja melanoleuca, 133–134, 145, 161–162, 163, 167–168, 281, 294–295, 317. *See also color insert*

Natural history museums, 7, 164, 166

Nerodia sipedon, 90, 92

Night adder. See *Causus*

Northern water snake. See *Nerodia sipedon*

Ontario, 80, 90, 93, 207, 238

Osteolaemus tetraspis, 34

Ouesso, 3

Owls, 114–115, 117

Pangolin, 246

Parasites, 122, 269, 275, 301–302, 304–305, 314. See also *Ascaris*

Permits, 19, 25, 26, 29–30, 32, 33–35, 40, 44, 49, 84, 161, 163, 164–165, 167, 168–169, 188

Phrynobatrachus hylaois. *See color insert*

Pierre noire. *See* Snakebite, treatment for